MILTON ACORN
IN LOVE AND ANGER

Portrait of Milton Acorn, by Brian Burke

MILTON ACORN
IN LOVE AND ANGER

Richard Lemm

CARLETON UNIVERSITY PRESS

Copyright © Carleton University Press, 1999

Printed and bound in Canada

Canadian Cataloguing in Publication Data

Lemm, Richard, 1946-
    Milton Acorn: In love and anger

Includes bibliographical references and index.
ISBN 0-88629-340-5

    1. Acorn, Milton, 1923-1986—Biography. 2. Poets, Canadian (English)—20th century—Biography. I. Title.

PS8501.C8Z76 1999   C811'.54   C98-900983-1
PR9199.3.A36Z75 1999

Cover photo: Milton Acorn, circa 1980, from the private collection of Mary Hooper.

Cover and interior: BCumming Designs

Frontispiece: *Portrait of Milton Acorn*, oil on canvas, 101.6 x 75.6 cm., 1985, by Brian Burke, from the Confederation Centre Art Gallery and Museum, Charlottetown, PEI. Courtesy of the artist.

Dig Up My Heart by Milton Acorn. Used by permission, McClelland & Stewart, Inc. *The Canadian Publishers.*

This book has been published with the help of a grant from the Humanities and Social Sciences Federation of Canada, using funds provided by the Social Sciences and Humanities Research Council of Canada.

Carleton University Press gratefully acknowledges the support extended to its publishing program by the Canada Council and the financial assistance of the Ontario Arts Council. The Press would also like to thank the Department of Canadian Heritage, Government of Canada, and the Government of Ontario through the Ministry of Culture, Tourism and Recreation, for their assistance.

for

John Smith

master poet & elegant scholar

&

Jack & Eva Bourne

CONTENTS

Illustrations *viii*
Foreword *ix*

Prologue	Vancouver, 1967	*1*
I.	In Love and Anger	*3*
II.	Forerunners	*11*
III.	I've Tasted My Blood	*37*
IV.	If You're Stronghearted	*67*
V.	On St. Urbain Street	*83*
VI.	Toronto and Marriage	*119*
VII.	Another Coast	*137*
VIII.	The People's Poet	*149*
IX.	The Figure in the Landscape	*185*
X.	A Bird in the Builder's Hand	*215*
Epilogue	Dig Up My Heart	*247*

Notes *255*
Works Cited *263*
Index *273*

ILLUSTRATIONS

1. Portrait of Milton Acorn — *frontispiece*
2. Robert Acorn, Sr. — *18*
3. Acorn's grandfather, E.T. Carbonell — *28*
4. Milton with his grandmother, Kate MacDougall Carbonell — *30*
5. Helen Carbonell Acorn — *34*
6. Milton at about age twelve — *43*
7. Acorn and Gwendolyn MacEwan — *121*
8. Helen Acorn in the mid-1970s — *154*
9. Acorn receiving the Canadian Poet's Award and his People's Poet Medal — *162*
10. The Working Class Poet — *172*
11. Acorn receiving his honorary doctorate in 1977 — *207*
12. Milton and Helen Acorn at the Convocation reception — *209*
13. Milton Acorn on PEI, 1982 — *217*

FOREWORD

> Since I'm Island-born home's as precise
> as if a mumbly old carpenter,
> shoulder-straps crossed wrong,
> laid it out,
> refigured to the last three-eights of shingle.
> — "The Island"

BORN AND RAISED in Charlottetown, Prince Edward Island, Milton Acorn rose to prominence as a poet and political dissenter in Montreal, Toronto, and Vancouver during 1953-68, and achieved national distinction and notoriety after 1968 as a literary figure and iconoclast while living primarily in Toronto. Yet his Island origins profoundly affected his poetic and political identity. Moreover, he often returned between 1953 and 1962 and after 1967 to "the fanged jaws of the Gulf" ("The Island"), walking along the "wave-lined edge of home" and on "the red loam," and immersing himself in his native Charlottetown. Prince Edward Island inspired many of his most accomplished and memorable poems and they in turn enrich the Island's history, landscape, and culture with a wealth of imagery, metaphor, critical vision, and passionate devotion.

Acorn was an important literary figure and influence in Canada for several decades, and his best poetic work has earned him a permanent place among the nation's cultural heroes. He was a forceful and sometimes irascible voice of social vision and conscience. Acorn's poetry, political impact, and coast-to-coast residencies earned him the title "People's Poet of Canada." Al Purdy, his great friend and fellow poet and another nationalist figure who, like Acorn, contributed significantly to the modern Canadian identity, wrote that "Acorn developed primarily off the Island. I think if he'd stayed there he'd have remained an insular parochial versifier" (Letter 30 September 1995). This may well be the case. But it is equally true that Acorn's unique and emphatic voice was substantially shaped by his Island experience.

It is impossible to separate Acorn's later growth as a poet or his political vision from their early formation on Prince Edward Island and their nourishment during his adult pilgrimages back home. A distinction must be made here between "parochialism" and "regionalism" in a writer. Parochialism implies an outlook which is narrowly confined to a region and its conventions and values, and which appears inaccessible or merely quaint or exotic ("local colour") to the outside reader. Regionalism involves a perspective which is grounded in the author's region and connects with readers in other places through a more subtle, complex, and richly inquiring perception of human conduct and of people's relationship with landscape and their home place. It may be argued that all good literature is essentially and inevitably regional. Without a doubt, the production of an impressive body of Canadian literature from the 1950s to the present has resulted from both regionalist and nationalist energies. This is especially the case with Acorn, a fervent nationalist and regionalist. A large part of his national achievement as a poet grew out of his rootedness in his particular region of Canada.

This book began as an exploration of Milton Acorn's years on Prince Edward Island and his Island identity and as an appreciation of his poems with an Island focus. This initial plan projected shorter sections that would summarize his years off-Island and the poetry which is not Island based. The intention was to provide a portrait of the Island poet who became known as the People's Poet of Canada. The result reflects that plan, though not quite so simply as originally conceived. Acorn's movements between Prince Edward Island and the mainland from the early 1950s onward were too frequent, and his personality was too much a blend of the Island and the mainland cities he inhabited during three decades, to compartmentalize his life and poetry rigidly into "Island" and "off-Island." A more extensive treatment of the off-Island periods became necessary to suggest how an Islander became a national literary and political figure, and how Acorn used his talent and public voice to enhance both other Canadians' awareness of Prince Edward Island and Islanders' appreciation of their own landscape, history, and identity.

Obviously, much work remains to be done on Acorn's life in Montreal, Vancouver, and Toronto. There are also his lesser-known stints in places such as Moncton and Dawson Creek to be researched. Anyone familiar with Acorn will know that stories about him—authentic and apocryphal—could fill several volumes. Indeed, some fine Island stories about him had to be left out. I hope this book will stimulate the discovery of more stories and information about Acorn's time on and off Prince Edward Island.

As well, there is ample room for critical studies of Acorn's poetry, since remarkably little critical writing has been devoted to his work. Perhaps the fascination with Acorn the public figure—the outspoken, long-suffering, rough-hewn, romantic, and romanticized poet of the people—has delayed scholarly attention to his major achievement: his poetry. This book is not an in-depth study of his poems. It does provide, I hope, sufficient introduction to certain poems, aspects of his poetry, and historical contexts that readers will be prompted to investigate Acorn's writing more thoroughly and to remedy the shortage of critical work on him.

Milton Acorn's life and poetic role have captured the interest of people well beyond the circles of Canadian literary studies. Many Islanders and other Canadians remember Acorn and, to borrow one of his poetic phrases, the figure he made in our landscape. This book was written equally for these people and for those readers who know nothing of Milton Acorn, but who share the growing interest in the lives and achievements of prominent Canadians.

Many people have helped with this book. First and foremost, Acorn's sister Mary Hooper, brother-in-law Garth Hooper, nephew David Hooper, and brother Robert Acorn have generously provided a wealth of information and support. I am deeply indebted to Acorn's Island friends whose voices are heard in this book: Hilda Woolnough, Frank Ledwell, John Smith, Reg Phelan, Andy Wells, George Steiger, Jim Hornby, Valerie LaPointe, Kent Martin, Sister Georgina Johnston, Joseph Sherman, and Gertrude Partridge. Acorn's mainland friends who provided invaluable information include Joe Rosenblatt, Patrick Lane, bill bissett, Cheryl Cashman, Al Purdy, Eleanor McEachern, and James Deahl.

Kathy Drummond, Marilyn Bell, and Charlotte Stewart at the Public Archives and Records Office of PEI were exceedingly helpful, as were Sgt. Greg Gallant of the PEI Regiment Museum at the Queen Charlotte Armories; Lynne Sherren and Pamela N. Brunt of Veterans Affairs; Karen Mair of CBC Charlottetown; Brooke Brady, principal of West Kent School; Jeannie Coulson, secretary of Spring Park School; Pauline Scott at the Garden Nursing Home; Edward MacDonald, Curator of History at the PEI Museum and Heritage Foundation; Leona Nicholson at the PEI Legislative Counsel; and Ken Mayhew of the PEI Department of Forestry. Other Islanders to whom I am grateful for information are Elaine Harrison, Eleanor Wheler, Bill Ledwell, Wanda Bourgeau, Don B. Smith, Brent MacLaine, Fred Pound, William Shields, Joe Flynn, Ray McCloskey, Cheryl Ann Savinant, Agnes Dickson, Peter Shama, Frank Turgeon, Walter Auld, and Helen MacDonald.

Anne Godard of the National Archives of Canada kindly facilitated my research in the Milton Acorn Collection. Henriette Levasseur and Diane Ally of The Canada Council provided assistance.

I also wish to thank Dan McLeod of *The Georgia Straight*, Glen Sorestad, Joan MacLeod, Dr. Robert J. Grimm, and Rosemary Sullivan. Cheryl McGuirk is the hero who transcribed the bulk of the taped interviews.

I would also like to thank all those who read the manuscript in its various stages and generously offered assessments and suggestions: Harry Baglole, John Cousins, John Crossley, Lawson Drake, Al Hammond, Michael Hennessey, Janice Kulyk Keefer, Deirdre Kessler, Patrick Lane, Edward MacDonald, Ken MacKinnon, Ian MacQuarrie, John Smith, and Andy Wainwright.

This book would not exist without the encouragement and expertise of Harry Baglole, Director of the Institute of Island Studies at UPEI, and Laurie Brinklow, coordinator of publishing for the Institute. They were the ones who suggested this project, who secured and funded the editorial guidance of readers, and who steadfastly envisioned this book as an appreciation not only of the People's Poet of Canada from PEI, but also of the Island's contribution to Canadian culture.

I also wish to thank the University of Prince Edward Island for granting me a research leave which enabled me to complete this project, and for research grants from UPEI and the Social Sciences and Humanities Research Council of Canada. Far more encouraging than money is the respect for contemporary poetry and Canadian writers to be found among my colleagues in the Department of English. I can't imagine a friendlier environment in which to write such a book. And if there were Governor-General's medals for department secretaries, one would go to Carol Francis. I must also thank Jack and Eva Bourne, Donna Bourne-Tyson and Jonathan Tyson, and Irene and Nigel Guilford for providing such gracious hospitality and conducive surroundings in which to work on this book during my sojourns in Ontario.

I am, of course, exceptionally grateful to Carleton University Press and to Jennie Strickland, whose elegant editorial direction and exuberant approach to publishing have been a godsend. I am indebted, as well, to Frances Rooney, whose copy editing was stunningly thorough, exact, and wise. McGill-Queen's University Press also deserves a note of appreciation for its partnership role with Carleton University Press.

Finally, thanks to Lesley-Anne Bourne and her amazing editorial and poetic eye, and for listening to enough about Milton Acorn to last her several lifetimes.

PROLOGUE

VANCOUVER, 1967

I FIRST ENCOUNTERED Milton Acorn in Vancouver one day in October 1967. A week earlier I had left San Francisco, where I had been working and attending university, and that morning, after saying goodbye to family and close friends, I boarded a northbound Greyhound bus in Seattle. A few hours later I stopped at the border, was interviewed by Canadian immigration officers, and was officially admitted as a landed immigrant to Canada. I checked into the YMCA in downtown Vancouver, and ate dinner in the Sportsman's Cafe—because my grandfather owned the Sportsman's Cafe in downtown Seattle.

After dinner I walked downtown. Around dusk I saw a man selling an underground newspaper outside the Hudson's Bay. It was the sixth issue of *The Georgia Straight*, which was stamped "BANNED BY THE MAYOR": police had seized thirty thousand copies of that issue. The vendor told me there was a rally at a union hall that night to raise money for the legal defense, and that I was welcome to come along. Soon a black Mercedes sedan pulled up, driven by a man in a well-tailored suit, and we climbed inside. In the front passenger seat a bulky man dressed in a plaid work shirt and tan work pants sat smoking a large cigar.

The newspaper vendor told them I had just immigrated from the States. The big man's head swung around toward me like a wrecking ball, and demanded in a voice resonant and surprisingly high pitched for such a rugged face, "Where do you stand on the Vietnam War?" I had been asked this question often enough in the States, sometimes in uncomfortable situations. Once, when I was hitch-hiking in the Sacramento Valley, a man picked me up at dusk, drove a few miles, then pulled off onto a side road by an orchard and informed me his younger brother had been killed in Nam. I had learned to be cautious. But here in Vancouver, in this company, I figured I could speak frankly.

The big man liked my response, pounded his cigar-clenching fist on the dashboard and exclaimed, "Damn those Yankee imperialists!"

"Do you know who this is?" asked the driver. "He's Milton Acorn, the poet."

That was the first and last time I saw Acorn until I moved to Prince Edward Island in 1983, after he had become the legendary People's Poet of Canada.

After we became acquainted on PEI, I asked if he remembered meeting me in 1967: "I was the guy who'd just immigrated from the States."

He stared hard at me: "You still might be CIA. We'll see." And scowled. Then broke into one of his huge embracing grins.

Acorn died in Charlottetown in 1986, and a few years later this person from Seattle was standing in front of a class at the University of Prince Edward Island, trying to talk about Acorn's "Island" poems, and asking his students if they had ever met Acorn.

IN LOVE AND ANGER

> I shout LOVE even though it might deafen you
> and never say that love's a mild thing
> for it's hard, a violation
> of all laws for the shrinking of people.
> I *shout* LOVE, counting on the hope
> that you'll sing and not shatter in love's vibration.
> — "I Shout Love" (1970)

ONE DAY IN THE LATE 1970s a young girl was riding with her mother through downtown Charlottetown. They stopped for a red light beside the Confederation Centre of the Arts. The girl was transfixed by the sight of a large dishevelled man with a craggy face standing in front of the entrance to the Confederation Centre of the Arts. He clutched a big black notebook and declaimed with a ringing and lyrical voice into the summer air, to the ravens and crows, to no one and everyone, to history.

"Look at that strange man," the girl said. "Is he a bum?"

"No. That's Dr. Milton Acorn, the famous poet."

"Why's he shouting?"

"He's reciting poetry. That's what he does."[1]

A decade later that girl was a young woman studying Canadian literature at the University of Prince Edward Island, which had awarded Milton Acorn an honorary doctorate in 1977. Every student at UPEI, native Islander or not, knew of the Island's most famous literary figure, Lucy Maud Montgomery, and her creation, *Anne of Green Gables*, with its lovable, adopted "come-from-away" Anne Shirley. A year after Acorn's death in 1986, however, too few students had heard of the Island's celebrated native son, the only person to be honoured by his peers as the People's Poet of Canada. Most students who *had* heard of him knew only enough to ask: Wasn't he a bit of a nut? Wasn't he a drunk? Wasn't he shell-shocked from the war? A few students old enough to have waited on tables in local restaurants during Acorn's last years remembered his generous tips and rousing appreciation of good service, but also had unpleasant memories of Acorn's sometimes unsavoury table manners and vociferous monologues. The poet was memorable as an eccentric, and no longer even the trendy kind.

Those Islanders who befriended him during his last few years alive on PEI knew that Milton Acorn, the larger-than-life poet of the people, was a problematic as well as an esteemed figure in his native province. He had been honoured in the province several times since the publication of his most famous book, *I've Tasted My Blood*, in 1969. Those who honoured him knew of his great love for humanity and nature— his "huge heart" as Island visual artist Hilda Woolnough calls it. These admirers were aware of his influence as mentor and friend to other writers. They acknowledged the courage—and the price—of Acorn's struggle to become an original poetic voice and a forthright social conscience and visionary.

Most of all, Acorn was saluted for his distinguished poems, and for his role in broadening the scope of Canadian literature and extending the range of poetic discourse. From the publication of his first chapbook in 1956, *In Love and Anger*, he became identified with these two dominant and interrelated motifs. He was celebrated for the refinement of his love and anger into poems about the Island's history, landscape, and sense of community; the working people of Canada and the modern era's revolutionary leaders; the inequality and oppression which earned his scorn; his bittersweet experience of sexual love; his devotion to nature; and his exploration of the Goddess motif and the existence of God.

And some Islanders, such as writer Deirdre Kessler, applauded Acorn's striking presence as a public poet, visible and audible amid the city's daily commerce: he "used to wander around Charlottetown, notebook under his arm, a handful of pens lined up in the pocket of his plaid shirt.... How many towns have you been in where a poet wandered the streets? Muttering to himself? Standing in the middle of a block, looking up?" (LaPointe 4).

Some of Acorn's fellow Islanders, however, found it difficult to admire him uncritically, and were put off by his untidiness, his reputation for cantankerousness and fervour, his inability to fit comfortably into the social world, and his frank expression of often unorthodox beliefs in a community with a long tradition of keeping one's political and ethical opinions private and of not being "different." In Vancouver and Toronto, Acorn's demeanour and appearance were less noticeable among the crowds and in the various circles of artists and politicos. But even in the big cities, this man, who could be a generous friend or valued mentor one day and, as one person noted, an "irascible bastard" the next, offended and made enemies with numerous people. On the Island, those unaware of his distinction as a poet and his stance as an iconoclastic social critic could regard him merely as a colourful character or shabby crank.

One scholar, Ed Jewinski, observes, "When Milton Acorn entitled his first short book ... *In Love and Anger*, his critics immediately recognized his two central themes. Virtually every reader, in fact, acknowledged that Acorn offered an outspoken, though paradoxical, vision of 'love' and 'anger.' Love, for him, was to be a full, impassioned feeling of fellowhood and brotherhood to man, a love which could repudiate all social rules that infringed on the dignity of mankind. Anger, too, was central, but it was a directed anger, an articulate controlled expression of outrage, as passionless as a clear thought and emotionless as direct, blunt honesty" (31). Sometimes, though, the seemingly uncontrollable anger in Acorn's poetry and his life resulted in versified polemic and diatribe, in mixed reviews of his books, damaged friendships, and alienated bystanders. Sometimes the love seemed dogmatic, stubborn, or incoherent. His importance as a Canadian writer and public figure and his stature as one of the Island's greatest citizens, however, rest on the fact that Acorn's love and anger found a unique and powerful voice in his best poems, in his most lucid and articulate public discourse, and in his often remarkable conversations with friends.

When Acorn returned permanently to the island in 1981, he encountered a much larger arts community and a considerably more receptive attitude toward the arts than when he left the Island in the early 1950s or visited during the 1960s. The cultural climate and socio-economic structures had altered markedly from the late 1960s.

In the 1970s a new generation of intellectuals and government advisors began a social analysis and policy formulation aimed to combine economic and cultural modernization with a reassertion and protection of traditional Island values—"the Island way of life." And, of course, the Island was rapidly absorbing the cultural influence of U.S. and global commercialism, consumerism, and technology-driven and media-transmitted values.

The Island was critically and dynamically confronting, and emerging from, a prolonged period of postcolonial, post-Confederation marginalization and stasis. In this context, artists and cultural enterprises were ceasing to be low-profile hobbyists or oddities in an "old-fashioned" and "out-of-the-way" region: they were becoming creators, entertainers, critics, entrepreneurs, and producers working in the "cultural sector"; they were important voices from and for the region; and their work commanded a more significant place in the lives of Islanders and other Canadians, helping to rediscover, redefine, and revitalize the region and the nation.

Along with these changes, recognition of Canadian literature had grown remarkably across Canada since the late 1960s, enhancing the status of writers. This development owed a great deal to the intensification of Canadian nationalism in the postwar period, and especially from the mid-1960s onward. With growing affluence and an increasing sense of accomplishment, the Canadian élite, the expanding urban middle class, and many rural communities took more pride in Canada's culture and history, and it became fashionable to support the formation of the country's own traditions. Institutions had been established to further this cause, such as the National Library in 1953 and the Canada Council in 1957. Other phenomena, such as the enhancement of federalism under the Trudeau government, regional development agencies, and substantially increased immigration, contributed to both Canadian nationalism and a corresponding regional pride and assertiveness. There were, of course, long-standing and newer tensions between regionalist and nationalist agendas; but regionalism and nationalism also strengthened one another. And both nationalism and regionalism were indebted to the growing ranks of Canadian writers who, overtly or implicitly, were helping to repossess and create Canadian traditions, to deconstruct the history of marginalization, and to generate a national and regional renaissance.

Many Islanders were proud of their province's contributions, especially the writings of Lucy Maud Montgomery. Another Island writer from the first half of the century, Sir Andrew Macphail, had earned a significant place in the Canadian literary canon with his semi-autobiographical memoir of PEI, *The Master's Wife*. In the postwar era, Milton Acorn was the first Island writer to play a notable role, nationally and regionally, in the advancement of Canadian literature, and he spent his last years on the Island reaping the benefits of that enhanced recognition, acknowledged as another principal contributor to the Island's heritage and Canada's identity.

In 1987, a year after Acorn's death, an extraordinary upwelling of interest in literary writing began on PEI; it continues unabated to this day. There had been literary readings on the Island for nearly two decades, organized primarily by the English Department at UPEI, by writer-professor Réshard Gool and Hilda Woolnough at the legendary Great George Street Gallery, and by poet and *Arts Atlantic* editor Joseph Sherman at the Confederation Centre. Gool and Elaine Harrison, a noted teacher and artist, had published local writers through their small presses, and Frank Ledwell had nurtured 20 years of aspiring creative writers at the university. Libby Oughton's Ragweed Press in Charlottetown had become an important Canadian publisher. A new generation of Island writers—J.J. Steinfeld, Michael Hennessey, Joseph Sherman, Deirdre Kessler, Frank Ledwell, and John Smith—was gaining regional and national stature. But it was not until 1987 that the literary community "caught fire" as it had in the Prairies two decades before or in Nova Scotia in the 1970s.

It was as if, with his death, Acorn's passionate and robust commitment to literature released itself into the community and helped *inspire*—literally, to breathe life into—the National Milton Acorn Festival of literature and music, an annual Island literary competition administered by the PEI Council of Arts and Theatre PEI, the founding of the PEI Writers' Guild, children's writing contests, *and* dozens of people emerging with poems, fiction, plays, children's stories, and feature journalism. The inspiration drawn from Acorn's life-work blended with the extraordinary interest in L.M. Montgomery's writing and renewed attention to Macphail's contribution. The accomplishments of Montgomery and Acorn had helped legitimize writers' work on the Island. If Montgomery's influence and acclaim have been greater than Acorn's, his place of distinction was granted more swiftly.

There is a romantic notion of poets as strange specimens on the borders of everyday life: rebels, bohemians, visionaries who reject our reality and want to replace it with their imaginative but improbable alternatives. Surprisingly few poets actually fit this romantic notion, which is colourful, but which allows the public to marginalize poets by ignoring their work and focusing on the entertainment value of poets who were exotic characters. In many ways Acorn did fit the romantic stereotype of the artist as outsider and eccentric, and this has unfortunately tended to obscure his more lasting achievements *within* our society.

Acorn, in fact, was a poet of our world, of what we call reality, of everyday life. As a critic and visionary, he attacked a good deal of reality: the greed, bigotry, and viciousness. His imagination called for transformations based on belief in equality, justice, and love. Whether the perspective of a particular Acorn poem seems accurate or not, he and his poetry were always of this world. There was no desire to transcend or escape reality. He wanted to improve it. He insisted that humanity remember its dreams and promises of a better world:

> Knowing that in this advertising rainbow
> I live like a trapeze artist with a headache,
> my poems are no aspirins...they show
> pale bayonets of grass waving thin on dunes
> ("Knowing I Live in a Dark Age")

The image of dune grass, so evocative of the Island's seashores, reveals how reliant Acorn was on his Island home, not only for imagery and other poetic elements, but even more for his sense of a "better world." As a poet of and from Prince Edward Island, he drew on his vision of the Island as a paradise in the Gulf, flawed by greed and tempered by strife ("bayonets"), of course, but as close to heaven as humans have thus far attained. His vision of the Island's pastoral and communal virtues and of the class struggles in its historical development was to a certain extent nostalgic, romanticized, and simplified by political perspective; but it also had a real basis in the Island's history, its rural and maritime character, and its undeniable beauty.

As well, Acorn's insistence on his Prince Edward Island identity left a lasting impression on many people across Canada. Acorn was a proud Canadian, too, fiercely nationalistic. But like so many Canadians, his first love and allegiance was to his region, his home province. In 1984, when asked by a journalist if he was "back home now for good," he said, "I'm never going to leave here. I'm never going to leave the Island. I know how to measure up every man that comes toward me. I know where I am here" (Burrill 7). "Home" for Acorn, as for other prominent Maritime writers, was not merely a sentimental projection of the author's nostalgia for an idealized, consoling past. According to Gwendolyn Davies, a noted Maritime literature scholar, "The 'home place' emerges as a symbol of cultural continuity and psychological identification in the face of fragmentation, outmigration, and a continuing hardscrabble economy" (194). As an image, the "home place" functions "as the nurturer not only of local tradition but also of a wider social universe" (Davies 195). This applies to the symbolic role of the Island in Acorn's poetry, and to Acorn's use of the island as a microcosm and "image" for the larger world.

Prince Edward Island's history, including Charlottetown's role as the site of the Charlottetown Conference of 1864 and the subsequent identification of Charlottetown and the province as "the birthplace of Canada," also enabled Acorn to combine his Canadian nationalism with his love of the Island. He drew on PEI's land struggle and tenants' revolt in the nineteenth century, the Island's and the Maritimes' fate within Confederation, and the battle for economic independence and social well-being in the contexts of British colonialism, first, then central Canadian and American domination, international capitalism, and the mixed blessing of tourists, "Pawns in a new still-just-brooding/ Struggle for the land" (*Selected* 153). PEI was foremost his home and, hence, the central land- and seascape where he envisioned the struggle of working people for freedom, dignity, camaraderie, and a decent livelihood. The Island also offered a pattern for the same struggles elsewhere and on a national and international scale.

The bond of Islanders with their home is abundantly evident in Acorn's poetry and life. No Islander was more loyal to his home and people, to the Island's physical beauty, to its rich history, to the goodwill and gutsiness of Islanders, and to his Island upbringing and identity. Growing up on an island, especially one distant from metropolitan centres, can also breed frustration with an island's limitations—geographic, cultural, economic, social. This was definitely true for a young man trying to write fiction and poetry in Charlottetown in the late 1940s and early 1950s, a young man whose political and economic views were left of centre and whose sense of morality and spirituality hardly fit the conventional wisdom. As in most of Canada at that time, the artistic community of the Island was small and kept a low profile, with relatively little support or recognition available for a mind and talent such as Acorn's.

Out of this experience Acorn developed, along with his loyalty, a sturdy critique of what he found stifling, complacent, hypocritical, opportunistic, and corrupt on Prince Edward Island. In his final years Acorn emphasized his love for the Island, but he had also over the years vented his anger toward what he viewed as its shortcomings. The ambiguity and ambivalence of Acorn's "love and anger" concerning the Island paralleled his love for Canada and anger at its exploitation by "the ancient rule of classes" and U.S. "imperialism." His criticisms, however, did not make him any less devoted, any less reverent. In fact, it can be argued that the greatest celebrants of a place, the worthiest patriots, are those who name their homeland's virtues *and* faults.

Some patriots spend time in exile. In 1984 Gary Burrill interviewed Acorn for the magazine *New Maritimes*. "What prompted you to leave the Island in the first place?" Acorn answered, "Well, I got kind of lonely" (4). It was the loneliness of a young writer and social visionary who had to leave home and develop his calling elsewhere to become one of the Island's eminent voices and one of its few mythic figures known across the land. He was, however, nearly 30 years old when he left the Island for the big cities of central Canada and became a "Canadian" poet. For the first three decades of his life, he developed as an Islander: sometimes lonely or set upon for being "different," yet often comfortably at home and imaginatively nurtured in his island world.

II

FORERUNNERS

> It's the last stormtime of winter. As if the ghosts of ancestors
> Forgetting even they are ancestors
> Were wandering. They cannot groan so the trees groan for them;
> The hiss of the snows is their wordless breath.
> — "It's the Last Stormtime"

JAMES MILTON RHODES ACORN was born on 30 March 1923, in Charlottetown. He was the oldest son of Helen Carbonell and Robert Fairclough Acorn. His sister Mary says Milton was "born in the old Charlottetown hospital and he died in the new one."[2] Milton was followed into the world at year-and-a-half intervals by his oldest sister Katherine, the middle child, Mary, his only brother Robert, and Helen. The Acorns were a modestly comfortable, lower middle-class family.

A hugely important feature of the Milton Acorn legend has been his "working-class" background and image. Many Canadians aware of Acorn's adult life and his poetry have assumed that his family origins and upbringing, as well as his young adulthood, were "working class." But this assumption about his family background needs a good deal of qualification and revision. It is also helpful, a half-century after Acorn began his metamorphosis into a proletarian, a worker-writer, and then the People's Poet, to examine the term "working class."

"Working class" had a more precise meaning in the nineteenth and early twentieth centuries, when socio-economic class lines could be more closely correlated to occupational strata. From the 1920s through 1950s in North America, "working class"—as used by most socialists and many writers—referred primarily to "blue-collar" workers such as skilled tradespeople, "unskilled" labourers, farmhands, and seafarers. The term "working class" grew less precise and reliable as the middle class grew substantially after the First World War, more of the traditional working class became unionized, the service sector expanded, and other transformations in production, occupational status, income, and ownership occurred. More recently, Tom Wayman, the chief advocate in Canada of "the new writing about daily work" and editor of several "work writing" anthologies,[3] has expanded the meaning of "working class" to include teachers, office workers, certain lower-income doctors, and others who once would have been excluded.

Who is "working class" and who is a "worker"? Which occupations and income levels qualify one as a working-class person? Many present-day writers would find these questions passé, and would abandon "working class" in favour of contemporary labels and gradations of class-structure: underclass, unemployed, working poor, low-wage service sector, techno-peasants, struggling middle classes, affluent professionals, small business people, corporate élite. These nuances were not lost on the older Milton Acorn, who could translate them into a traditional socialist analysis of capital and labour, the owner class, bourgeoisie, petit bourgeoisie, and proletariat. But Acorn insisted on the existence, virtues, and future triumph of the *working class*: "When the ancient rule of classes is hit / And hit again. History's greatest change / Is happening.... And I'm part of it" (*Selected* 149). He also insisted on his own working-class origins and experience, his membership in the proletariat.

Acorn's family laughs gently at this claim. "Milton liked to think he was working class," says his brother Robert, "but that's not the way it was. Dad wore a suit and tie to work." His sister Mary states emphatically, "We were middle class. Maybe Milton was working class for a few years there between the army and when he became a poet. But not when he was young." Being middle class in the 1920s and 1930s, of course, did not entail the same level of material well-being and leisure options that the term "middle class" has implied since the mid-1950s. Moreover, then as now, "middle class" included a range of income levels and lifestyles. While the Acorn family was not at the affluent end of the middle-class spectrum, it was secure enough to be, as the saying went, "respectably middle class."

The Acorn ancestry, in fact, includes traders, the landed gentry, and entrepreneurs, as well as a civil-servant father and stenographer mother whom traditional Marxism might have labelled "petit bourgeois." The ancestors celebrated in Milton Acorn's public poetry and private discourse were real enough: farmers, soldiers, a sea captain, and a carpenter. But his bloodlines were rich, too, with capitalists and inheritors of accumulated land and wealth.

Milton Acorn's family name is an anglicized form of the German name Eichorn. Milton was enthralled with his ancestors, including John Eichorn (1761-1857), later John Acorn, immigrant to PEI and transitional figure between German-American origins and Anglo-Canadian identity.

David Hooper, Milton Acorn's nephew, inherited his uncle's interest in the Acorn ancestry. A university chemist, David left teaching to assume responsibility on the farm of his parents, Mary and Garth Hooper, in the Island community of North Milton, where Acorn spent a good deal of time during visits to the Island, especially in his final years. The coincidence of his Christian name was not lost on the poet. Reliant on taxis for much of his commuting, Acorn was fond of phoning City Cabs and requesting "a cab for Milton in Milton." There at the farm, David Hooper spent many hours both as a child and as a grown man with Acorn, and has a strong acquaintance with "Uncle Milton's" ancestral mythology: "Milton supposedly traced all this himself, one time or another," says David, "although he used his imagination."

According to David's research, the Eichorns were millers or connected to millers in Hesse-Darmstadt, Germany. Matthias von Eichorn arrived in the American colonies, David says, "by way of a Hessian regiment working for the British Army."[4] After his discharge from the British Army he settled in Waldoboro, Maine. His eldest son, also named Matthias, drowned while canoeing with an aboriginal companion, and left behind a wife named Mary, a son, John, and possibly another son named Richard who vanished after his father's death.

Milton sometimes insisted that Mary, the mother of John Eichorn/Acorn, was a "native Indian." This bolstered his claim that he had aboriginal ancestry—a background that suited his poetic persona and political self-image. He usually declared a Mi'Kmaq connection through another branch of his family, the Musicks. But the mysterious figure of Mary also allowed him to imagine a blood connection with aboriginals' ancient rootedness on the continent and the Island; with their history as noble peoples oppressed by colonialists, imperialists, and capitalists; and with their struggle for survival, freedom, dignity, and their very land. There is, however, no hard evidence of Mary's ethnicity. After his son's death, Matthias Sr. took his grandson John into his home to raise. There is no further record of Mary. She vanishes from this German-American family, and reappears in Milton Acorn's affinity with First Peoples and wishful thinking.

John Eichorn was not only raised by Matthias Eichorn, but also named sole beneficiary in Matthias's will. Matthias had become a substantial landowner. The right of primogeniture meant that John, eldest son of an eldest son, should inherit his grandfather's estate. Unfortunately for John, Eichorn had other children, who were neither so respectful of primogeniture nor so generously inclined toward John. With the rebellion of American colonists against British rule under way, John's uncles conspired to have him pressed into the British army. Meanwhile, they joined the American rebel army. As the smoke of war cleared, the uncles—on the winning side—secured their father's estate, disinherited John, and spread the rumour that John had abandoned his wife and run away without cause. Meanwhile, John was fleeing the victorious rebels and his uncles, one of thirty thousand Loyalist refugees who emigrated to the Maritime colonies.

In May 1782 John arrived on the Island of St. John (formerly Ile St-Jean under French administration, and renamed Prince Edward Island in 1799). About a fifth of the Island Loyalists were, like him, of German descent (Zimmermann 9). Like many Loyalist newcomers John was promised a grant of land. He waited four years until Governor Patterson deeded him one hundred acres in Vernon River in 1788. The same year he married Eleanor Williams (1771-?), the daughter of Captain Williams of the British Navy in Pictou, Nova Scotia.

In 1795 John purchased two hundred acres of land in the Pownal area, "and for many years ran the grist and saw mills ... referred to as Acorn's Mill and the Mayflower Mills" (Jones and Haslam 15). This is the ancestor to whom Milton would approvingly refer in his writing and in interviews as a "Red Tory," miller, and farmer, and not as a colonialist landowner or mill-owning capitalist.

John and Eleanor had 13 children, most of them male. Their son George Acorn (1800-72), who married Anne Sentner (1805-89) on 20 December 1824, was Milton's great-great grandfather.[5] John Eichorn gradually became John Acorn. "The change in name from the German Eichorn to Acorn was a gradual English phonetic evolution. On leafing through old papers one comes across Eachorn, Achorn as well as the original Eichorn. The Acorns on Prince Edward Island, who are all descendants of John, are the only ones who spell their name as 'Acorn'" (Jones and Haslam 15).

According to a family legend, another branch of Milton's ancestry on his father's side can be traced to a forebear right out of an historical romance novel. As David Hooper tells the story, during the American Revolution a cabin boy named Peter fell overboard, swam ashore, and went to live with an aboriginal tribe: "The events as we heard them occurred in the Gulf of St. Lawrence, but in the Loyalist history off Cape Cod. He went to live with the natives who didn't speak English, and they didn't know where he was from. He was a very good singer. So they called him Peter Musick." This legend, unfortunately, lacks documentation. A Loyalist reference work attests that Peter Musick was a sergeant in His Majesty's First Battalion of King's Rangers and arrived on the Island in 1782, but offers a different version of his surname: "Some say the name Musick is a German name, others Dutch and still others claim it is Welsh. There is also a question in regard to Musick being an adopted name. A very familiar legend is the story of a boy picked up from a shipwreck by a German boat and being so fond of music that he was given the surname Musick with the German spelling" (Jones and Haslam 201).

Some of Peter Musick's descendants settled in the China Point area of PEI and lived with the Mi'Kmaq, where a branch of Milton's family on his father's side, the Faircloughs, had a farm. Mary Musick married Robert Fairclough, and one of their seven children was Mary Fairclough (1868-1948), Milton's paternal grandmother. Milton claimed Mi'Kmaq ancestry through the China Point connection of the Mi'Kmaq, Musicks, and Faircloughs. And once, in his need to identify with peoples who have struggled against political, economic, and racial oppression, he asserted, "There's some Acadian in me, you know" (Meyer 127).

"There wasn't anything exciting about the Acorn side of the family," says Mary Hooper,[6] and David refers to the Acorns as "a bunch of non-entities," while Garth adds that "Milton's father was just ordinary people." Presumably, they refer to the Acorns after Matthias Eichorn, John Acorn, and Peter Musick. But the generations between them and Milton were not entirely commonplace.

Charles Acorn (1841-1907), John's grandson and Milton's great-grandfather, married Caroline Sabine (1842-1917) on 5 August 1867. Caroline's mother was Martha Jago, the first woman preacher on PEI.

"She used to spout and harangue on the street corners. She caused no end of trouble. She'd go into the schools from time to time, just pick a school at random and go in and deliver a sermon. 'Go preachers' they were called at the time" (D. Hooper). Martha Jago arrived on PEI in 1828 from Plymouth, England. She was a member of the Brienites sect. This is how an Island reporter in 1829 described her: "Among the marvels of the week, one not the least remarkable is the advent of a Female Preacher, who has been holding forth to crowded and we have reason to think, admiring audiences.... Her countenance had nothing in it peculiarly intellectual, neither could it be said to be devoid of expression.... She mounted the pulpit with the greatest composure and without betraying the least appearance of embarrassment, gave out the hymn" (*P.E.I. Register*). It is no stretch of the imagination to see the spirit of Martha Jago, his great-great grandmother, resurrected in Milton Acorn, another kind of preacher, who often held forth without embarrassment.

Gilbert Chester Acorn (c. 1869-1948), Milton's paternal grandfather, "worked for people minding stores" (D. Hooper). Chester's career as a storekeeper took him to several Island communities and to Sydney, Cape Breton. In *McAlpine's Prince Edward Island Directory, 1900* there is a listing for "Acorn G.C., mgr. Singer Mfg. Co." in Charlottetown. In the 1909 *McAlpine's* he is listed as a clerk. But in *Balingall's Directory of Prince Edward Island, 1914* there is "Acorn, Chester, Vice-Pres. Maritime Fox Exchange." The silver fox fur industry was significant on PEI, and Chester became a partner in a fox ranch. While Chester was selling shares in Halifax, his partners back home failed to tell him that the mother fox had eaten her pups. Chester gave back the investors' money and, as a result, had a falling out with his partners. This "non-entity" was also a member of the 1894 Crescents Rugby team and served as a quartermaster sergeant overseas during the First World War.

Mary Fairclough (1868-1948), whom Chester married in 1895, was, according to David Hooper, "a very gentle, kind woman, almost revered. That's where the family's psychic ability comes from, the ability to communicate with one another through psychic means. Prescience, the ability to see what's coming before through dreams, that's what they claimed." Mary Hooper says that her father "told of Grandmother Fairclough coming to him in dreams to warn him of oncoming danger, such as Milton smothering with diapers that he'd wrapped around his head." In the 1970s Acorn claimed that he was psychic, and toward the end of his life, several of his friends complained that Acorn was becoming "mystical." Any psychic or mystical proclivities in the poet had their family antecedents. Mary Fairclough was also a devoted follower of the Church of England, and helped solidify the Anglicanism on the Acorn side of Milton's background.

Among the Acorns, then, there were a German-American colonial soldier and prosperous landowner, a betrayed, disinherited orphan fleeing revolutionary radicalism who became an established Island miller and farmer, a cabin boy with a beautiful voice, the first woman preacher on PEI, a grandmother with psychic powers, and a storekeeper. This was a legacy rich enough for any writer mining his heritage. For a writer who would be proclaimed the People's Poet of Canada, the "storekeeper" legacy is as intriguing as Peter Musick; curiously, however, Acorn would absorb neither that part of his ancestry nor the occupations of his parents into his poetic perspective.

Robert Fairclough Acorn, Milton's father, was born in Charlottetown in 1896, and attended West Kent and St. Peter's Cathedral schools. Robert served as a signaller in the local militia before the outbreak of the First World War. His unit, the No. 3 Battery, 4th Canadian Garrison Regiment of Artillery, sailed from Charlottetown on 5 August 1914, for Canso, Nova Scotia, where he was posted for 13 months, guarding the Commercial Cable Company's underwater cable station at Hazel Hill. When the unit was disbanded, he re-enlisted for overseas duty in the 105th Canadian Infantry Battalion, and sailed as a corporal from Halifax to Liverpool in July 1916. He was promoted to sergeant in November of that year. That same month, however, Robert requested a drop in rank to private so that he could join one of the units being ordered to the front. He was assigned to the "Black Watch," the 13th Canadian Infantry Battalion, Royal Highlanders of Canada, and was stationed in Belgium, France, and Germany until the war ended. Along with all campaigners in France, he received the British War Medal and Victory Medal.

Robert Acorn was injured at the front, and suffered from the trauma after the war. "Shell shock," David says. "Robert Sr. was under fire a long time at Vimy Ridge and Passchendaele. And gas." Mary says, "He spent a lot of time in the trenches. He said he saw somebody split right in two next to him. He never got a scratch. But he was shell-shocked. When he came back from the war, every time a car backfired he would be down on his face and he would be screaming at night. Sometimes he would get talking about the war and would just get white. Just the

Captain Robert Acorn, Sr., leading his troops in Charlottetown during the Second World War.

odd time he'd tell a story. Very gruesome. He couldn't stand to talk about it that much."

But Robert's memories of the First World War did not prevent him from joining the 17th (Reserve) Armoured Regiment as a lieutenant during the Second World War. He was promoted to captain in command of the Reconnaissance Squadron, with troops stationed in Charlottetown and Summerside, and later in command of Charlottetown's "A" squadron. Stanley Bryant, Milton's uncle, was his lieutenant, and Garth Hooper served under him. Upon retirement he was promoted to major.

The battlefields of Europe may have had another, long-delayed effect on Robert: "The alcohol problem was always attributed to this. During the Second War his drinking problem was quite bad. He did not drink when he came back from the First War, at least that's what the family said" (D. Hooper). Robert's "drinking problem" sheds more light on Milton's abuse of alcohol during the 1960s and 1970s. Robert Jr. remembers that his father's "drinking was noticeable or serious for only about four to five years. I was about 13 and a boy scout, and my father was a scoutmaster. I had that problem with the other boys of my father being the scoutmaster, and now I had the problem of his being drunk. Dad got drunk the first time he drank. He was in the squadron, around men who were drinking. A padre offered him a drink and he at first refused. 'Aren't you the good boy,' said the padre. So he went out and got drunk. He got sick every time he drank. But he never staggered around. He always wore a suit and tie and did his job well."

The drinking began in 1940 or 1941 and ended abruptly in 1953. "He went cold turkey," says Robert, and Mary adds that "he never drank again for the rest of his life." Robert Sr. joined Alcoholics Anonymous, and a letter to one of his children beams with enthusiasm for the AA environment and his own sobriety. In an undated 1950s letter, Milton wrote to his mother, "Probably the AA has saved Dad." Milton was home, however, during most of the "four to five years" of serious drinking, and Robert Sr. was still drinking after the war when Milton lived with his parents and argued strenuously about politics and economics with his father. There is a distinct possibility that Robert Sr.'s alcoholism contributed to the tension, anger, and disapproval that developed during this period between father and son—a wounded relationship that, understandably, did not begin to heal until several years after Robert Sr. stopped drinking. As well, his father's alcoholism was quite possibly a risk factor underlying Milton's own self-destructive drinking and psychological distress in later years.

As a young man Robert Sr. had had ambitions of becoming an Anglican priest. "The war and consequences put an end to that. He didn't have the means or the nerves," says Mary. "I was always proud that my father worked for the government. Mother never belittled his work, but felt sad for him that he did not fulfil his dream."

After the war Robert was hired in the Charlottetown office of what was then the Inland Revenue Department, which united in 1922 with the Customs Branches to form Customs and Excise, which, in turn, was blended in 1927 into the Department of National Revenue, Customs and Excise. He began his 38-year career in the Charlottetown office of Customs and Excise as an examiner, then worked as a computing clerk for over two decades. "Dad was considered an expert as far as customs regulations were concerned," says Robert Jr. "He was proud of his job and so was mother. Anytime I visited him at the office he was cheerful and engrossed in his work." At home, he engaged some of the intellectual energy that might have been employed in the priesthood.

"Milton's father was a voracious reader," says David. "If he read a book once he could pretty well spill it back to you. Very intelligent. He could compose something and say it in his head, but not put it on paper. At work he could fill out forms: German descent would take over." Mary, however, remembers reading a paper her father wrote on his family history, and that it was well written. His difficulties were with civil service exams: he mastered the material but had trouble committing it to paper. Milton recalled that "My Dad was a real storyteller. Truth and fantasy. He would talk about his experiences in the war and all of a sudden would wander off into complete fantasy. Yet he was afraid that *my* imagination would lead me to madness" (quoted in Meyer and O'Riordan 128).

In 1947 Robert Sr. became a cashier at Customs and Excise. He was promoted in 1949 to supervisor in charge of Excise, and held that position until his retirement in 1958. After his retirement he worked as a commissionaire in various Charlottetown locations until ill-health made work impossible. He died in 1968.

The maternal side of Milton Acorn's family, the Carbonells, rivals the Acorn side for colourful characters: an English remittance man, who was a political dissident and cultured, globe-trotting entrepreneur; an Island sea captain of Scottish descent; and a raconteurial grandmother.

Captain Neil MacDougall (c. 1846-1914), the master mariner immortalized in Milton's 1982 sonnet sequence, *Captain Neal MacDougal & the Naked Goddess*, spent his early years in Belle River, a community east of Charlottetown. His family was involved in the shipping business, and Neil MacDougall later became a mariner, shipowner, and merchant. He was the sole owner of two schooners, the *Edwin A. Grozier*, built in 1862 and condemned and broken up in 1915, and the *Elizabeth*, named after his wife and built in 1875 and broken up in 1896 (*P.E.I. Registry of Ships*). In one of Acorn's finest short poems, "The Schooner," his skill with the descriptive lyric complements his subject: the poem's smooth and sharp-edged strokes, taut monosyllabic lines alternating with cresting phrases, bring to life the vessel and craftsmanship which the shipping trade relied on:

> Keen the tools, keen the eyes,
> white the thought of the schooner
> lined on a draughting board,
> fine the stone that ground the fine blade
> and skills, the many fingers
> that stroked and touched it surely
> till, intricate delicate strong
> it leans poised in the wind:

> The wind that has its own ways,
> pushing eddying rippling invisible
> in light or darkness;
> now no engineer or engine
> can guide you but
> only the delicacy of touch against touch
> underneath the breathing heaven.
> (*Selected* 33)

Celebrating the romance of the schooners, shipwrights, sea captains, and sea trade, Acorn preferred to view this ancestor not as a merchant capitalist, but as a master mariner entrusted with the people's cargo.

In 1873 MacDougall married Elizabeth Stewart, a friend's daughter, who Helen Acorn claimed was descended from royalty. The captain was 10 years older than Elizabeth. According to David, Neil MacDougall's father and Elizabeth's father joined in the locally famous upheaval known as the Belfast Riot of 1847. Of that disturbance, historian Andrew Robb writes, "Divisions between ambitious local leaders and absentee landlords, between Protestant and Catholic, between Scots and Irish, ran very deep. It was not uncommon for these tensions to surface in violent fashion. Electoral riots were endemic in a deeply divided society where open voting and district by district polling was the rule. The Belfast Riots of 1847 are merely the best known of these affairs: an admixture of ethnic, religious, and political tensions in the context of the movement for responsible government, the Belfast violence took several lives and left scores wounded" (Robb 74-75). Another Island historian, H.T. Holman, takes a more circumspect approach to these riots, downplaying the occurrence of violent strife in Island history: "If it is difficult to explain just what happened at the Belfast riot it is even more difficult to explain why. Yes, we know that there were Scots and Irish, and Catholics and Protestants, and landlords and tenants, and Tories and reformers, but so were there at almost any election at that time in the colony. Why should these factors have combined at Pinette Mills on 1 March 1847 to cause this bloody era in the otherwise relatively peaceful history of the colony?" (7).

Robb's version would have been more appealing to Acorn, who nurtured and promoted his own view of a passionate, politicized, and sometimes turbulent legacy in his Island heritage. Along with his celebration of "the spirit of the dreamlike Island landscape" (*The Island Means Minago* 64), Acorn maintained that he came "from an Island to which I've often returned / Looking for peace, and usually found strife" (*The Island Means Minago* 14). He was more than willing to acknowledge, and perhaps exaggerate at times, the turmoil in the "Garden of the Gulf," and to connect himself with tales of struggle as well as maritime lore and pastoral beauty.

Acorn recreated Grandfather MacDougall in "Daddy," a poem published seven years before the *Captain Neal MacDougal* sonnets:

> "Daddy" in our family means just one man;
> Six generations ago, since two have followed me.
> On other lines we trace our ancestry
> Farther back, but "Daddy"
> Seems to start with himself, like Adam.
> * * * * *
> He went to sea as a carpenter,
> Became the master of his own schooner
> And for a while owned a little fleet
> All of which was lost in one storm;
> Begged bought or borrowed another schooner
> To sail safely the rest of his life.
>
> When winter came and ice
> Floated and ground, crashed back and forth across
>   the Gulf
> He'd sail his swift lateen to the Caribbean
> Leaving supplies and one instruction
> "NEVER TURN AN INDIAN FROM YOUR DOOR..."
> Which Great-Grandmother interpreted
> As he would've, getting down to situations
> : — "Never turn ANYONE from your door..."
> When Spring came our folks were always poor.
>
> Describing wicked men is easy...
> In good men you've got to look for a flaw; otherwise
> It's painting a picture without shadows.
> Daddy didn't drink, smoked sparely,
> Didn't save his love, only his money;
> Spoke with such a clear modulation
> He could be heard from poopdeck to prow, masthead to
>   wheel.

Only a hurricane could make him yell;
In short was perfect—except one thing:
At visiting time he'd sometimes climb the roof,
Use his cane to knock on the door
To say in a voice so polite it was sinister
"Would ye be the kind of man to let me in?"
(*Selected* 164-65)

Here, Acorn mythologizes his grandfather, creating out of family lore and his own imaginative needs an iconic character with multiple value. "Daddy" allowed Acorn to identify with a maritime heritage and lineage he could reconstruct in vigorous and virtuous terms. "Daddy" is also one of the numerous portraits in Acorn's poetry, several of well-known historical figures (e.g., "For Mao and Others," "Lumumba Arrested," "One Day Kennedy Died and So Did the Birdman of Alcatraz"), and others of ordinary people, the unsung heroes of the working class. "Daddy" is also an addition to Canadian myth.

Much has been said about the dearth of myths and mythic figures in Canadian history. Canada, of course, benefits from the wealth of myths of its First Peoples. The dearth, then, refers to the Euro-Canadian legacy. This opinion that Canada has an insufficiency of mythic events and figures—an opinion which has been challenged in recent years—no doubt grew out of an awareness of European and Middle Eastern mythologies, contact with indigenous myths, and exposure to the mythic traditions of newer immigrants from Asia, Africa, and other regions.

Living next to the United States has also aggravated the Canadian sense of mythic inadequacy. The U.S. historically has seemed to generate myths much more energetically than Canada, and the gigantic American advertising-and-entertainment machine is a hyperkinetic corporate myth factory, glutting Canada and much of the world with its output.[7] During the resurgence of Canadian nationalism in the 1950s-80s, however, Canadian institutions—from broadcasting and the arts to sports, businesses, and governments—generated with much more vigour those psychosocial processes, commercial-political energies, and artistic motifs that transform history into myth, people into mythic figures.

Acorn was a prominent mythmaker of the 1960s-80s period. Some of his mythic figures are fellow workers, comrades in labour unions and poetry, war veterans, boarders in his favourite cheap hotels. One of his most important books, *The Island Means Minago*, which won the Governor-General's Award for poetry in 1975, includes a mythic-historical treatment of the nineteenth-century land struggle and tenants' revolt on PEI. Moreover, Acorn would become a mythic persona in Canadian literature—perhaps he himself was his greatest mythic creation. The mythic elements in his poetry and his own evolution into the People's Poet, though, were a far cry from the kind of mythologizing he condemns in President Kennedy: "the image-man, / his very soul wired / and tugged into shape / by advertisers, his words / so evidently sincere / and false" (*Selected* 123).

Jewinski writes that "Acorn often changed, altered, or exaggerated parts of his life and family history to impress upon his readers man's need to be socially and politically responsible and, therefore, to be politically self-conscious. At every opportunity, Milton Acorn dramatized his own life as an inescapable commitment to politics. By mythologizing his life, his family heritage, and his personal history, he hoped to counter public complacency" (21). Jewinski tends to glorify Acorn's "deep purpose": "Acorn deliberately entwined facts and fictions to give force to his vision of social justice and responsibility.... He wanted to reveal that his feeling of identification with the poor and the oppressed and the outcast was profound and sincere and 'natural' to the blood" (21). Much of what Jewinski says is true, but it also reduces Acorn's poetic and political mission to the kind of motivational purity and simplistic agency bestowed on public heroes in patriotic speeches. Moreover, mythologizing figures such as MacDougall serves other worthy purposes, for example, the enrichment of a community's identity, not only "social justice and responsibility."

When Jewinski turns to the "facts," he writes that "Acorn's 'conventional life' is, however, as interesting as his 'mythological one'.... His father was a ship's carpenter, and his mother, a homemaker.... The working-class background influenced much of his writing.... As a young man he managed only a grade 8 education" (22). Did Acorn tell people his father was a ship's carpenter? If so, was this only to impart a vision of social justice? Or was there also some embarrassment, anger, or longing concerning his civil servant father? Such questions are not intended to deflate the mythic stature of a figure such as Acorn. In fact, our mythic figures become more fascinating and impressive when we can see their accomplishments as outcomes of complex personal and social histories.

At the same time, when searching for the reliable facts of a life such as Milton Acorn's, and sorting through his autobiographical statements, it is wise to balance the political and cultural rationale for mythologizing with the observation of Island historian Edward MacDonald, curator of history at the PEI Museum and Heritage Foundation. He greatly admires Acorn's poetry, but notes that "if I were to say the whoppers that Acorn told, I'd just be lying, but because he is a poetic genius with mythic pretensions, he is 'mythologizing' or 'adjusting history'" (Letter). In other words, some of Acorn's misrepresentations may be viewed as self-serving prevarication: the image of a "working-class" poet from the Maritimes required a shipwright father rather than a civil servant with Customs and Excise.

As for the mythmaking in his poetry, Acorn was engaged in a process that owes a great deal to a writer's responsiveness to a society's needs, that is, to the requirement for myths that can reinforce, revitalize, and transform cultural values and identity. It would be easy to be critical of Milton's mythologizing and to find fault, for example, with his portrait of Captain MacDougall as another romantic archetype of maritime tradition. Yet there is value in the artistic reformulation of that archetype and tradition. The past is revitalized and ennobled by Acorn's vision of the schooner captain's life, and the present is enhanced by a laudable past (as viewed through the poet's eyes) where skill, courage, fortitude, canniness in the face of dishonourable adversaries, generosity, and other virtues mattered.

Moreover, the figure of the captain reestablishes the Island as a vital site in that historical nexus of commerce and culture that included the British Isles, the West Indies, and the Maritimes and the "Boston States." Acorn moves the Island out of its postcolonial marginalization and back into a more central place in history. The myth becomes transformative. In this regard, it is enlightening to view Acorn's mythopoetic writing as a project shared with writers in other postcolonial and marginalized regions, for instance, the Caribbean poet and historian, Edward Kamau Brathwaite, one of the most influential figures in Caribbean literature and culture. In an essay on Brathwaite, J. Michael Dash, a professor at the University of the West Indies, writes, "At this point Brathwaite the poet upstages Brathwaite the historian, in that he feels the need to go beyond the formal recorded history to a more open and speculative view of the New World experience. This is one way to avoid the knowledge that falsifies, to rediscover in myth a new, liberating sense of self and of possibilities in the Caribbean. When this intense moment of revelation is attained, the poet begins to see his community and landscape for the first time" (202).

Mytho-poetic renderings, indeed, often do not conform to historical evidence,[8] and the sea captain of Acorn's poetry differed substantially from his grandfather, the real Captain Neil MacDougall. After moving to Charlottetown, in his early married years Captain Neil was infrequently home. Even so, his wife Elizabeth gave birth to 13 children. Amazingly, she also pursued a career as a schoolteacher, which was unusual for a woman then. Acorn's poem says nothing about MacDougall's absences from home or Elizabeth's role in the family.

Nor does "Daddy" reveal that the captain fell into a desperate financial position in the early 1890s. According to a family tradition and Milton's own account, Captain Neil lost all his money when one or more of his ships (Milton later claimed it was his "fleet") went down in a storm. This tradition even suggests that the ship(s) should not have sailed, and hence that MacDougall was partly responsible for the destitution that followed—another element not included in Acorn's portrait of a nearly "perfect" ancestor. The *P.E.I. Registry of Ships*, however, provides no record of McDougall's ships being lost at sea. Other circumstances, then—perhaps related to the demolition of the *Elizabeth* in 1896—were responsible for his reduced financial prospects, and prompted him to forge the MacDougall-Carbonell connection. E.T. Carbonell was a moneyed friend of Captain Neil, who arranged a marriage between E.T. and one of his daughters, Catherine.

The Carbonells "came as Huguenots to England in the 1600s," says David Hooper. The Carbonell family home was in Croydon. "I suspect E.T. was tutored in private schools, given the family background and summer home in Wales." Carbonell's obituary in *Maple Leaf Magazine* states, "Deceased was a native of Wales." E.T. Carbonell had angered his father by taking a different political stand, most likely, that of a reformer with democratic socialist sympathies. "They made him leave [England]," Garth says. "He'd embarrassed the family. They gave him so much money and sent him overseas." In short, he was a remittance man.

Milton had his version of Carbonell's political difference: "My grandfather, Carbonell, was one of those who helped set up the first modern communist state in Paris, which lasted only a few months" (Barker et al. 171). Acorn later acknowledged that his grandfather's participation in the 1870 Paris Commune is unproved: "I've romanticized that a lot—can't find any basis for it, you know," but he insisted that E.T. "wrote a response to a very official version of Prince Edward Island's history. He contradicted as much of it as he could. The whole pamphlet has disappeared.... He was a man of mystery—erased from the history books. All his papers, that I went over as a young boy were on topics like 'Class Struggle and Equality,' 'Class Struggle and the Tourist Question'" (Meyer and O'Riordan 128).

Milton's maternal grandfather was, according to David, very learned and literary: "I have a few things he wrote, and they're quite well done. E.T. expounded his ideas like Milton, as far as I understand, and therefore probably never agreed with anybody for long. Very forceful in his opinions, and very certain as to the right way things should be done." David Hooper believes that Carbonell may have published a newspaper while in Paris, and there are suggestions that he briefly worked as an editor or publisher in the Maritimes.

Acorn wrote his poetic version of this grandfather, "E.T. Carbonell," late in life, and it is included in the unpublished manuscript, *The Bare-Eyed Birdwatcher* (c. 1981). Carbonell, he wrote, was "an English gentleman / Banished away for sundry offenses; / Sympathy for workers, other innocences." He "felt himself not inferior / To any worker in the matter of hands," yet he handled "cutlery with such elegance / That he made eating a sheer act of grace." In spite of Acorn's ideological and emotional rejection of the privileged élite, he was pleased to include an aristocratic strain, as well as proletarian affinities, in his ancestry.

Carbonell travelled extensively in Europe and America and "didn't stick at any one enterprise for a great length of time," says David. He lived in the United States for many years. In fact, two of his four wives were American. He was in Truro, Nova Scotia, in 1895, just before going to the Island.

Carbonell arrived in Charlottetown with a handsome monthly income. "He didn't have to work, but then things started to go out of the wallet. He used to get into different things, like raising foxes, but never worked any steady job. He was quite a character. A busy bee" (M. Hooper). "He was saved like Milton, he had a lifetime pension," says David, alluding to Milton's war-related disability pension. But Carbonell wasn't content to subsist on that income. According to David, the "busy bee" was engaged to an extent as a merchant and trader. E.T. brought ships in from the West Indies. He imported molasses and other goods. On signed documents he usually referred to himself as a publisher. For example, his shares in the Cape Breton Fish and Trading Company list him as a publisher for Arichat, Nova Scotia, in 1893. Unfortunately, the PEI business and residential directories

E.T. Carbonell, Milton's maternal grandfather, in the regalia of the Royal Arch Chapter of Free Masonry.

prior to 1909 contain no listing of a Carbonell. If he had been a prosperous merchant and trader in Charlottetown, he left no trace of his success. He first appears in *McAlpine's* 1909 directory as a "game inspector," and then in the 1914 *Ballinger's* as "retired" and living on one of Charlottetown's better streets. "Since he was from a well-to-do family," says David Hooper, "Milton's mother, Helen, was a bit aristocratic in the way she talked about her background." But E.T.'s income was shrinking around the time Helen reached adulthood, and she found their diminished financial situation difficult.

Of E.T.'s arranged marriage with his fourth wife, the much-younger Catherine (Kate) MacDougall (1878-1968), David says, "Her father was destitute and needed a place to live, and E.T. took a fancy to her. Kate's sweetheart and first love was, most likely, John MacInnis, a farmer in Glenwilliam, near Murray River on the eastern end of PEI." Kate dutifully married E.T., however, and had several children, including Helen.

Kate MacDougall was 16 in November 1895 when she married Carbonell. According to records in the PEI Archives, he was born in 1843, which would have made him 51 at the time of their marriage. Helen Acorn claimed he lied about his age and was sixty. "Papa," as Helen called E.T., was a kind but distant father and husband. David recalls the story "that when E.T. sat down to dinner nobody addressed him, especially the girls. He was quite old-fashioned that way, although in other ways he was quite progressive. Supposedly, he let women have more freedom than they were used to, but still had that trait of the dominant patriarch. When he went off to his business interest he wore his top hat. When he'd go out the front door, Kate would hang out the bedroom above and try to knock his hat off. She probably never loved him, but got along with him."

"There were many things about the Carbonell-MacDougall connection," says David, "that helped mold some of Milton's personality, along with some of the Acorns, too, of course. Very outspoken, very intelligent, perhaps a bit flighty in their pursuits. Perhaps never hammered down to anything that made them famous, but all kinds of potential."

Grandma Kate had "quite an influence" on the Acorn family, and certainly on young Milton Acorn. Part of that influence was the stories she told about the neighbourhood in the South End of Charlottetown adjacent to the harbour, where she was born and raised. She first lived in the captain's home on King Street until 1888 or 89, and then on Dorchester Street. After she married E.T., Captain MacDougall moved to Water Street. Robert Acorn Jr., speaking of Milton's attachment to this neighbourhood, says that "Milton's people, like Captain MacDougall, came from there. Grandma's stories came from Dorchester Street, so he could feel the vibes on Dorchester Street." As a

Grandmother Kate MacDougall Carbonell (left), with two neighbours and a frail, eight-year-old Milton.

young veteran discharged from the Second World War, Milton worked at the harbour, on the wharves and in the railroad yard nearby. Milton was living in an apartment on Dorchester Street, his final home, when he died.

E.T. Carbonell died in 1929, and Kate remarried in 1931. Her second husband was John MacInnis (1878-1968), the man who may have been her youthful sweetheart. She joined John at his farm in Glenwilliam. There, she raised chickens, cows, and horses. Milton's family spent parts of their summers at the farm. "We'd stay a couple of weeks. Milton wasn't there as often as Robert Jr. was. At the farm the girls could do what they liked but the boys had to work. Milton didn't work as hard as Robert" (M. Hooper). As for Kate's second husband, "I don't think any of us said two or three words to John, which was what we called him. He never said anything, stayed in the background" (D. Hooper).

Kate Carbonell, also known as Grandma Carbonell and Grandma MacInnis, was an exceptional storyteller, used her imagination extensively, and quite likely was a strong influence on young Milton, who shied away from farmwork, but who began practising storytelling with fervour at an early age. Kate's stories were often about old-time Charlottetown and the Belfast area. Kate could also sing in Gaelic and had a keen awareness of Gaelic tradition. She was not a reader, and relied heavily on memory and imagination—on the oral tradition. There were other ways she may have influenced Milton: she was "very outspoken. Would say whatever she thought, right to you, possibly to her regret later" (D. Hooper).

The matter of "psychic ability" appears, too, on the maternal side of Milton's family. His mother's "psychic ability has mainly been said to come down from the Stewart connection, that is, Neil MacDougall's wife, although Helen always added that E.T. Carbonell's mother, Sarah Mary Rohde [1813-71], had it too. Given that Scot and Welsh mix, the Celtic tradition of female powers shouldn't surprise anyone" (D. Hooper). Mary Hooper talks about the alleged "psychic ability" which Kate and Helen had in common: "Grandma Kate and my mother had dreams of disaster to come or warnings which prevented disaster. Mother always knew when someone in her family was going through a crisis, even when they were not near and did not tell her about it" (M. Hooper).

When David Hooper remarks that "Milton's mother was the driving force in her family," one can imagine her drawing her forcefulness from Kate's example. For instance, Kate looked out for her family by "saving part of the grocery money to beat old Carbonell when he came up short" (R. Acorn). E.T. "showered her with new gadgets, which she never used and kept giving away as gifts to others" (M. Hooper). When her own children were young, Kate was more interested in her sons than in Helen, made excuses for their "discrepancies," and had little time for her daughter. It was Helen, however, to whom Kate turned when she was older. When Kate and John left the farm and returned to Charlottetown they lived with Helen.

Helen Carbonell was born in 1900. She married Robert F. Acorn in August 1922. Helen was the closest person to Milton throughout his life—a devoted mother, mentor, and amanuensis, friend, fan, correspondent and, finally, housemate. She passed away at the age of 84, only two years before her son.

Helen Acorn became one of Canada's most famous literary mothers because of the images shaped in Acorn's best-known poem, "I've Tasted My Blood":

> But my mother's look
> was a field of brown oats, soft-bearded;
> her voice rain and air rich with warm lilacs:
> and I loved her too much to like
> how she dragged her days like a sled over gravel.
> (*I've Tasted My Blood* 1)

Proud and admiring as Helen was of his poems, she was not entirely thrilled by the last line in the passage above, nor by certain lines in "Poem," which also appeared in the famous 1969 collection *I've Tasted My Blood*:

> My mother goes in slippers
> and her weight thumps the floor,
> but when I think of her I think of one smile
> when she was young
>
> and to me was a goddess of green age
> tho now I remember her young
> with hair red as a blossom.
>
> I remember the whole room full of that smile
> and myself scampering across the edges.
>
> Now she lives on cigarettes and wine,
> goes from potted plant to flower,
> knowing the time and manner
> of each one's tending. (30)

In the 1984 NFB film about Milton Acorn directed by Island filmmaker Kent Martin, *In Love and Anger: Milton Acorn—Poet*, Helen said she liked "Poem," "All but the last four lines, which I wish he would change. Some people were kind enough when they quoted it to put dots at the last four lines." Helen was a non-drinker most of her life, and was distressed by her husband's drinking during the 1940s. She grew fond of wine only in her later years.

In the fashion of many girls and young women early in this century, Helen's thick red hair flowed to her waist. Often she "dry-cleaned" it with cornstarch and oats because it took too long to wash and dry, especially during the winter. She proudly told her children how she once represented the sun in a Dominion Day parade, "her red hair flowing around her" (M. Hooper "Red Light!"). Also in the manner of her era, she cut her hair short just after she married. "The red hair ended up in a box, preceding my mother by 62 years. Dad told her that he wouldn't marry her if she cut her hair. So she cut it! I always had the feeling that she was the one that lost" ("Red Light!").

With each of her five pregnancies, Helen hoped for a red-haired child, but with no success. "My earliest memory of my mother's red hair was at Rocky Point. Mother fell and sprained her ankle. I can see in my mind a very large woman bravely and determinedly tracking her way to the boat, her short red hair shining golden in the sun. This could have been the fall that started the labour for her fifth child—her last chance to have a redhead. The doctor told her that she dare not even have this one. This time she had a beautiful blond baby girl, and so gave up the idea of having a redheaded child. She now pinned her hopes on her grandchild" ("Red Light!").

Milton's bittersweet poem, "Letter to My Redheaded Son," suggests that his mother's wish was granted in her fourth grandson (the Hoopers had three boys and one girl first) or more likely—given that none of Helen's other grandchildren or great-grandchildren has red hair—that Milton absorbed her longing for this emblem. For Helen, it was the red hair of her youth. For Milton, red hair was an emblem of his mother, his Scots ancestry, and his fiery passion—and, no doubt, the red of rebellion, of workers' blood, of the people's revolution and communism. And there is Milton's declaration that "I am from what you might call a red Tory breed" (MacFarlane 4). In a profoundly metaphorical sense, Helen Acorn's first-born was a "redhead" in passion, temper, and ideology. And this may be why Island artist Brian Burke, in one of his two astonishing portrait-visions of the poet, painted Milton with, as Mary writes, "the wildest red hair I had ever seen. Mother finally gets her wish!" ("Red Light!").

Helen Carbonell Acorn, Milton's mother, just before she married and cut her red hair short.

Before her marriage and the birth of her five children, Helen trained as a stenographer and bookkeeper, and worked for the federal Department of the Marine.9 "She was quite brilliant at her work," says Mary. "Garth and I used to laugh at her when she said she made 99 and 9/10ths in her class exams. And she said the only reason she lost that tenth was because her typed page went too far down. She was paid as much or more than the men in the office, and in those days they didn't do that. Some of the male employees were really wild when someone got wind of it."

In the 1940s, Helen's doctor advised her not to do any more housework, so she went back to work in Charlottetown as a stenographer and bookkeeper with Custodian Trust Company, a subsidiary of Royal Trust, and then she worked with Hughes Insurance. In the 1950s she ran a successful business out of her house for about ten years. "I used to go in the summertime into Helen's—Grandma Acorn's—place, and help her with her mimeographing," says David. "I used to turn the Gestetner for her and stamp envelopes. Kate, her mother, always called her 'the devil's printer.' That gives you an idea of the interplay between mother and daughter. Helen used to do all this work for these men around town out of her home. She had quite a business."

Helen was a creative person, Mary recalls, and quite an entertainer. She acted in plays and read humorous poems and dialogues. "We used to get so embarrassed when she got up on stage doing these things, but people really enjoyed them. She could keep a roomful of people entertained for hours. She had a regime of stories which she told over and over again.... Every time she would entertain new company with old stories we would say to ourselves, 'Oh no! Not again!'" ("Memoirs").

Milton owed no small debt to Helen's imagination, her stories, and her expressive vitality, as well as to her care and devotion. Many years later, as a celebrated writer, he told interviewers that he inherited his bardic calling from a multi-branched ancestry, including a Loyalist rebel, the Welshman Carbonell, a Mi'Kmaq princess, a Scottish-Canadian sea captain, Grandma Kate, and even the spirit of an Acadian fisherman. But it was his mother, Helen, more than those ancestral and mythologized figures, who endowed him with the legacy he transformed into his poetic voice, into the language and vision of his poems.

III

I'VE TASTED MY BLOOD

> To be born on an island's to be sure
> You are native with a habitat.
> Growing up on one's good training
> For living in a country, on a planet.
> — "I, Milton Acorn"

AS A SMALL CHILD Milton Acorn—or "Mickey" as he was called by his brother and sisters—was often sick. Mary describes him as "very delicate. He almost looked like a starving child. He didn't seem to gain weight at all. He was just skin and bones." For his first 15 years, Helen worried about his weight and health. "He was a very delicate child until he was fourteen," she says in Kent Martin's film. "That's when he first showed the signs of health coming back.... He was a healthy enough baby ... and then when he was three he just faded away into a shadow, practically."

For a long time Helen's favourite remedy was to feed Milton figs. "We were often told that Milton's drugs cost us more than our groceries," writes Mary. "There was need for extra economy in spite of the fact that our father worked for the government. Even though Mother found it necessary to cut corners, we were never deprived of the proper vitamins. Oranges are something we didn't see very many of, but we almost swam in tomato soup. Mother was a self-taught nutritionist" ("Memoirs"). Milton later gave his mother the nickname "The Little Red Hen," who made sure her family had the necessities of life.

The fig remedy, however, did not work miracles. Eventually, their doctor convinced Helen to forget about Milton's table manners, and to let him eat in whatever way would get food into his stomach. This wasn't easy in a family where, Mary observes, the "parents were very particular about how we handled a knife and fork. We could either use the English method (Mother's way) or the Canadian method (Dad's way). We ended up with a mixture of the two. Dr. Seaman told Mother, 'Just make sure that he gets the food to his mouth'" ("My Brother Milton").

Milton's earliest literary endeavour was deconstructive. A lot of Grandfather Carbonell's books were classics and English novels such as *Lorna Doone*. Before Milton could read the books he tore them up. Helen remembered him "tearing up these books and making men out of them, men in his army or something. Then he finally decided he should read them. He read all that remained" (Martin *In Love and Anger*). Milton enjoyed books about King Arthur and the Round Table, but his biggest interest as he grew older, according to Robert Jr., was science fiction, for instance, the Buck Rogers tales. Milton's devotion to literature began at an early age, nurtured by Carbonell's library, Grandma Kate's storytelling, and Helen's recitations and skits.

Mary says, "We had a wonderful childhood. An awful lot of time was spent at the beach." During most of Milton's childhood the family lived close enough to the shore in Charlottetown that they could easily walk to the beach. Before that, when Milton and then Mary were born, Helen and Robert lived downtown at 102 Fitzroy Street, in a triplex tenement next to Garden City Dairy. The Acorns moved to Park Terrace, a quiet lane in Brighton, Charlottetown's old wealth neighbourhood, where Robert Jr. was born in 1927. In their rented house, they were a few minutes' walk from the harbour and one block from Victoria Park, the city's exquisite preserve of woods, picnic grounds, and playing fields.

In 1927-28, the Acorn family was back at 102 Fitzroy Street. The Acorns then rented a house from 1929 to 1933 at 103 North River Road, a main boulevard leading from Victoria Park, through the comfortable homes of the élite interspersed with more modest dwellings—such as the Acorns' rented residence next door to Lt.-Governor Charles Dalton's home—and then into the country, the farms which long since have vanished under urban development. During those years, Mary says, "Mother used to dress us up every day and take us down to the North River to swim. We'd take our lunch and Dad would come out after work and have lunch with us. We had a lovely, free childhood."

Milton's childhood was not entirely lovely nor his teenage years free of distress. But his earliest years were spent in a close-knit family which encouraged reading, singing, and outings in the countryside.

During 1933-36 the Acorns lived further out North River Road, in the farmland outside Charlottetown. Their home was next to Cudmore's Fur Farm. This is now a residential area of the city. Then, it provided Milton with three crucial years—age 10 to 13—of rural life. The city was not far away, but, as Mary writes in a memoir, the Acorns had traded their indoor plumbing for "an outdoor two-holer, a creaking cantankerous pump in the back porch, a ten-gallon water tank attached to the side of the wood stove with a large steaming kettle on top.... Bath time was my first experience of the assembly line. Mother washed and Dad dried.... This might seem like a step down the ladder to many, but to us children the place was a beautiful all-around pleasure resort. We had wonderful snowbanks in the winter for skiing and tumbling on, and a skating pond across the road. Inkerman Shore on the river [North River, which flows into Charlottetown Harbour] was just a couple child leaps away. This provided marvellous swimming, cliff-climbing, clam-digging, and shell-hunting all summer long" ("The Assembly Line"). Milton had nothing but gratitude, and no regrets, regarding this upbringing. But in the Kent Martin film he does claim that "for a person destined to be a natural man, I picked a bad time to be born because nature was just going out of fashion. Most of my chums weren't the least bit interested."

Living in Montreal in the mid- and late-1950s, Milton composed his most familiar and beloved poem about PEI, "The Island":

> Since I'm Island-born home's as precise
> as if a mumbly old carpenter,
> shoulder-straps crossed wrong,
> laid it out,
> refigured to the last three-eighths of shingle.
>
> Nowhere that plough-cut worms
> heal themselves in red loam;
> spruces squat, skirts in sand;
> or the stones of a river rattle its dark
> tunnel under the elms,
> is there a spot not measured by hands;
> no direction I couldn't walk
> to the wave-lined edge of home.

> In the fanged jaws of the Gulf,
> a red tongue.
> Indians say a musical God
> took up His brush and painted it;
> named it, in His own language,
> "The Island."
>
> (*Selected* 52)

This poem is informed by Acorn's work as a carpenter, and metaphorically bonds the Island's agrarian life with a skilled trade common to farmers, fishermen, the shipping trade, and the construction industry in rural and urban areas. It alludes to the fact that PEI truly is "the garden of the gulf," the only Canadian province where every "spot" of land is layered in human history. "The Island" also shows that years before the renewal of interest in aboriginal spiritual traditions and before his own gesture of respect for the First Peoples in *The Island Means Minago*, Acorn revered the Island's Mi'Kmaq heritage. It is also worth noting that this poem's popularity on the Island results not only from what it lyrically says and imagistically shows, but also from what it does not say: the hard, painful truths found in a poem such as "I've Tasted My Blood," or the social realism and political radicalism of "I, Milton Acorn." "The Island" is an exquisite poem of pastoral beauty and serenity.

"The Island" was written well before Milton's various trips back to PEI in the 1960s and 1970s, during which he made day-trips through the farmlands and woodlots "measured by human hands" to his favourite beaches, and sometimes rented a cottage near the sea for two or three weeks. "The Island," then, is a distilled memory of the Island he knew as a child and young man.

"The Island" is also a prime example of what has been called the "poetics of place," a "sense of place," and the "literature of the home place." In a poetics of place, the poet's home provides, to quote again from Gwendolyn Davies, a symbol and image of "cultural continuity and psychological identification" (194). It also offers a site for communal and individual transformation. The home place becomes more than a setting. It is the context for personal and social realization; even more, the context itself—the home place—is inextricable from the poet and the poet's investigations of self and society. The poetics of place is found prominently, for instance, in Robert Kroetsch's long poems out of the Canadian prairies, *Seed Catalogue*, *The Ledger*, and *Stone Hammer Poems*; Daphne Marlatt's *Steveston*; and Ralph

Gustafson's treatment of Quebec's Eastern Townships. It is also found, distinctively, in Acorn's Island poems of the 1950s and 1960s and in his 1975 volume, *The Island Means Minago*.

Anne Compton, a Maritimes poetry scholar, writes that "Acorn's early Imagist Island poetry rises naturally from a landscape ... intricately and minutely patterned" (1). Stressing the poetics implied by "The Island," Compton notes that "Acorn's Imagistic precision is directly and self-referentially linked to Island landscape.... The precision of home demands an exactitude in language" (2). Yet, as Compton explains, his early Island poems are not mere exercises in Imagist representation: "Everywhere his Island landscape bears 'reminiscences' of the lives lived there, the labour accomplished" (13); "Acorn's early poetry is a record not of things but of the apprehension of the sensation of things.... He was so permeable to the sights and sounds of his place, he was in effect the province of their expression: he translated the elements and physical attributes of place into language" (5).

Acorn's desire to reinvent his home place in language and to locate his realized self in that context was stimulated, according to Mary, during family outings, including picnics and holidays in rented cottages at Rocky Point across Charlottetown Harbour. "We used to spend the day swimming and lazing on the beach," writes Mary. "We usually closed the day singing as a group. All the uncles, aunts, and cousins were there with us. I didn't realize then that most families didn't do this sort of thing. Perhaps this is where Milton first learned the freedom of expression which later showed in his poetry" ("My Brother Milton").

Mary remembers another event that reveals the family's creative freedom and atmosphere. Living near the beach, the Acorn children used to play with the wet clay. "I went up to visit my cousins one time in the North End and I introduced them to pottery clay, and I got my cousin to bring hers home with her. Her mother made us take it right back to the shore where they lived and dump it. But we were allowed to do things like that. We were very free. I think that is one of the reasons Milton was so creative. He realized other parents didn't allow their children to do things we did."

Robert and Helen were strict disciplinarians when it came to the values they felt were important. Mary says, for instance, "My dad was so honest that he cracked, we used to say. Anything to do with morals, they were both very strict about." Mary was a very timid child. When she was about thirteen, she took a bottle back to the store to get a refund of two cents. But the store wouldn't give her the money. When

Mary returned home, her mother sent her back to the store to demand the refund. "She made us do things that she thought were important. But they didn't make us do things that other people thought were important."

Encouraging creativity in her oldest child, the sickly one she nurtured closely for years, was exceedingly important to Helen. And Milton responded in literary ways: a hunger for all kinds of books, an obsession with telling stories at home, an inability to suppress his imagination in order to be socially acceptable at school and on the street, and, of course, writing.

"I can't remember Milton being a little boy. He was a little old man, that is until he became a poet, then he was a little boy," Mary wrote in "My Brother Milton." She relates one of their sister Katherine's memories:

There was mother sitting in front of the bay window in our living room, with the sun shining through her beautiful red hair. She was holding this tiny premature baby. My sister Helen. The rest of us were peeking from behind doors and corners at this wonder. Milton was a little more curious than the rest of us, so he edged a little closer. Mother said, 'Come on Milton, come and see the new baby.' Milton came up to mother's knee and looked at the baby in astonishment. 'Mother! Did God make that baby?' 'Yes Dear,' said Mother. 'Well,' said Milton, 'He sure must have run out of skin.' There was Milton always ready with an answer, be it right or wrong.

A note from his kindergarten teacher informed his mother that she had a genius on her hands. There were no formal arrangements for "gifted" children in those days, and there is no further evidence of teachers recognizing exceptional intelligence or imagination in Milton Acorn.

He attended Spring Park School through eighth grade. His only close friend apart from his family during these earlier school years was Bill Hine, the son of C.F. Hine, a vice-principal and principal at West Kent School, where Acorn attended grades 9 and 10. Acorn and Bill Hine went skiing together, the only sport in which Acorn had success. "Milton felt badly that he never learned to skate," says Mary. "He lacked coordination." At West Kent he also made friends with Harold Dougan, whose tragic fate overseas during the Second World War contributed to Acorn's poetic response to the horror and injustice of war. Apart from these friendships, Acorn was a loner at school, and

Young Milton Acorn, about age twelve.

his academic career appears to have been undistinguished.[10] Chris Gudgeon, in his 1996 biography of Acorn, *Out of This World: The Natural History of Milton Acorn*, claims that "the bedridden boy ... missed a lot of school" and that "inside the classroom Mickey was disruptive" (29). Mary Hooper and Robert Jr. have no memory of Milton being troublesome at school. He missed more school than normal, but was not "bedridden." He did refuse to learn French and Latin, but this was hardly abnormal behaviour.

Charlottetown native Fred Pound, who attended West Kent the same years as Acorn, recalls that "Milton Acorn was a very odd child. He certainly would've been voted the kid most likely to get beaten up on the way home from school. He bore the brunt of an awful lot of teasing, and he was a loner." There is an all-purpose word favoured by Islanders for behaviour, fashions, movies, music, food, and other things that don't catch on or fit in with Island habits and tastes: "different" as in "that's different" and "he's different." Milton Acorn was different.

Not only was he scrawny, sickly, physically weak, and a loner, Acorn had a tendency to talk to himself. On the way to and from school he would make up stories, while kicking a can or swinging a stick, and neighbourhood kids would tease and torment him. Certain schoolmates, not appreciating that the future People's Poet of Canada was absorbed in his formative perceptions and early apprenticeship with language and narrative, often harassed or assaulted him after school, and there was one particular bully who preyed on him for several years. Acorn often fought back, though his size and weakness left him at a serious disadvantage.

He was, however, sometimes the author of his misfortune. There may have been occasions when Acorn verbally goaded other kids. "His mouth would get him into trouble," says Robert. Mary adds, "He felt so badly that he couldn't do some things other kids could do, such as skating, and that other kids bullied him." Mary remembers her mother saying that other kids started the fights, but Robert believes that he "brought a lot of it on himself." Milton did not, however, "mouth off some bigger kid, luring him into a fight" during family outings, as Gudgeon claims (33). Nor did he "stammer" (33). Robert remembers that his brother would often pause, saying "uh uh uh," when he was excited and speaking fast.

Acorn's newspaper route was another early experience that informed his poetic persona and political stance, as he explains in his essay, "I was a communist for my own damn satisfaction":

I'd got my papers and, being a studious young fellow, had made my first stop King's Square ... where I'd stretch myself with my rump on a patch of grass and my legs on a brown trodden place and started to read. I read like an antelope drinking at a desert hole.... One moment with my head down, gulping in the stuff of life, the next with my head up watching out for danger.

Danger approached. A boy, ragged and with half the week's history smeared over his face, was watching me from the sidewalk.
I looked up again when I felt his shadow, then bunched myself for a jump.

"Give me five cents," said rags.
"Why should I?" said me.
"Give me five cents," he said again....
"No," I said.

Little rags stuck his chin out fiercely at me and threatened: "I'll hit you."

At this point the conversation came to an end. I had sprung to my feet and hit him.

Limping and swaying under my load I can't confess I made myself a harmless curiosity by deciding not to hit anyone in the future. But I decided that when I grew up and became a man I'd be damn careful who I hit and why. (37-38)

In this story, as in so many, Acorn allegorizes his past experience in order to bring to the foreground those characteristics he wants readers to associate with Milton Acorn, working-class poet and judiciously truculent communist. The young Acorn had to learn to defend himself, including his "working-class" responsibility as a newspaper boy and his emergence as a "studious young fellow" investigating and "gulping" life. The working-class kid, however, is threatened by "rags," a desperate child of the poorest class. Defending himself against a threat from the impoverished lower class, the working-class Acorn resolves to be "careful" in his choice of enemies to defend himself against. The real enemy, according to the older Acorn, the oppressor responsible for the condition and behaviour of "rags," is the owner class, the capitalists, and other privileged people who exploit the working and lower classes. End the exploitation, and the newspaper boy would not have to hit a "rags" or come home with his clothes torn and nose bleeding.

Acorn also allegorized the fact that he suffered from frequent nosebleeds, which made self-defense more difficult and necessary, and which underlies the most famous image, metaphor, and line in his poetry. "He'd get into fights so easily," says Mary. "Somebody would always be at the door saying, 'Come and get Milton, he's in a pool of blood.'" His brother Robert remembers, "He had so many nose bleeds, just bleeding all the time, nothing but blood around our house. Mother said to Father, 'For heaven's sake, Bobby, get some gloves and teach that boy how to box!'" And of himself, Acorn writes:

> If this brain's over-tempered
> consider that the fire was want
> and the hammers were fists.
> I've tasted my blood too much
> to love what I was born to.
> (*Selected* 130)

When Island broadcaster and writer Helen MacDonald in a 1969 interview asked about the book and poem title *I've Tasted My Blood*, "What does it mean?," he replied with surprising, matter-of-fact restraint, "Means that in my youth I had a lot of nosebleeds."

The poem and the line, "I've Tasted My Blood," allude to and evoke much more than childhood fights, bullies, and nosebleeds. It is about surviving, defending and strengthening oneself, suffering and challenging oppression, upholding one's difference, honouring fallen comrades, and more. The line creates one of those exquisite moments in poetry that allows us to focus on vividly specific images that take us wherever we need to go in our own experience. These images and this discourse of suffering and resistance, tempering and temperament, were first forged on the streets during Acorn's youth.

Years later, much stronger and more imposing, he writes gratefully of those and other times in "I, Milton Acorn":

> The Island's small...Every opinion counts.
> I'm accustomed to fighting for them.
> Lord I thank Thee for the enemies
> Who even in childhood tempered me.
> (*Selected* 149)

Some who experienced Acorn's adult manner of discourse describe it as argumentative, hot-headed, feisty, pugnacious, ornery, intense. Some who did not enjoy their debates with Milton, including those who had a falling-out with him, have called him stubborn and belligerent. Others who happily sustained their long discussions with Acorn, and who cherished an ardent exchange of opinions with a man they regarded as uniquely gifted, remember his discourse as beautifully passionate, deeply informed, and intensely engaged. There are plenty of stories of Acorn's friendships—in left-wing political circles, in the writing world—ending in bitter arguments. There are also lasting friendships, such as the one with George Steiger, a long-time labour activist and socialist in Montreal, Toronto, and PEI: "In all those political debates in the fifties and sixties, and they could get nasty, sometimes with fights, Milton never got violent. He'd argue, sure, but you knew he'd never physically attack anyone over their opinions." And Reg Phelan, an Island farmer and close friend from 1968 until Acorn's death, says that "Milton was always so intense. Some people didn't know how to handle that. Yet if he respected you, if he thought you knew what you were talking about, he'd listen and talk with you for hours." But other accounts suggest that Acorn, when angry and feeling hurt or betrayed, could lash out physically as well as verbally.

One can only speculate to what extent the adult Milton Acorn, especially his poetry, politics, and disputatious relationships, was shaped and motivated by those childhood adversities resulting from his physical fragility, his reputation as a "very odd child," his isolation outside the family, his victimization as a neighbourhood scapegoat, and his need to fight back, nosebleeds and all. His sister Mary attributes his commitment to socialism and liberation movements largely to these childhood struggles: the oppressed kid grows up identifying with oppressed peoples and their struggles for survival, equality, dignity, and, above all, the strength to resist oppression and secure a just existence. This is a valuable insight as long as it does not ignore other sources of Acorn's political beliefs. It is safe, though, to say that these struggles were powerful elements in the development of the persona in "I've Tasted My Blood" and "I, Milton Acorn," and of the passionate or pugnacious man with whom so many people locked minds.

Acorn's poetic ability to thank his childhood enemies owed a great deal to the warm, supportive, and creative ambience of his home, where Milton was able both to develop and to be appreciated for the "difference" that made his life troublesome elsewhere. "He was always writing, always scribbling," says Mary. And with his mother, Helen, he took a wide variety of books home from the library and devoured them.

Anyone who knew Acorn later in life recalls that he was constantly writing: on napkins in restaurants and bars, in notebooks while visiting friends or sitting on park benches, on scraps of paper if nothing else was handy. Reg Phelan, who as a farmer is familiar with hard work and devotion, speaks of Acorn as "an intensely disciplined writer." One could also say that he was compelled from within or "called" to the craft by whatever circumstances breed a poet. It is possible, now, to think of PEI as the land of Lucy Maud Montgomery and the People's Poet, as if it were a hotbed or paradise of literary creation. But for a long time it was not. Montgomery was no longer an Island resident during Acorn's youth, and there was no literary community to encourage a boy who was "always scribbling" or a young man who wanted to write and publish literature. If anything, the desire to be a writer was one more proof of how "odd" he was. It is all the more remarkable—and a tribute to his family—that his need to write emerged and was sustained.

Another manifestation of Acorn's literary calling was his need to tell stories to his family, primarily to his younger brother Robert. "He started out telling Katherine stories. I don't know whether she put up a fight, but one day when I was five he grabbed me by the scruff of the neck and said, 'You're it from now on.' He threw me on the bed and asked, 'What story do you want me to tell?' I wanted The Lone Ranger and Ghost of the Spanish Main. He'd push Doc Savage, Buck Rogers, and Tarzan. But I could choose. I think I learned storytelling from him. It was the days of those old serials, and he knew how to stop at the exciting points. He could start right where he'd left off."

Milton also made himself the commander of his younger siblings during playtime. "He would be right in the middle of everything and he'd order us around, sort of like his little army. He was the ringleader" (R. Acorn). The storytelling and ringleading traits he displayed with his younger siblings extended to other younger children in his neighbourhood. When in late 1936 or early 1937 the Acorns moved back to the triplex on Fitzroy Street, Milton organized his siblings and other younger kids in a corps of "cadets," using wooden laths from cellar walls for rifles and swords. He marched his "cadets" around in imitation of the real cadets and militia.

The younger kids knew Milton was a loner in his own age group. Some of them thought he had fallen out of his highchair when he was young, and that was why he was "different." Even so, they looked up to him. And there was his prowess as a storyteller, perhaps enhanced by his peculiarity. The tenement cellar was divided in three by partitions the kids could climb over. They gathered in the Acorns' cellar and Milton told them ghost stories. One was about the rocking chair in the

Acorns' attic, which would rock at night all by itself, back and forth, audible in the bedrooms below, until one night blood began to drip through the ceiling. His "cadets" were suitably scared and enthralled. When the family moved a year later to 219 Hillsboro Street, he continued to be a storyteller for the neighbourhood kids.

Milton was the favoured child when it came to writing. "I saw the support our mother gave him," says Robert. "She wouldn't even know I had any desire to be a writer. I always doubted my own writing because I thought I was being a copycat. So I'd stifle it at home because my brother was a writer." Robert did show some of his writing to Milton: "He said, 'It is good, I'm not kidding you.'" But Milton was Helen's promising young storyteller and writer, and Robert's primary role was as captive audience.

Milton also read avidly, and Helen encouraged his devotion to books and stories. Around age 14 or 15, his interest shifted from historical and epic adventures to science fiction, and he devoured issues of magazines such as *Astounding* and *Fantasy*. Gudgeon speculates that "Mickey had developed a fertile imagination, flights of fancy fuelled by his passion for pulp fiction magazines.... Science fiction appealed to him most of all, perhaps because it was essentially optimistic, the triumph of imagination and intellect over humanity's darker tendencies. This romantic outlook seems to go against the rough and cynical exterior Mickey was developing" (41). This seems based on Acorn's later account, in politicized hindsight, of why he fell in love with science fiction as a teenager. His brother and sister remember the fertile imagination and romantic outlook, but no "rough and cynical exterior" (R. Acorn) at that stage in his life. Rather, he was a "sensitive" and "shy" lad with frequent "flights of fancy" (M. Hooper).

He also began to read *Ring*, the premier boxing magazine. Referring to Acorn's keen interest in boxing reports, Gudgeon states, "Mickey lay awake longing for the day he would step into the ring as a professional boxer" (35). According to Mary and Robert, Milton had no desire to become a boxer. "He knew he had a soft nose," says Robert, who does remember Milton's fascination, for a time, with professional fighters. Milton would also tell stories about his own fights, and even make up cowboy stories for Robert: "Milton didn't like cowboy stories, but he knew I would, and he'd make himself the hero of cowboy fights." But that was as far as his imagination went with boxing.

Gudgeon suggests that Milton was also becoming acquainted with populist, working-class Maritime verse, and mentions Dawn Fraser, a populist labour poet of the 1920s and 1930s in Cape Breton: "It's unlikely—but not inconceivable—that Milton Acorn ever heard Dawn Fraser recite his verses. But there's no doubt that young Mickey would have come in contact with Fraser's kind of populist troubadour, and that his own earliest poetic yearnings were influenced not by the university-anointed literary greats, but by the voices and cadences of the oral tradition" (38). At present, however, there is no evidence that Milton had any such contact with "populist troubadour" or labour poetry in the 1930s. Robert states firmly, "He didn't read any poetry until well after the war. I don't think he read any poetry until 1950, until after he started writing poetry." As for poetic influences, Milton's anti-institutional stance as a poetic persona did not interfere with his devotion to the "literary greats." His poetic innovations clearly grew out of a strong traditionalist and formalist base. His exposure to the oral tradition, with its voices and cadences, was less likely from populist Maritime poetry than from his own family, including Grandma Kate Carbonell, and especially his mother, with her humorous verse recitals and skits.

Milton prospered from his relationship with his mother, but his connection with his father was not so congenial, even though it may have been one of those attachments that "tempered" him, and which prefigured his later testy relationships. "There was a lot of conflict between his father and Milton right from day one, because Robert Sr. and Milton were two different kinds of people. Milton, if his Dad told him to do something, he'd just say 'no,' and his Dad would get angry and there would be a shouting match. Robert Jr. would please his Dad by saying 'yes,' but do it in his own time. Milton had a lot of conflicts in that he would never do what he was told, and I suspect it was impossible to discipline him also. And being under the wing of his mother, and being so ill when he was young, led to a favoured position" (D. Hooper).

According to Gudgeon, Acorn "developed a potent imagination and a quick tongue ... a gift that could always bring a smile to his mother's face, and an angry word to his father's lips" (29). This may be an exaggeration, since, according to Mary and Robert Jr., their father was angry with Milton only occasionally in the years before the war. "Milton didn't have unusual anger," says Mary. "He refused to do things, and Dad could be upset, for instance, on a family outing when Milton refused to go swimming. But there was no vendetta. Milton played hookey once, and Dad had to talk to him. But he was no rebel in the family. He would toe the line when he had to." Milton's imagination was not, according to his sister and brother, a cause of paternal anger.

His relationship with his father eventually was dominated by the other central passions in Acorn's life: politics and economics. "Milton always talked a lot," remembers Mary, and when his political consciousness developed, "Milton and Dad argued a lot about politics. They might've enjoyed it, but that wasn't the impression we got. We had to listen!" (M. Hooper).

At age 15 and 16, Milton began to develop his lifelong devotion to socialism and communism. Mary and Robert are unaware of any individuals, such as teachers, who stimulated "his boyhood fascination in 'Communist plots'" and "serious, adolescent interest in political theory, and in particular, the work of Marx, Engels, Lenin, and Stalin" (Gudgeon 41). Again, they suspect he was drawn to socialism by his childhood experience as a bullied underdog. Gudgeon asserts that "this attraction to politics was as natural as eating" (41). Both views beg the question of how Acorn discovered political texts and tracts. Unfortunately, at present, there are no specific accounts of how Acorn became acquainted with left-wing materials and thought as a teenager. Did this voracious young reader stumble upon these texts in the library? Was there a significant teacher at West Kent School or a closet socialist in the Acorn clan? Certainly, by 1939 Acorn was expounding on the virtues of Lenin to his father, who counter-attacked on behalf of capitalism.

In Kent Martin's film, Acorn admits that he practised being "tough" on his father. This practice took the form of heated disagreement. "Milton had to try himself out against the world," says Robert. "And he would make outlandish statements. Milton and Dad were wide-open thinkers, and Milton would bullshit what Dad had to say, and Dad didn't take that too lightly. This was when Milton was a teenager, the coming-out years."

Gudgeon surmises that "Mickey enjoyed the battles he had with his father, and perhaps it was one area that he felt he could adequately compete. Although short in stature, Robert was extremely strong.... A scrawny, sickly child, young Mickey felt inadequate in the shadow of this 'epitome of masculinity' ... I wonder, though, if Mickey goaded his father because it gave him a sense of control ... it allowed Mickey to feel heroic, David against Goliath" (31). As intriguing as this conjectural analysis might be, it appears to be based more on Acorn's own self-romanticized writings at a much later date, than on his siblings' recollections. No doubt Acorn had a problematic relationship with his father, which influenced his writing—including *both* the "anger" and the "love"—and his adult personality and behaviour. When compared with Mary's and Robert's memories, however, Gudgeon's account seems overly dramatized and simplified, drawing on the Acorn myth of "the tough little man proving himself almost every day" (31) against the figure of oppressive authority.

In fact, Milton's political awareness and feistiness began to emerge as he started to develop physically. Robert says that "the tussles with his Dad began when Milton was robust and at least 15." These political tussles were probably a psychological proving-ground for Milton, but he selectively and metaphorically magnified them as an adult writer, ideologically glossing over issues of authority and resentment, emulation and respect, self-assertion and inadequacy, self-realization and rejection of parental models. There are also the issues of Milton's role as the oldest son—who should have set an example for younger siblings, yet who was the first to express rebellious views—and of the father's expectations and possible worries, frustrations, or disappointments concerning his oldest child.

In order to keep Robert Sr. and Milton from fighting, the family sat Helen, the youngest child and their father's favourite, between them. The conflict may have been fed by his father's drinking, which began when Milton was 16 or 17. Even though Robert Sr. "never staggered around or anything like that" (R. Acorn), Milton's mother, who did not drink then, was not pleased by his father's behaviour, and it is possible that Milton, too, was distressed.

A more benign development occurred during Milton's fifteenth year: he turned from a skinny, delicate child to a large, muscular, and impressively strong young man. With this radical transformation in his physique, he began lifting weights. This "new" Milton challenged people's expectations. "There was a weightlifting contest. They were giving a prize for whoever could lift the weight. Milton went up on stage and lifted it up, and they said, 'Oh no, you've done it the wrong way.' They refused to give him the prize because he'd used the wrong technique. There was apparently quite a hullabaloo" (D. Hooper). Once the prey of neighbourhood bullies, Acorn became their scourge. By age 16, he was respected and feared for his strength and size.

Once a dreamy runt, Acorn was transforming into the larger-than-life person who would write, in "Self-Portrait":

I've got quite a face, thank God
for smiling or scowling;
tho the smile doesn't earn me much
(so knowingly innocent

and forgiving of all
they bewilderingly find themselves to be
people wonder what they've done
and edge away from me)

:but the scowl—that's different!
especially when I stick a cigar in it.
If they have any plans
for bringing me crashing down on it

They give them up. Either way
no one believes in the puddle of mother's milk
that almost floats my heart, or how
the miracle of a human being's existence

disarms me. I guess I see enough evil
as it is, without it being tossed like acid
into my eyes
—the way most people get it.
(*Selected* 119)

Several of Acorn's central poetic concerns appear here, in characteristic juxtaposition: the potential for victimization by the dominance of "evil" and the need to defend one's soft-hearted, "smiling," and "forgiving" self with an imposing "scowl"; his "knowingly innocent" belief in the essential "miracle" of human existence, and his experienced knowledge of others' bewildered suspicion and hostility.

In 1938 Acorn matriculated from West Kent School. He failed the entrance exam to enter Charlottetown's Prince of Wales College[11] for grades 11 and 12 "because he wouldn't learn Latin. He didn't figure a person should have to learn Latin," says Mary. This put him in the company of a another future poetic luminary, Irving Layton, who might have failed to graduate from high school in Montreal, if he had not agreed to be tutored in Latin by a brilliant young poet and scholar named A.M. Klein.

On 12 July 1939, the imposing physical presence that helped Acorn develop his metaphorical and literal "scowl" also enabled him to enlist, along with his close friend Harold Dougan, for active service in the 1st Battalion, Prince Edward Island Highlanders, having convinced the army he was old enough to be a soldier. "They were the first two to enlist in Charlottetown during the Second World War. As soon as they heard it on the radio, they marched down to the armories and enlisted," Mary says. On Acorn's "Attestation Paper" for the Canadian Field Force, dated 29 September 1939, at Sydney Mines, Nova Scotia, his birthdate is listed as "31st March 1920." Three years underage, and listing his "Trade or Calling" as "Student," he had gone with his unit to Cape Breton. On 29 February 1940, he was discharged in Dartmouth, Nova Scotia. His discharge paper notes that his conduct had been "Fair," and gives as the reason for discharge that Acorn was "not likely to become an efficient soldier." In fact, he was discharged because his father finally succeeded in convincing military authorities that his son was too young to accompany his unit overseas.

Acorn was home from March 1940 until his re-enlistment on 23 June 1941, in the Canadian Armoured Corp, unit 62 C.A. (B) T.C. The new version of his birthdate is 30 March 1921, two years short of the truth. During his time back home, Acorn may have again unsuccessfully attempted the entrance exam for Prince of Wales College. He attended Union Commercial College in Charlottetown and obtained a bookkeeping certificate. Robert and Mary recall that Milton successfully wrote the civil service examinations "between his two stints in the service" (R. Acorn).[12] Returning to active service, Acorn continued to list himself as a "student" on military forms.

He was first stationed with his unit in Charlottetown, then posted to a military training camp in Ontario, on 26 August 1941. "I was taken down to Toronto on a troop train and I went to Camp Borden" (Deahl "Acorn" 4). His unit was ordered overseas on 22 January 1942, and embarked on a troopship in a convoy on February 28. During the passage, on March 5, Acorn was injured onboard ship.

There has been much speculation about the nature of his war injury and its impact on his later behaviour. Medical records are not available from Veterans Affairs or in the National Archives; therefore, the cause and nature of his injury and the medical treatment cannot be determined with any certainty.

Drawing on Acorn's accounts, Gudgeon writes, "The convoy encountered a pack of German U-boats, and the two sides engaged in an agonizing game of cat and mouse" (43). Acorn usually explained that he was standing on deck, near the rail, when a depth charge exploded near the ship. "There is no record of the depth charge incident, but Milton mentioned it often. I remember some discussion about it when they were applying for Milton's pension. This was probably what started the mastoid infection" (M. Hooper, Letter). Mary says, "He was in the wrong place at the wrong time, as usual, and it deafened him." Acorn told one interviewer:

It was a blast, just a pure blast. I didn't have enough sense to cover my ears. Typical story of the young intellectual. I should have been an officer, but they made me a sergeant instead and there was no one behind me to say "Put your hands over your ears." I looked at the depth charge and said to myself: "The blast from that charge is going to reach me in nineteen seconds," so I started counting but never thought to put my hands over my ears. It happened while I was standing on a troop-ship going over to England. The nervousness of the Canadians in that situation was just incredible. It was a near-death experience. There's lots of things I'm terribly afraid of now, but not death. (Meyer and O'Riordan 129)

He was obviously not afraid to mythologize his rank, which was, in fact, the lower rank of "trooper," and never sergeant.

There are three other problems with this story. First, troopships were usually unescorted, and normally did not carry depth charges, depending instead on speed and maneuverability for their safety. Second, depth charges are designed to explode underwater, and it is therefore highly unlikely that a blast would damage the inner ear and hearing of someone on deck. Third, a delay of "nineteen seconds" would mean that the ship had travelled a considerable distance from the underwater explosion.

If, however, his ship was equipped with depth charges, and this was the cause of his injury, there is a possible explanation. A depth-charge is launched through the air some distance from the ship before it hits the water and has a time-delayed fuse set to explode the device at a desired underwater depth. But under combat conditions, and with armaments hurriedly mass produced, devices did not always function as designed. Depth charges sometimes exploded too soon, in the air. For example, an otolaryngologist with No. 15 Canadian General Hospital in the Mediterranean theatre, documenting injuries in Sicily, reported that "thirty-five ear drums were evacuated," and that one of these injuries was caused by a "depth charge" (Feasby 321-22).

Other explanations have been offered for Acorn's injury: he was standing too close to a ship's guns when they fired; he fell down a ship's ladder and landed on his head; he was struck in the ear during a fight. But there is even less support for these suggestions than for the story that Acorn was injured by some sort of blast. One legend, that his ship was torpedoed, is untrue.

There is also the question of shell-shock. Indeed, the widespread notion that Acorn was shell-shocked during the war has been used to account, partly or in whole, for his idiosyncrasies. Without any medical evidence, however, and without any reliable information about the cause and nature of the injury, it is difficult to attribute psychological trauma to a putative blast. Certainly, his injury was serious enough to keep him hospitalized, first in the ship's hospital, then at Hairmyres Hospital near Glasgow, from March 9 to June 16, and then at No. 7 Canadian General Hospital at Marston Green near Birmingham until 27 July 1942 (Feasby 104). "Some of the time we didn't know whether he was living or dead," says Mary. "That hospital he was in was bombed out, I think. And he didn't write very much then." The bombing of the hospital may have added to his trauma. Robert Sr. read about the bombing in a Charlottetown paper, and kept the news to himself until the family heard from Milton that he was safe.

According to his family, he underwent surgery and was placed on a heavy regimen of sulpha drugs for many months. "From what I remember, Milton's scar on his face was from a Mastoid operation. His nerves were damaged through the use of excessive sulpha drugs" (M. Hooper, Letter). There is, then, Acorn's story of a blast injury, his record of hospitalization, and his family's recollection of a mastoid infection and sulpha drug treatment.

He was hospitalized again, on November 11, in No. 1 Neurological Hospital in Britain, and discharged eight days later. He was assigned clerk duties when he was not in hospital. On December 12 he returned to Halifax, posted to No. 6 District Depot, and was discharged from the army on 11 January 1943, "being unable to meet the required military standards," according to his discharge document. "I can't see that he changed that much, except perhaps he might have been more depressed," says Mary. "His nerves, we always figured, were caused by the sulpha drugs." He had also suffered hearing loss.

Dr. Robert J. Grimm, a neurologist with an interest in the inner ear, writes that "high blast forces ('barotrauma') can damage the cochlear portion of the inner ear (that part devoted to hearing) to produce either transient or long-lasting deafness." Considering the possibility that Acorn was injured by a blast, Grimm notes, "It is also entirely plausible that the force of the blast either ruptured the eardrum(s) or worse, the round or oval window membranes of the bony capsule of the inner ear with the middle ear space (behind the ear drum), the latter productive of a leak of fluids out of the inner ear, a condition called a perilymph fistula. The latter is a condition characterized by vertigo, nausea, tinnitus, pain with loud sounds, and the inability to think straight. It would have made Acorn a candidate for hospitalization for several months until the ruptured membrane had sealed over" (Letter).

Commenting on the long-term effects, Grimm adds, "That it affected his 'nerves' is a point in favour that the blast produced a perilymph fistula (PLF) syndrome with its vertigo, disequilibrium, tinnitus, nausea, and disorganization of first-order cognition, e.g. concentration, short-term memory, as well as perceptual disorganization. The fallout on emotional stability as well as the ability to think can be devastating ... and qualifies for damage to 'nerves'" (Letter).[13]

Relying on testimony from Milton's sister Katherine, Gudgeon writes, "Kay recalls that he was 'very paranoid,' and was convinced that government officials and others were watching his every move." Gudgeon adds that Milton "talked openly of suicide, and like many veterans, turned to alcohol for relief" (44). Robert and Mary insist that Milton was not paranoid in the first few years after his discharge. "It wasn't until much later," says Robert, "that he thought the RCMP were following him. And there was no alcohol then. Not until he got to Montreal. Not until he got into taverns and talking with poets." As for suicidal tendencies, Robert says there was "no incident, no evidence." Mary agrees, but says that "He was in anguish a lot of the time." All his siblings agree that his "nerves" involved depression.

Focusing on Milton's "competition with his father," Gudgeon ironically writes that "when he got the chance to test himself in battle, Milt literally 'lost his nerve,'" and insists that "it was a blow to his own rigid perception of what it meant to be a man.... He never even saw active duty, yet he came home even more emotionally scarred by war than his father had been" (45). There is, unfortunately, a lack of evidence to support these assumptions about Acorn's perception of manhood at the time or the comparative damage Robert Sr. and Milton experienced from their wars. Was Milton's depression—his "nerves" and "anguish"—strictly a byproduct of his physical injuries? Or was a sense of failure or inadequacy in relation to his father and his own emergent sense of masculinity also a causal factor? Milton's later tendencies toward gross simplification, ideological revision, and mythologized construction of his past offer little help. In his writings and interviews we have, along with declarations on the horrors of war, his pride in his military service, however limited, and in the sacrifice he made through his injury and disabilities. With occasional bravado, he admits disappointment that his soldiering was foreshortened; but he does not probe any "blow" to his manhood or rivalry with his father in this regard.

The war did deliver Milton another devastating blow. "He had one good friend, Harold Dougan," says Robert Acorn. Harold had become engaged to Milton's sister Katherine when she was thirteen, and their relationship was serious when he embarked for Europe. "His ship was torpedoed and he drowned. And Harold's brother died of liver disease. Milton was friends with the two brothers. Harold was his buddy, but all the other ones in his age group were gone too." This, also, is essential background and stimulus for "I've Tasted My Blood":

> Playmates? I remember where their skulls roll!
> One died hungry, gnawing grey perch-planks;
> one fell, and landed so hard he splashed;
> and many and many
> come up atom by atom
> in the worm-casts of Europe.

Here is Acorn's personal loss and anguish. Here, too, in the poem's final stanza is political and moral outrage fleshed out with intimate pain and intensely personal hope:

> My deep prayer a curse.
> My deep prayer the promise that this won't be.
> My deep prayer my cunning,
> my love, my anger,
> and often my forgiveness
> that this won't be and be.
> I've tasted my blood too much
> to abide what I was born to.
>   (*Selected* 130)

These lines, with their near-religious quality of litany, connect to more than Acorn's war experience. They are also a testament that he will not "abide" the economic and political oppression of unjust social systems, an oppression he first encountered, according to the allegories of his youth, on the streets of Charlottetown. But the brutal blood-letting and the deaths of his friends in the Second World War are among the notes in the powerful closing chords of this poem.

Two other poems reflect the political and philosophical hindsight of an older poet looking back on that war. In "The Second World War" (1972) there is no trace of the teenager who couldn't wait to join, no attempt to explore whatever motivations—patriotism, the romance of heroic adventure, youthful masculine aggression, an urge to take on the bully, father-son tensions, the lure of male camaraderie, the attraction of having allies and enemies, a reaction against fascism—might have prompted Acorn to enlist so eagerly. The older poet, instead, wants us to dwell on the ironies of war, of recurring conflicts, of successive generations of onlookers, recruits, veterans, and casualties—and on the whims of the élites responsible for war. The poem begins on Great George Street, leading from Charlottetown harbour to Province House, the route walked by the Fathers of Confederation on another historic occasion:

> Down Great George Street, up to the station;
> The skirl of the pipes the very thrill of your nerves
> With the pipemaster (only man who has the Gaelic)
> Ahead with his great baton, his strut and toss proud
>   as any man who's ever walked.
> This is where we came in; this has happened before
> Only the last time there was cheering.
> So few came back they changed the name of the regiment
> So there're no cheers now. Tho there are crowds
> Standing silent, eyes wide as dolls' eyes, but brighter
> Trying to memorize every face
>
> This is where we came in. It happened before.
> The last time was foolishness
> Now's got to be done because of the last foolishness.
> In the ranks, perfectly in step (with the pipes
>   even I'm perfectly in step)
> I'm thinking of *Through the Looking Glass*:

> The White King's armies marching while he sleeps;
> We are his dream....At least it seems that way.
> They're so clumsy the front line topples
> The second line topples over it; and on it goes
>   —line after line, eyes glazed straight forward
> Shoulders back, spines held stiffly unnatural
> Toppling over the line before
>
> So few came back they abolished the regiment.
> I was lucky—sickness and bad marksmanship.
> Man by man we'd sworn to take our guns back,
>   man by man we didn't.
> One man—one war—that's all he's usually good for.
> Now a strange short-haired subculture
> Glares at us out of the TV set
> Snarling the news, every phrase or disguised opinion
>   as if it was a threat, which it is.
> This is where we came in
> It's happened before.
> This last time was right
> But ended in foolishness.
> It has happened before, could happen again
> Despite the fact that stuff is out of date.
>   (*Selected* 134-35)

    The soldier is a kind of Alice in Wonderland. Acorn's allusion to Lewis Carroll's metaphorical realm alerts us to the confounding occurrences—duplicities, lunacies, contradictions, sinister capriciousness, authoritarian ruthlessness, and egomania—that the soldier experiences once he follows the white rabbit down the hole or steps through the looking-glass. The nature of the looking-glass changes, from old-fashioned patriotic parades to the manipulative "subculture" of TV news, but the armies keep marching and toppling in service of "The White King's ... dream" and in the historical dialectic of "foolishness" and "right." The final line brusquely dismisses the binary question of "just" versus "unjust" wars: "that stuff is out of date."

    In "The Bronze Piper" (1975) Acorn contemplates a monument in New Glasgow, Nova Scotia, which honours local men who died in the wars. Among those named on the monument are Islanders, for "Many Islanders fought the Second World War in the North Nova Scotia

Highlanders," writes Acorn in the poem's epigraph. In the first half of the poem we hear again his sardonic treatment of war's recurrence—the "war to end all wars" leading to the Second World War leading to the next conflagration—but thinly disguised by his offhand domestic wit:

> This was put up by the citizens
> and of course most of the names are Scotch;
> survivors Scotch too for they calculated
>   to a nicety in 1930
> ...how large a plinth for how many names.
>
> Ten years after came another war
> so behind they had to put up another stone
> for names of the new born new dead; but
> this time took precautions;
> left a blank square yard and a half on the
>   back of the stone.
>   (*Selected* 174)

Acorn then shifts his attention to the capitalism and commercialism for which these soldiers fought and died:

> But...again but...when you look round the stone
> you find this is not a monument
>   but an advertisement.
>   for the names of two entities
>   living in law
> that of a monument company
> and a firm of architects
> are there ...
>   (Selected 174)

This leads to the larger question of "What exactly did they fight for?"—a question that erases the false line drawn between the political and personal:

> In a park by the river in New Glasgow
> stands a kilted piper playing a dirge
> all in bronze, though not kept shone

>   :
>   all in silence
>   Still you know it's a dirge
>   for the dead, some of whom could be husky today
>   :and for...
>   some of them hoped...
>   What exactly did they fight for?
>   Yanks?
>   to claim their victory?
>   as if it was over themselves?
>   their nation prisoner?
>   May the poem not end here;
>   the last note
>   not be a dirge....
>   (*Selected* 174-75)

Obviously, Acorn in the early 1970s was not preoccupied with the struggle against Nazis and Fascists. He wasn't celebrating or critiquing the defense of democracy or capitalism. He wasn't even paying elegiac tribute to the sacrifice of European socialists and communists and of the Russian people in their contribution to the victory over fascism. His interrogative answers to the question, rather, refer to the postwar era and contemporary concerns about Canadian independence and U.S. domination. The answers refer, too, it seems, to his own, his buddies', and his countryfolks' "victory? / as if it was over themselves?" That victory is still a dirge for the Harold Dougans of his youth and, vicariously, for the poet who once lay in a military hospital, no doubt contemplating his "victory" and near-defeat. As Timothy Findley so brilliantly showed in his novel *The Wars*, the external conflict is a stage setting where soldiers enact personal dramas. Acorn knows this, and wants us to ask the question, "What exactly did they fight for?" within historical, political contexts. We must not uncritically rely on received interpretations of history but use our own ability to interrogate, interpret, and imagine the causes of war and the motives of individual soldiers.

The reference to "Yanks" bridges the postcolonial era of British dominion and the postwar era of American domination. Some readers may recall *Barometer Rising*, Hugh MacLennan's classic novel set in Halifax during the 1917 Halifax Explosion, and written in 1939-40. MacLennan's perspective on English Canada and Anglo-Canadians in

1917 is an implicit comment on the nation's identity at the start of the Second World War: the Anglo-Canadian élite's mentality had been dominated by anglophilia and British cultural hegemony. In 1940 anglophilia remained strong, but American hegemony was appearing and would be the next challenge, the next source of economic and cultural control. If MacLennan was the prophet, however, Acorn was the astute revisionist: Canadians thought they were fighting for Canada, Britain, the English God and King; they were fighting and dying more, suggests Acorn, for the rising power and imminent supremacy of the "Yanks." In "Rabbie Still Be With Us" Acorn writes,

> "There'll always be an England as long as Scotland's there"
> And always a U.S.A. so long as Canada's friendly;
> The trouble being the Yanks have no friends, only suckers:
> Can any nation live with such external cares?
> (*More Poems For People* 13)

MacLennan and Acorn might well have agreed that they fought for their nation, "prisoner" both of a fascist threat in the short term and of their two "great" democratic and capitalist allies in the longer historical span.

Acorn speaks of his state of mind as an enlistee and about the enemy in "The Dead," a poem published in 1956 in his first collection, *In Love and Anger*:

> I see the smiling faces of the dead.
> I was a boy in nineteen-thirty-nine;
> a thousand whirling visions in my head
> but death in none of them for me or mine.
> (*I Shout Love and other poems* 32)

His poetic touch still callow, and prone to moments of mawkish grandeur, he writes, "The thrilling pulse of youth ran through their veins," and describes a comrade's "frank and rareless gift of heart and soul." But the poem toughens up when he speaks of the tacit enemy:

> But brains and virtue didn't count at all.
> A Nazi with the morals of an ape
> shot him dead against a German wall
> for his plain duty...trying to escape. (33)

There is, however, another enemy, equally sinister:

> Was their sentence signed and sealed? I say
> that while they played their games and paid no heed,
> those who ruled them pawned their lives away
> to satisfy their foolishness and greed.
>
> They nursed the beast, the grey wolf-bitch that strives
> to burst out, ravening, from its Prussian den,
> and now that freedom's bought with brave young lives
> they turn around and nurse the beast again. (33)

Leaving aside the note of anti-German racism which was not uncommon in 1956, Acorn reveals the fate of the ordinary soldier, trapped between the "foolishness and greed" of two sets of rulers, one the nominal "enemy," the other one's own leaders.[14] It is in "The Dead," too, that Acorn appears to acknowledge directly Harold Dougan's death:

> Yes...One of them, a loser in all strife,
> quick-grown, bull-throated, comical and proud,
> counting himself defeated soon in life,
> could read his fate, and trumpet it out loud:
>
> and his was a destroyer that was struck
> by a torpedo between wind and wave.
> He died below in such a bloody muck
> they laid him and his bunk-mates in one grave.
>
> I don't want to idealize and say
> that they were innocents and had no sin;
> the cynic's creed that mars our youth today
> was known to them, too. But—What might have been? (32)

In this early poem Acorn formulates and confronts two of his lifelong concerns: the "foolishness and greed" of "those who ruled" the lives of ordinary people, and the violence of exploitative systems, with its immediate effect in the destruction of Acorn's friends and others "pawned" to "satisfy" those who possess economic and political power.

The poem also labours, awkwardly, to glue together elements of narrative, allegory, elegy, political discourse, and moral declaration and to sustain the effort with a lumbering, but energetic, iambic pentameter rhythm. Acorn was 33 when this poem was published, and it shows that he was not one of those poets who burst brilliantly on the scene in their early adulthood with dazzling technical facility and astonishing figures of speech. Rather, it is evidence of a slower, tenacious effort by a writer who, while working at manual and clerical jobs in the Maritimes and Montreal, had developed largely on his own, assisted by family and political-activist friends, not by practising artists or academic mentors.

IV

IF YOU'RE STRONGHEARTED

> If you're stronghearted look at this Island;
> red gouges of creeks at low tide and
> the stronger red which spreads behind plows.
> Don't hold your tongue too long, it'll swell
> with so much good and so much bad to say.
> — "If You're Stronghearted"

FROM THE MID-1950s ON, poetry was so central to Acorn that he seemed to have been born with metaphors in his mouth. Hilda Woolnough says, "He was always a walking poem-in-progress." Few, if any, would disagree. It is natural, therefore, to assume he was writing poems before or immediately after his military service. For example, Valerie LaPointe, a close friend late in his life, repeats a familiar refrain: "He learned carpentry but knew from an early age that his vocation was to be a poet" ("Celebrating" 4). Even better, here is Acorn speaking to a Charlottetown reporter in June 1968, three months after he returned to PEI from his years in Vancouver: "I can remember writing poems since I was 20, but people tell me I was writing them when I was much younger" (MacIntyre). This contributes to the Acorn myth. But his apprenticeship began differently.

Likewise, when one reads Acorn's poems and articles about him, it is easy to picture him as an apprentice and journeyman carpenter from 1944 or 1945 until he sold his tools, in a dramatic gesture and declaration of poetic vocation, in Montreal in 1956. Moreover, he played up the image of a man called to the time-honoured vocations of poetry and carpentry, and torn between them, until one craft prevailed over another, the proletarian tradesman following his muse.

Here is part of a profile from *Books in Canada* in 1981: "Acorn's sleeves are almost always rolled up, carpenter-style. His forearms are broad and strong-looking. He had, in fact, worked as a journeyman carpenter until 1956, when he decided to sell his tools. He was thinking too much about poetry to be doing good work, but then he had always been thinking about poetry. His voice rolls like an old-time sermon. 'One thing that has followed me all my life,' he says, 'is the poetry.' But carpentry had helped him roam around a bit, and he felt at ease working outside. 'Carpentry was my grand tour,' he says" (MacFarlane 4). It is difficult not to think of another carpenter who put down his tools to speak the word, especially when Acorn claimed that "Jesus was a proto-Marxian, an early Marxian" (Burrill 7)—thus casting Jesus as a forerunner, the archetypal tradesman turned prophet and radical, preaching liberation to the masses with inspired language and parables.

Another writer constructs a melodrama from unreliable accounts of Acorn's wartime experience and poetic salvation: "He was on his way to fight in the Second World War when his ship was torpedoed crossing the Atlantic. He suffered a head injury so debilitating that he collected a military pension the rest of his life. After his release from hospital, his fate seemed set in stone: he would be poor, wounded and adrift. What could not be imagined was that poetry would rescue him as he had been scooped up from the burning sea surrounding the sinking ship" (Wayne 14). His ship was not torpedoed. He did not fall into burning seas. He did not apply for a disability pension until the mid-1950s. The hyperbole and inaccuracies may be partly owing to Acorn's need to have a legendary launch for his poetic voyage, and not just to his admirer's need for a tragic hero rescued by the Muse.

And here is an excerpt from a tribute published after his death in *Canadian Dimension*: "As one who was not left as a 'worm-cast of Europe,' he became a carpenter by trade, but he left construction carpentry in the late 1950s to become a full-time poet" (MacKay 41). Acorn sometimes encouraged people to think that he strapped on his carpenter's belt from time to time after 1956, when the poet needed more cash. This is Acorn again in 1968: "A carpenter by trade, Mr. Acorn says he has not done much of that type of work lately. 'In my travels I have found that having a trade sustains me economically. I also draw a war pension from the Canadian government'" (MacIntyre). While this aspect of Acorn's persona is attractive and vital, the reality was somewhat different, and no less fascinating or worthy. After his discharge from the military, he lived for several years with his middle-class parents, hardly poor or adrift. His parents' economic support, Uncle Stanley Bryant's construction business, several labourer and civil service jobs, his mother's emotional and literary support, and his brother's literary advice and encouragement enabled him to spend nearly ten years discovering his poetic voice.

According to Robert, Milton was visited at home soon after his discharge by two men from the government. They inquired about his injury and whether he wished to apply for a pension. "He told them he didn't want a pension and that his nerves had always been bad. He didn't know at the time how difficult it would be to earn a living."

When he came back from the war, Acorn's first job, from 31 January until 1 March 1943, was at the Charlottetown airport where he worked as a fireman's helper for the Department of National Defence. He also briefly worked at the Provincial Hospital in Charlottetown and as a stevedore on the Charlottetown wharves during this first year back from the war. "There used to be a wharf called the fertilizer wharf," says Robert, and Milton was "loading and unloading fertilizer ships. He'd come home covered head to toe in fertilizer, only his mouth and eyes showing. You had to be in the union to work on the docks." There are no records indicating when he worked on the wharves or at the hospital, but he almost certainly held these jobs between March 1 and the Christmas season of 1943, when he was a temporary clerk at the Charlottetown Post Office.[15]

In February 1944, Acorn went to the CNR freight yard on the waterfront looking for work. He came home and told his father, "The man said I wasn't good enough for the job," which involved "lugging stuff around" (R. Acorn). But Acorn was in excellent physical shape, except for his hearing, and prodigiously strong. Perhaps Milton misheard the man, for when his father went down to the freightyard, he returned with a different story: "The man said the job wasn't good enough for Milton." But Acorn wanted the job, and his father, middle class or not, wanted him working: "He wasn't going to hang around the house. Dad would tear on him for not being able to support himself" (R. Acorn). So Milton returned to the railroad sheds and signed on with the CNR.

Before Acorn arrived at the sheds on his first day of work, some of the men were discussing their new workmate. One of those men just happened to be Acorn's old nemesis, the neighbourhood bully most responsible for mistreating him during his childhood. When this man heard the new worker's name, he dropped his tools, took to his heels, terrified, and never returned. Acorn worked there as a freight porter into June of 1944.

Apparently these kinds of jobs did not entirely please Acorn's father, nor did the first signs of his inclination to "hang around the house" working "on his typing," says Robert, who explains what was expected of a middle-class child returning from the war: "In those days if you were from a middle-class family, you automatically got a middle-class job. There were no ifs or buts about it, it was there for you, practically came to look you up. Milton was going to all these weird jobs." Milton showed no signs, however, of settling into a career as a labourer or clerk. It is likely that a combination of his restlessness and his lifelong "dreaminess" or self-absorption—his concentration on "stories," rather than on the movement of fertilizer or mail—were steering him away from a "regular" job and toward his literary vocation.

On 22 July 1944, however, he began a remarkably long stint as a civil servant, working as a clerk with the Unemployment Insurance Commission in Moncton, New Brunswick. Mary recalls that he was a stockkeeper in Moncton: "He was a really good stockkeeper because he'd remember where everything was in his head. I guess it nearly drove him crazy, being cooped up in a nine-to-five job. But he received a really good letter of recommendation from there." As Acorn's months in Moncton turned into years, his father might have indulged in relief and satisfaction that his oldest son was getting established respectably. But Acorn would not follow in his clerk-father's or his bookkeeper-mother's footsteps. He held this position until 7 July 1947—almost three years, the longest he would stay at any job other than writing throughout his life. In fact, given the testimony of his family and the lack of hard evidence of extended carpentry work, it is quite possible that Acorn spent more time working as a civil servant, as a clerk in an office job, than he did as a carpenter.

His carpentry work began sometime after his return home from Moncton in July 1947. Mary says, "He came back in good spirits. He took a carpentry course and he had carpentry jobs. He worked a lot for his uncle, Stanley Bryant. Stanley used to do contracting, build houses. Uncle Stanley was the main person Milton worked for. He didn't work at carpentry for a long time. Milton was always glad to go to work when he could get it. He was probably happier when he was able to stay home and write. Some of his jobs didn't last long. I guess he was too much of a dreamer." Later in life, Acorn once claimed he had been more of a rough carpenter, not a highly skilled craftsman. Mary remembers his workmanship differently. "Mother told us the story about Milton working with a carpenter on a house. The carpenter was installing windows in the holes Milton had prepared, and was amazed to find that the windows went in perfectly." Milton helped the Hoopers build their house: "He did a little bit. He was quite thorough. He was a fussy carpenter. Garth was a rough carpenter, and Milton would come out to work and want things exact. Milton was upset when he noticed that some of the measurements in the framework were not exact. He wanted to correct mistakes made by the foreman carpenter. This made him slow. We couldn't afford him."

Acorn sometimes referred to himself in later years as a union carpenter. Unfortunately, there appear to be no existing union records for the building trades on PEI from that era, and no Revenue Canada records for the "ordinary citizen." Mary says, "I don't think he ever belonged to the union. Uncle Stanley didn't have union connections for his construction business." A retired member of the Labourers' Union, Leo Arsenault, remembers a labourer named Milton Acorn, but points out that there were plenty of non-union work sites which employed non-union labourers in those years. William Shields, a Charlottetown carpenter and union man from that time, remembers Acorn on a job: "He was a labourer, and he didn't last too long. It seemed his mind was somewhere else. I suppose, being a poet and a man working on a construction job is two different minds. He appeared to be lost. His mind didn't seem to know what he was doing in construction as a labourer. It likely was a union job. The only way he could get a job there was to join the union." Many other poets have, indeed, managed to keep their minds on their money-paying jobs, including jobs as carpenters and construction workers, but apparently not Acorn.

His own testimony supports Shields in general, but shows how Acorn could work in his political message: "All the time I was taking my carpentry course I couldn't do things right because my mind was always thinking, always thinking, saying, 'communism is right, communism is right.' There was a strike on in town, then, and it was odd how my mates just couldn't get the political implications. They were all for the workers, of course, but when it came to a vote they voted for the man who broke the strike [Premier Walter Jones]" (Meyer and O'Riordan 130). In a 1969 interview he offered a view of his carpentry skills which differs from the Hoopers' recollection: "I wasn't a good craftsman. I was a good rough carpenter. I knew I wasn't going to make the best carpenter, which sort of kept me looking for something else which I would be best at" (MacDonald).

We will likely never know to what extent he was not, in spite of his attempts, cut out to be a skilled tradesman or labourer. What we know is that writing took over, and that as a writer Acorn needed the image of a carpenter. And as Mary says, "He didn't like people destroying his image." In addition to other reasons for this need, it was no doubt more acceptable in some circles to say, "I'm a carpenter," than, "I'm a writer, a poet." When necessary he could avoid the stigma of being "one of those artsy types" or a writer in an ivory tower; he was a "real" worker, too, a labourer, a skilled carpenter.

Years later, the carpenter image and the question of its authenticity or substance is much less important than the writing which emerged from that period in his life and his preoccupations as a "worker." One of his finest poems about work, "Why a Carpenter Wears His Watch Inside the Wrist," has become an exemplary text, not only for its superb focus on the nuances of a skilled trade, but for its canny treatment of power relations on the job. Published in 1969 in *I've Tasted My Blood*, this poem shows the mastery of diction, detail, cadence, sound textures, and narrative focus which Acorn achieved in the 1960s. Language, tone, and perspective blend smoothly and exactly:

> They say it's guarded better
> there, from the bumps of the trade.
>
> I disproved this, and
>
> guessed first those patched people
> stuck up like chimneys
> in high places, fix them
> there so's to look at them
> with no long upsetting armswing,
> just a turn of the wrist,
>
> but the gruesome truth is
> that with the gargoyle-pussed
> boss watching, they
> don't worry much about balance;
> which led me to the real reason

they wear watches tucked so close
bouncing and scratching
among all their tools...

it's so they can look quick
out of the lefteyecorner
without the foreman seeing.
(*Selected* 37)

Vivid and delightful as this poem is, it lacks the psychological depth and sociological reach of another work-based poem, "I've Gone and Stained With The Colour of Love." Also published in *I've Tasted My Blood*, it draws not only on his work experience in the late 1940s and early 1950s, but also on a later period in his life, after his marriage and divorce in 1962:

I've gone and stained with the colour of love
The two-hundred-and-fifty-pound road foreman
Gone on his liquor, who sits
On my wicker armchair and strains it
So much in every binding point it can't even creak.

I've known him as laugh-cursing soldier;
I've known him posed decisively as a statue
Out on the road, telling them what to do.
I've known him so much sufficing himself
Carrying his lunchpail....
      But here he sits
And his eyes are like a bull's except
A bull's eyes don't hurt and his do....

Or does a bull cast such a poignant hurtful look
At the slaughterer between the blow and his collapse?
I've gone and stained with the colour of love
Bulls too; and this man is called Bull...
He says to me, "Milt—You old bastard!"
And I say, "Bull—You old bastard!"
We've told each other about all our nicknames:
But his life was this—His Childhood and the War;
And all that followed was a disappointment

> I've gone and stained with the colour of love
> Life:—Well here is a man who knows life....
> We tell each other about our wives
> His dead, mine lost, his lost before her death:
> And I say, "Bull, you old bastard!"
> And he says, "Milt, you old bastard!"
> It being the admission of manhood
> That each has done wicked things.
> So we pitch arguments back and forth;
> But sometimes he just sits and watches me work.
> *(Selected* 108-09)

Here, two workers' camaraderie within the human condition obliterates the conflicts of hierarchical relationships. There is the blustery affection and vulnerability of men toughened by work and war, and wounded in love. There is the sad dignity of Bull, whose competence on the job and masculinity do not compensate for the "disappointment" life has dealt him. The poem also shows Acorn's rough-and-tender sensibility—what Tom Wayman called his "surprisingly tender feelings" (38)—a prominent feature in many of his strongest poems.

His carpentry mentor appears in "The Retired Carpenter" (1963), one of Acorn's tersely effective cameos:

> Tools, grips sweat-polished,
> in a dinted box, loose
> at all angles,
> half of them vanished.
>
> No gripes today if
> old Stan stops too often
> to fire up his pipe.
> *(Selected* 26)

Uncle Stanley, in this portrait of a craftsman taking well-earned breaks toward the end of a long career, seems to age more contentedly than the road foreman. There is none of the pathos Acorn bestows on Bull, no hint of victimization. But, then, Uncle Stanley was a self-employed tradesman and small businessperson.

"The Retired Carpenter," with its taut sentiment, can be linked with "Charlottetown Harbour," another poem about an "old" worker.

Milton's time spent on the wharves underlies this well-known early poem (1960):

> An old docker with gutted cheeks,
> time arrested in the used-up-knuckled hands
> crossed on his lap, sits
> in a spell of the glinting water.
>
> He dreams of times in the cider sunlight
> when masts stood up like stubble;
> but now a gull cries, lights,
> flounces its wings ornately, folds them,
> and the waves slop among the weed-grown piles.
> (*Selected* 50)

The picturesque figure, the nostalgia for the maritime past, the final line's lament for the harbourfront's decay as well as of a storied "tradition"—these are three familiar themes in modern Island and Atlantic Canadian culture, and they recur in much of Acorn's Island poetry, especially in his poems related to traditional Island occupations.

The lament can be found in the songs of Stan Rogers ("Make and Break Harbour," "Fisherman's Wharf"), in the socio-economic analyses of the magazine *New Maritimes*, in George Elliott Clarke's poetry about Black Nova Scotian communities, and in the Cape Breton fiction of Alistair MacLeod, which often highlights the tension between tradition and change. The elegiac aspect also embodies a classic mythic motif: humanity's fall from a state of grace, from Eden or a golden age. In Acorn's view, that fall from grace was not due to original sin, but to the wickedness of power brokers who exploited, betrayed, and abandoned the Maritimes. Through this classic motif, political and economic indictment blends with nostalgia for a golden past.

In the late 1950s, with the "old docker" and the "weed-grown piles" Acorn captured the long decline of the Island and the Maritimes as a shipping and merchant centre with "masts ... like stubble" symbolizing importance and wealth. Acorn was familiar with the reasons for the decline of the Maritime provinces' economy and social status. Before Confederation, the Maritime colonies relied on their Loyalist affinities and connection with Britain, their close ties with the New England states, and their mastery of the Atlantic Ocean and its trade routes. But "at Confederation in 1867, the Maritime provinces had little in common with Canada," and "it may be argued that the Maritime provinces never fully recovered psychologically from the traumatic experience of Confederation and the sudden end of the golden age of 'Wooden Ships and Iron Men'" (Rawlyk 1306). Maritimers' sense of their region as a privileged place within both the British Empire and North America was permanently lost as the Canadian economy developed westward, as immigrants bypassed the region, and as the Maritimes found itself without the natural resources, geographic location, population base, and political clout to compete with central Canada or the American northeast. Nothing during the century after Confederation removed that sense of loss, although it was mitigated for brief periods, for instance, during the boom years and patriotic fervour of the First World War.

In 1986, the year Acorn died, the Charlottetown waterfront still reflected the Maritimes' economic limitations: the CNR yard was about to be dismantled, with the railroad ceasing to exist on the Island; freighters loaded potatoes from the potato warehouse on the government wharf; giant oil tanks dominated the harbour. Only one decade later, however, the waterfront had been radically transformed, as the Island's economy and social outlook adjusted to new realities. What would Acorn think today, the freight sheds torn down and oil tanks moved, and the waterfront redeveloped for tourism—with Confederation Landing National Monument—and teeming with people, a new kind of entrepreneurial spirit, and new plans for prosperity? Freighters still load PEI potatoes at the wharf, but these boats are dwarfed by cruise ships. The traditional "workers" who remain on the waterfront are far outnumbered by employees and customers of restaurants, hotels, art and craft galleries, the yacht club, and souvenir shops.

A decade before "Charlottetown Harbour," when Acorn was toiling off and on as an Island labourer and carpenter, his politicization was well advanced, hardly limited to nostalgic laments for a vanished tradition and the heyday of Island prosperity or to poignant appreciations of gnarled old-timers. His family, however, were largely unaware of the details of his political education and radicalization. Mary does remember "the Russian books Milton brought home from the library, even when he was in his teens. That's where he was learning communism from." After the war, says Robert, "Milton kept his friends to himself. I don't know any of the friends he had at that time. He was working with these union types and he'd hang around the union office. He worked so much on his typing, anyway, that he wasn't socializing." The old Labourer's Protective Union (LPU) Hall on Water Street has been gone for years, and it is difficult to find "union types" who remember Milton Acorn on the job or hanging around a union office.

There was precious little political activity of the left-wing variety in the late 1940s and early 1950s on PEI. Mary says, "I don't think he went around preaching anywhere but home. It was mostly us had to listen to him." Then there were his arguments with Robert Sr. over politics and economics. Acorn himself claimed that his Uncle Stanley was a political confidant: "Oh, there were a few old guys who weren't afraid to talk. My Uncle Stanley, for instance, his wife would laugh at him and say, 'Stanley's going to join the red army.' If you talked to him, he'd say, 'No, I'm a Conservative, but communism is best for them.' We had lots of interesting talks" (Burrill 4).

Milton liked to trace his radicalism back to John Acorn, that is, his fabulous version of this first PEI ancestor: "I am from what you might call a red Tory breed. John Acorn was a miller, witch, rebel, and pirate, running blockades for the Yanks in the 1770s. But they sold him out ... so, a red Tory" (MacFarlane 4). Acorn became thoroughly "red," a communist and member of several left-wing organizations, and relegated the red Tory stance to his New Brunswick counterpart, Alden Nowlan, the only other Atlantic Canadian poet to achieve major stature in the 1960s and 1970s.[16]

Nowlan worked his way from poverty into the middle class as a journalist and as writer-in-residence at the University of New Brunswick. Acorn needed to replace his petit bourgeois background with a proletarian identity and a socialist faith: "I have to impress upon people [that] my concern is the working class. And of course that includes, in fact, all the poor people, and those of the rich who are honest" (Burrill 6). Acorn's attraction to the proletariat and socialism, though, may have owed as much to the repression of local movements as to any left-wing conversations on the Island.

There was union activity on PEI during the late 1940s, but the local atmosphere was a strike-breaking one. Premier John Walter Jones (1943-53) was a union buster. Nicknamed "Farmer Jones," his political ascent owed much to his support of farmers and rural interests. In 1947, using "the farm interest" as his pretext, his government halted a Canada Packers strike by taking control of the plant, hiring scab labour, and passing legislation to outlaw unions affiliated with national or international labour organizations, effectively banning all unions on the Island. Fortunately, this legislation was short lived, and union affiliation resumed before the end of the decade.

In 1984 an interviewer asked Acorn, "What was it that prompted you to leave the Island in the first place?" He answered, "Well, I got kind of lonely. During the regime of Premier Jones ... virtually every socialist was driven out of town. They weren't going to throw me out of town—in those days, I could have picked them up one by one and thrown them into the harbour.... But you got awfully lonely, hearing nothing but the rankest reactionary argument. You don't know what that does. When I joined the Carpenters Union, the organizer was filling out a form for me, and he came to the question, 'Are you a communist?' He said, 'You're not a communist are you?' Of course he knew I was a communist, but he just didn't want to hear me say it" (Burrill 4). Since Acorn did not join the Communist Party until after he moved to Montreal, he could only have been referring to his convictions or sympathies, and not to official membership. "I just had the URGE, URGE, URGE! I didn't even bother with sex! My first driving urge was to get into political action" (Meyer and O'Riordan 130). It is hard to know whether Acorn displayed such political spunk in the late 1940s, or whether he was swaggering in hindsight.

He was apparently telling the truth about "sex": the absence of any amorous involvements during these years in Charlottetown raises the question of whether Acorn's sexual development was problematic, and if so, why. Lacking evidence in Acorn's writing or family speculations, one can only consider the possibilities. Was his sexuality suppressed by the physical and emotional traumas stemming from his war experience and medical treatment? Did his close relationship with his mother somehow inhibit or delay his sexual development and attraction to other women? Did the mother-son connection generate a problematic sexuality? Is it even possible, as some people have wondered, that Acorn was gay or bisexual: were his gruff masculinity, assertive heterosexuality, and bonding with men from the late-1940s onward, along with his vitriolic homophobia in later life, symptoms of confused, repressed sexuality? Or did he, in the 1940s and early 1950s, experience sexual desire and deal with it privately, as was required of countless people in a more sexually restrained, tight-lipped era and community? If so, why was he apparently not drawn sexually and amorously to women until he was almost thirty? It would be convenient to say that he was too shy, but "shy" is a polite euphemism for psychological constraints or preoccupations. Whatever the combination of psychological, physical, and societal reasons, Acorn was fully absorbed—one might say "sublimated"—in his writing, in his family and especially his relationship with his mother, and in the development of his working-class persona and political engagement. It was this persona, so passionately engaged in the making of literature and of a socialist society that he couldn't be bothered with sex, that Acorn the People's Poet wanted his public to remember.

Although Acorn was writing stories as early as 1947, he was more preoccupied with politics than literature during his first year back home from Moncton. Referring to the period, roughly, of 1944-48, Mary says, "He never in his wildest dreams thought he'd be a poet, or even a writer. He wanted to be a revolutionary."

Acorn did have two other significant interests in the late 1940s apart from politics and becoming a revolutionary. One was acting. Peter Shama, who was prominently involved with two important theatrical groups in Charlottetown, the Anglican Young People's Association (AYPA) Players in the late 1940s, sponsored by St. Peter's Cathedral, and the Little Theatre of Charlottetown in the 1950s, remembers that both Milton and Robert Jr. were active with the AYPA Players, and that Milton continued acting with the Little Theatre. "We were exceptional in those days," says Peter Shama. "We studied hard and worked hard. We did a lot of original skits and improvisations. And we won a lot of drama awards at festivals. Milton was a keen member of the AYPA Players." Another supporter of the Players was Agnes Dickson, whose husband Stuart Dickson was a broadcaster and news editor for Charlottetown's CFCY Radio. He directed many plays for the AYPA Players and the Little Theatre. Agnes remembers Acorn's first role, in *The Bishop's Candlesticks*: "He played the thief, that was his start. People wondered where he got the talent to play the part so well. He was a born actor." He was in several AYPA productions after that.

In the early 1950s, the Little Theatre offered Islanders serious productions of Shakespeare and other masters, as well as modern hits, and local material. Although Acorn moved to Montreal in 1950-51, he made lengthy visits to the Island throughout the decade, and while at home, "Milton was in several plays. He excelled himself. He really should have been an actor" (Dickson). A review in the local *Patriot* newspaper lists Acorn as the actor playing Sganarelle in a 1955 Little Theatre production of Molière's *Love's the Best Doctor*, and comments, "Milton Acorn gave a splendid performance as the rascally old 'Sganarelle'" ("Little"). The play was directed by Father Adrien Arsenault, also a visual artist, poet, and professor of fine arts, whom

Acorn later sought out for companionship during his visits home to the Island. Shama also tells of the time Acorn built the set for the Little Theatre's production of *Charley's Aunt*: "He was a carpenter, but he wasn't the world's greatest. The set was rough, but it did the job."

The other interest was, of course, writing. Milton began with a serious effort at drafting short stories, and his mother was his audience, secretary, editor, and cheer leader. Mary says that "Mother always said he was going to be a writer and she encouraged him. She read his stories, typed them for him, and he sent out a lot of stories. They came back. She'd listen to them too. It didn't matter what time of day or night. She didn't criticize too much. She told him she especially liked something. But he never actually had anything published that I know of."

"I tried to break into the science fiction field," Acorn said in the 1969 interview with Helen MacDonald. "I wanted to be able to do what I could do in Canada. I didn't want to go down to New York to discover what the ins and outs of the trade were in science fiction."

Robert remembers that "whenever they [the stories] came back he'd rip them up and throw them in the fire. He had fabulous ideas, but the trouble with Milton's stories, there were no normal people. Any character was a fabulous character. Of course, he was only young, but there were no normal people at all. They'd all be out of Walt Disney or Robert Louis Stevenson movies." Milton continued to write science fiction throughout the 1950s, and wrote to his close friend, Montreal poet Louise Harvey in the early and mid-1950s, and to Al Purdy in the late 1950s, about his ongoing study of the genre, his desire to gain an audience and income from science fiction, and his determination in the face of repeated rejection.

"As to when I started writing poetry," Acorn told Helen MacDonald, "I don't know that.... I don't remember writing poetry in school, but I've met people who went to school with me and who said I was writing then. I submitted a poem first in 1945, and I think the next poem I submitted was in 1952. The first poem or two poems was [*sic*] rejected without comment, and the poem I submitted in 1952 was not only accepted by that magazine but as far as they were concerned it was sensational.... I wanted at any cost to stay in Canada. So I went into poetry where you could do it in Canada, although the reward at that time was zero." Mary recalls Milton switching to poetry in 1950. The author's note in *I've Tasted My Blood* states that Acorn "has been writing poetry since the 1950s." According to Robert, Milton may have begun writing poems before 1950: "He was talking about free verse and he was struggling, getting more and more frustrated all the time, and I said, 'Maybe so Milton [attempting free verse], but that's not the way it's done.' He started writing four-line stanzas. I said, 'Yeah, the imagery is there, and the stanzas and lines fortify the image.'" Robert then suggested the sonnet form, "and he'd get off into sonnets. Poems were coming out of my ears. He'd hand me this bloody poem and I'd read it: 'Yeah, not bad.' 'You don't like it,' he'd say. And I'd say, 'No, I didn't say that,' and he'd take it and work on it again, then he would finally get it so I would say I liked it."

In a tape recording Acorn made in Vancouver in the mid-1960s he says, "I started to write in iambic patterns, taught by my brother who went to college.... I used the iambic meter because I thought it was popular, it would reach people; but I became uninterested in reaching people if I had to present my work in terms such as they didn't use themselves, in their own speech" (Livesay 33-34).

Peter Shama remembers Acorn's attempts at short fiction and his transition to poetry. "He wrote lots of stories and they seemed good enough, but I guess they weren't what was wanted, because they kept coming back rejected. Then Bert Foster showed him how to write poetry." Foster, who died in 1993, worked in the Canadian National Railway office, and later for the Charlottetown *Guardian* newspaper. He directed and wrote plays for the Little Theatre. Bill Ledwell, an Island journalist who died in 1996, remembered that Foster's "great consuming love was poetry" and that he was "a great admirer of A.E. Housman." If Foster did have a critical impact on Acorn's choice of poetry as his métier, his role in Acorn's development is all but forgotten.

Helen Acorn's contribution to Milton's artistic development is far better known. Her support for her oldest son's writing is still in one respect a sore point for Robert, who on occasion took home school compositions for Helen's comments and, he hoped, encouragement: "All the support Milton was getting. I never got any." If this is true, it is a sour note in the story of Acorn's literary apprenticeship and success. Robert acknowledges, however, that "I wouldn't have done what he did: send something away and have it come back rejected. And not know where the food was going to come from. You have got to be up with the saints or something to take that kind of life." Milton was able to sustain his writing through that period of rejections. He also, according to Robert, experienced "good success with the poems. It wasn't very long before he got the odd one published."

From mid-1947 through 1950, Acorn spent long hours at the typewriter, read voraciously, and relied heavily on his mother and brother for encouragement, advice, and an audience. He startled the community with his theatrical talent. He was also becoming a political radical, a socialist, a communist, and perhaps "hanging around union types," while working just enough as a labourer and carpenter to address those needs in himself and to appease his father.

As valuable as the local theatre group may have been for that part of Acorn which needed public artistic performance, and as important as Robert and Helen were for the development of his writing, they couldn't provide what he would find in a large urban centre, among writers and other artists and intellectuals who would help define the future of Canadian literature. The local political scene could not begin to offer him the left-wing environment of cities such as Montreal and Toronto. The need to leave the Island and the region for a more cosmopolitan scene must have been brewing for several years. Unlike Alden Nowlan, who moved from Nova Scotia to New Brunswick, Acorn opted for a radical change, one that would immerse him in the centre of Canadian literary creation and left-wing political ferment.

He also needed—for all his love of the Island—to distance himself from its conservatism and the limitations of a small artistic community which had not yet been significantly influenced by modern aesthetic movements. Acorn took the time-honoured path of exile—a necessity for countless artists, especially those raised far from the major metropolitan centres. This was essential for Acorn's creative development, both to broaden his artistic consciousness and to sharpen his perspective of his home place. Finally, he needed to throw himself into urban, cosmopolitan life, to be part of the metropole. He headed for the city where modern Canadian poetry had been born.

V
ON ST. URBAIN STREET

> Knowing that in this advertising rainbow
> I live like a trapeze artist with a headache,
> my poems are no aspirins....
> — "Knowing I Live in a Dark Age"

IN THE EARLY 1950s Acorn established the pattern of restless movement that would characterize the rest of his life. He moved to Montreal sometime during late 1950 or 1951. His first visit to Montreal, in 1949, had been prompted by officials at the Department of Veterans' Affairs, who sent him for observation to the military hospital in St. Anne de Bellevue. Back in Charlottetown, he considered but did not act on his Uncle Stanley's advice to apply for a disability pension. In his twenty-seventh or twenty-eighth year, compelled by his artistic, political, and psychological needs, he joined the Island and Maritime tradition of out-migration.

The earliest dated letter from Montreal in the Milton Acorn collection at the National Archives is addressed to his sister Mary. As well as distancing himself from his past, primarily in the form of his father, he conveys the growing agility of his rhetoric and wit: "I'm not coming home, either for a vacation or to stay, not for many years; Mother seems to expect me to and I'm afraid it's up to you to undeceive her. I'm not coming home on account of the Old Man!... If you feel resentment at being made the conveyor of unpleasant tidings I'm afraid you'll have to get used to it. To avoid it is simple—change your personality. Become carping instead of sympathetic. You'll find then that people will no longer trust you with such tasks" (17 March 1952).

Acorn did not exactly settle at first in Montreal, nor did he stay away from PEI "for many years." He began his lifelong pattern of travelling between the Island and central Canada. For instance, in Montreal he worked again for the Unemployment Insurance Commission as a clerk, from 5 January 1952 until some time the following month. He then worked as a carpenter in Sept-Iles from March to July 1952, and as a carpenter for County Construction Company in Charlottetown during September and November. He returned to Montreal and worked as a packer and helper with the Department of National Defence from 21 November 1952 until 16 July 1953.

According to one profile, "He spent some time in Sept-Iles, sharpening chainsaws, before ending up in Montreal" (MacFarlane 4). There is no documentation of chainsaw sharpening, but we do have evidence of his carpentry employment and his poetic testimony in "They've Murdered Two Workers":

> Wandering around Sept-Îles
> With seven cents in my pocket
> Down the other side of the street
> Came an Acadian I knew,
> And within an hour I had
>
> > a job
> > a place to eat
> > and a place to sleep
>
> It wasn't so much a company
> As a co-operative gang of carpenters,
>
> * * * * *
>
> They've murdered two workers in Sept-Îles
> Where I was treated better than anyplace else in my life.
> (*More Poems For People* 28-29)

Acorn's reference to his treatment in Sept-Iles strikes a plaintive chord that recurs throughout the rest of his life. It is, of course, a rhetorical stance for the sake of the poem's perspective; but it also suggests an undercurrent of self-pity.

Acorn's 12 April 1953 letter to Helen encapsulates his "dilemma" as a person compelled to the craft of writing, yet concerned both about his ability to make a living *and* his need to be a genuine worker filled with "working-class" esprit de corps:

Now I'm up against my old dilemma. On one hand I need leisure to do my writing—on the other I need work to keep me in trim and filled with the joy of life which makes for writing. I've often thought if I was somewhere, on a farm where I could pitch in and help when I felt like it ... I'd be better off. I've often thought of broaching the subject to Garth and Mary. Perhaps I could do that on a temporary basis while I was working on trying to get a job in the freight shed. I know such a course puts the idea of marriage and a decent life away into the future but after all a happy life is a happy life.

His reluctance to move back to the Island had obviously moderated, for he did write the Hoopers: "What I'm asking is this. Just a place to hang my hat while I'm preparing my book. A place where I could earn my keep with my work and still be able to do my writing. Home is barred to me because of my politics." He reflects again about his dilemma: "Actually work, which keeps the creative wheels turning slowly when the mind is not producing is a necessary stimulation to me. When I'm working in congenial surroundings I feel full of the joy of life and able to create. When I'm absolutely out of work I sink into a sort of lassitude. Existence loses its meaning. On the other hand, when I'm working the hours are always too long. At the end of the day I'm exhausted. What contradictions!" (undated).

To what extent was Acorn genuinely torn between the life of a labourer-writer and that of a full-time writer? To what degree was he rationalizing his desire to write full time and his discontent with steady employment? The evidence suggests that he was temperamentally unsuited to a long-term career as a skilled tradesman, labourer, or clerk, and that the primary cause was not any kind of psychological "weakness" or personality dysfunction which prevents some people from a commitment to a career. On the contrary, the strength of his commitment to writing—his devotion to a literary career—was the determining factor in his need to resolve the "contradictions" by choosing writing over other kinds of work. As well, his determination to be a political activist, although it required in his mind a "working-class" background, was another factor that urged him, ironically, away from the paid employment he variously took pride in and bemoaned.

As a packer and helper at the Department of National Defence, he worked in the "stores" where his boss was "an army major and a little god" (Letter to Helen, 7 May 1953). After July 1953, there were no more jobs with the government. In late September and early October of 1953 he did odd-job carpentry on a non-union basis for a Montreal man (Letter to Helen, 1 October 1953). He was glad to be working, but felt exploited and verbally badgered by his employer. He wrote to his brother Robert on 8 May 1954 from Verdun, "I'm working in a truly immense shop, making railroad cars," insulating passenger cars and grinding off welds. In this sporadic manner, he worked as a labourer and carpenter in Montreal and on the Island for the next two years.

In 1952 Acorn began a correspondence as a worker-poet with the Nova Scotian poet Joe Wallace (1890-1975), a dedicated communist and devout Catholic, who had published five poetry collections and suffered imprisonment when the Communist Party was outlawed. He wrote to Wallace when the latter was ill, "Seriously, Joe, try to stick around for at least another decade and a half. We've begun a friendship which is going to loom large in the annals of Canadian, even world literature. A lot is going to come out of it" (11 May 1955). Their correspondence lasted until 1957, and Wallace stuck around for two more decades, but was largely forgotten by the time Acorn took his place in the "annals" of Canadian literature.

Acorn's first poetry publications appeared in *New Frontiers*. Historian Ivan Avakumovic explains that *New Frontiers*, "the literary periodical launched in 1952 ... owed its existence to the fourth LPP [Labour Progressive Party] convention.... Its contents reflected the concerns of the LPP: the struggle for peace and socialism, strong opposition to many aspects of American culture, and criticism of those whom the Communists held responsible for the neglect of literature and art in Canada" (205-06). Acorn was duly encouraged that his work was accepted by a magazine under the impressive literary editorship of Margaret Fairley and with strong left-wing and nationalist credentials.

Of his *New Frontiers* poems, one of his later editors remarks, "His early verse ... exhibits a conventionally clumsy rhyme" (Wayne 14), and Jewinski concludes, "The occasional poems published in magazines like *New Frontiers* were usually highly romanticized 'ballads' in quatrains which pounded out the theme of social injustice" (38). Accurate as these observations are, they have the benefit of aesthetic hindsight, and overlook the narrative energy and early appearance of Acorn's rambunctious, sinewy, cagey, and compelling voice.

"Grey Girl's Gallop," Acorn's first published poem, appeared in *New Frontiers* in 1953. It is a philosophical and political allegory set in the colourful environment of a harness-racing park. Harness racing is a central institution in Island life,[17] and this verse-narrative of a mare who breaks free from the traces shows how the young poet was finding his way with traditional poetic form, the innovations of "free verse," political analogy and commentary, and, especially, his background and *material* as an Islander:

> Oh joy what a gallop! What a wonderful gallop!
> Lovely to hit the ground with a wallop;
> Flying, feeling my muscles contracting,
> Shaking the soil with a fearful impacting,
> Then hurtling on in delirious bounces,
> Whole body exploding in power-surging jounces;
> Not the prim gait of civilization
> But a passionate rout—pure barbarization!
> What a glorious gallop!
>   ("Grey Girl's Gallop" 38)

Evident, too, is the persona of Milton Acorn, thinly disguised as the Grey Girl, dedicated to "a passionate rout," not the "prim gait of civilization."

The publication of "Grey Girl's Gallop" boosted Acorn's artistic confidence. On 12 April 1953 he wrote to his mother, "My Grey Girl's Gallop is arousing lots of comment. There was a very good review on it in the Trib. The writers here seemed to miss its allegoric content but spoke of its 'lovely rhythm' and much more along that line. Oddly enough I wrote the first verse in a disciplined iambic and then slammed away from then on in a sort of trochaic doggerel. They seemed to think the slam-bang verses were better." Acorn's growing awareness of craft is apparent, and his satisfaction is balanced with astute self-criticism. His demanding approach to his writing appears again in a 7 May 1953 letter to Helen: "I'm glad you like my poem. Robert liked the opening verses when they were shown to him over a year ago. He said he was reminded of Keats. I'd hardly read any Keats at the time. Your comments seem to imply criticism of the fourth verse—about the wave. I thought the analogy was very clear, but maybe it'll take some more bringing out. Please let me know if I'm correct in my assumption."

Meanwhile, his belief in his innovative role as a poet is expressed in an undated letter to the Hoopers: "My trouble is complicated by the fact that I'm a trail-blazer. Grey Girl's Gallop was not simply a narrative poem. It was a short story in verse.... Now the trouble with trail-blazing is nobody understands it." Acorn, however, preferred the stance of successful revolutionary to misunderstood genius, and tells his family in another letter that "People are rereading it and getting at the deeper meanings.... I've found a metier which combines the features of the modern introspective short story with those of poetry. Thus making the story easier to take and the poetry more gripping" (5 July 1953). The doggerel quality of the phrasing and rhythm in much of the poem, however, signals the fact that "Grey Girl's Gallop" is largely derivative of old-fashioned ballads, and that its "trail-blazer" qualities are limited to the poem's narrative and emotional vigour.

During 1953-54 Acorn spent a lot of time at the El Cortijo coffee shop on Clark Street in the heart of Montreal, where the clientele was a combination of students, artists, and working-class residents. Acorn immortalized this scene and experience in his memorable poem, "At El Cortijo."

He also became a member of the principal Communist organization in Canada: the Labour Progressive Party, founded in 1943 as a replacement for the Communist Party of Canada, which authorities had increasingly persecuted and suppressed since the late 1930s. This is likely the "Communist Party" to which Acorn refers when mentioning his formal membership. Later, looking for an alternative to the Communist Party, with which he had become disgruntled, he participated in meetings of the Socialist Forum of Montreal in 1958 and contributed to their pamphlet, *Canadian Democracy and the Struggle for Socialism* (Wayne 14).

Jock MacKay writes that "all poets are concerned about injustice, but very few see the class contours of problems. Milton made no bones of his Marxism—he was a communist and proud of it. But he was a PEI communist and poet-communist, the 'Minago' wordsmith" (42).

MacKay makes several important points. First, he points to a lack of awareness in Canadian poetry of class relationships and conflicts. Poets do not, of course, have to be Marxists to see, and to include in their writing, "the class contours of problems." They only have to realize that poetry cannot afford to ignore or to give lip-service to such profoundly central aspects of our lives: work, wages, property, capital, relationships between employers and employees, material needs, economic privilege and inequity, class differences, and the power and powerlessness that grow out of "class contours."

Since the 1970s increasing numbers of Canadian poets have incorporated an awareness of economic and class realities in their poetry. This is partly due to the growing prominence of women poets, aboriginal poets, and poets with backgrounds considered "ethnic," "immigrant," "visible minority," or "regional": writers who are often attuned to their own groups' legacy of exploitation, disadvantage, and marginalization; who often target the privileged position of the élite; and who evoke in their poetry the need to end injustice. This change in our poetry also owes a great deal to poets such as Milton Acorn.

Acorn was hardly the first Anglo-Canadian poet whose verse was politically and economically charged. In fact, he was part of a lineage which dated far back to the satirical verse, anti-Yankee and pro-Tory, published abundantly in the Loyalist era. He was an inheritor of Alexander McLachlan (1818-96), the "Burns of Canada," who honoured the labours of the common man and the spirit of democratic brotherhood. Before Acorn, for example, there was F.R. Scott (1899-1985), a radically different personality (an eminent law professor, scholar, and social philosopher), but a socially conscious poet prominent in Canadian left-wing political movements. Dorothy Livesay and A.M. Klein were two of the strongest voices of socially committed and socialist-inclined poetry in the 1930s.

Closer to home, there were the Nova Scotian poets Joe Wallace and Kenneth Leslie (1892-1974). Leslie was a Christian socialist who won the Governor-General's Award for poetry in 1938, and who was lumped together with Einstein, Chaplin, and other suspected "fellow travellers" by *Life* magazine during the anti-communist hysteria of the McCarthy era. In the 1950s, 60s, and 70s Acorn was joined by his great friend Al Purdy, by Raymond Souster and Alden Nowlan, then by a younger breed including Patrick Lane, David Donnell, Tom Wayman, Erin Mouré, Lorna Crozier, Al Pittman, George Elliott Clarke, Rita Joe, and others poetically aware of the "class contours of problems." These poets may not share Acorn's ideological solutions, but they do share Acorn's politically and economically sharp concern for "the people."

Acorn was a "poet-communist," writes Jock MacKay. In his introduction to *I've Tasted My Blood*, Al Purdy says that "Milton Acorn is a dedicated Communist, in the same way that some of the best Christians are not formal members of the Church. But with him Communism is more idealism than Marxist philosophy" (xi). The ideals included: an end to economic inequality, especially the grosser divisions of capitalist wealth, working-class subsistence, and poverty; support for genuine democracy, not contests among factions of the élite; an end to racism and bigotry; the overthrow of imperialism by local autonomy movements; and the ideal of "brotherhood" in place of ruthless competition. These ideals informed his poetry.

Literary critic Michael Gnarowski, assessing Acorn's maturation, strengths, and weaknesses as a poet in a 1963 review, wrote, "While he excels in the depiction of Prince Edward Island life and has a sure hand in the sympathetic portraiture of man, he gets into serious trouble with the poetry of ideology. Here, even though the poetry may be born of a genuine socialist anger, and although Acorn may expend great reserves of energy and talent, he founders consistently. He is safe only if he harnesses his anger long enough to allow its energy to infect some sharp picture of social abuse or inequity" (121).

Acorn did write some bad or mediocre "political" poetry, as most critics have remarked. But so have many other prominent poets of various political and aesthetic persuasions. Those who use failed political poems as justification for dismissing all political poetry should remember that there is a great deal of inferior poetry—by accomplished and master poets, as well as lesser artists—focusing on nature, love, family, spirituality, language, and other subjects. At his best, Acorn drew on political ideals and critiques in his production of an impressive body of socially-conscious poems—including "portraiture" and the "sharp picture" of social inequities—with lasting artistic *and* political value.

Among the most valuable of his socially-conscious poems are those associated with work and the lives of workers. His short poem "In Addition" is an example of Acorn at his class-conscious best—ideology an invisible inspiration, idealism strengthened by irony, political message embodied in details of ordinary life:

> In addition to the fact I lost my job for a nosebleed
>
> In addition to the fact my unemployment insurance stamps
>   were just one week short
>
> In addition to the fact I'm standing in line at the Sally Ann for
>   a breakfast of one thin baloney sandwich and coffee
>
> In addition to all that it's lousy coffee.
>   (*Selected* 46)

This is the kind of poem that prompted Wayman to say that "Acorn was one of the first people to show me it is possible to write about work and working life" (Wayman 38).

Finally, Acorn was a "PEI communist." As much as he tried—and usually failed—to be part of political associations, Acorn was not an organizational type, and his impetuous personality made effective membership difficult. Rather, he was a rebel in the spirit and tradition of the Island's land struggle. Like the tenant farmers who revolted against the rent collectors and absentee landlords, Acorn's temperament was individualistic rather than collectivist.

Acorn commented on his communist stand and its reliance on his Island roots and experience. As with any Acorn "version," it is useful to keep in mind the words of poet and editor James Deahl, one of his closest friends and collaborators from 1972 until Acorn's death: "Milton, as you know, was an A-1 bull shitter" (Letter, 16 August 92). The facts may not always be reliable. Fortunately, we can relish an account such as "I was a communist for my own damn satisfaction" as an allegory of his heritage, development, and philosophy. It shows that Acorn was prone to outrageous humour as well as earnestness:

I well remember when I was first contaminated by the international plot to spread bad Kremlin architecture and other foreign innovations across our fair blot of land. I was young, idealistic, just out of college. Oh sirs, may I in humble apology bow and kiss your oh-so-discreetly perfumed ases [sic]? I was young.... So, so young.

Eleven in fact. As I was saying I was just coming out of the yard of the College Coal Company with fifty pounds of their main product on my back. I'd managed to obtain, I forget how, 25 cents to buy a sack of coal for my cousin Effie (who was merely freezing to death) but vehicular transport was beyond me....

How come I had twenty-five cents to buy the coal? How come I had the strength to lift it? Obviously I was well-fed. And how come *my* mother didn't need the coal and I was able to carry it to my cousin Effie's?... I'm a fraud. My coal-carrying wasn't a case of desperate need but an altruistic one. In other words messy and anal and guilt-ridden as all hell!

As a matter-of-fact my old man worked every single day, except Sundays and holidays, all through the depression. The Communist Marx once said that the Communist Prudhon was an example of the *furor aristocratus*, or some such Latin phrase like that. If that's what I've got I'm proud of it even if it's tearing me apart. If aristocratic qualities like courage, pride, vision, have combined with proletarian realism—another word for it is truth—have combined in me and produced a state of raving sanity, then that's what I am and I'm going to enjoy it.

One of my great-great-grandfathers was a carpenter. He was also a nobleman. He spent ninety percent of his adult life in a backyard corner of his estate, building boats. A great-grandfather on a different line went to sea at a young age as a ship's carpenter. Before he was through he was a skipper. Before he was through that he was owner of a fleet. Before he was through that all his ships were wrecked and he died poor. I was born poor. I also became a carpenter....

I was carrying a sack of coal to my cousin Effie who was freezing and nearly starving because her man had been fired, presumably for buggery, actually because someone else would work cheaper, and I had profound thoughts....

My fine sardonic enlightened gentlemen. Shall I go on and tell you the usual tale of enthusiasm and disillusionment? Shall I tell you that I eventually became an enemy of Communism and made my peace with you? Unfortunately I can't. I haven't made peace with you. I'm an enemy all right ... but of Capitalism. I found certain sections of the Communist movement difficult to work with.... That's true. But you see I believe in three things that you will probably find absolutely hilarious. I believe in freedom. I believe in it finally and absolutely. I believe in equality ... finally and absolutely. I believe in a rational mode of life directed toward human happiness. I'm sure you'll agree with me that these beliefs make me absolutely and irrevocably your enemy. ("I was a communist" 32-38)

Acorn wrote a number of such allegories, conflating politic stance with local colour, anecdote, and wishful thinking. For instance, in a Charlottetown alternative paper, *The Broad-Axe*, Acorn wrote in 1971 about fishing with his father in a public stream that had been illegally dammed by a "bourgeois" landowner. Twice the "bourgeois" drives Acorn and his father away with threats of arrest. The third time, Acorn's father kills the "bourgeois," father and son bury the body, and they return to town, righteous citizens ready to proclaim that another owner-class criminal has received his just reward ("On the Wheel"). Allegorically, Acorn transforms his petit bourgeois father into a working-class hero—the same father who, in the late 1940s, vehemently argued over politics with Milton, and who wanted Milton to find respectable and secure middle-class employment.

In Montreal one of Acorn's most important political and artistic companions was the poet Louise Harvey, a single mother. Gertrude Partridge, an Island resident whose late husband Glen had been a native Islander and a friend of Acorn in Montreal, mentions that Harvey was "Acorn's girlfriend." James Deahl writes that she was "the first really important 'girl' in Milt's life. Louise was much older (had two children) and taught Milt a lot about love and sex. She also taught him a lot about poetry (she was a much better poet at the time they were together). And it was Louise who introduced Milt to the Communist writers in Montreal. She was part of their circle and also helped Milt get published in the left-wing lit. mags. of the day. She died around the time he died" (Letter, 12 November 94).

Their friendship began before 1953. The correspondence between Harvey and Acorn during 1953-56 reveals a relationship cemented with political and poetic affinity. Expressions of emotional intimacy, however, flow one way. Harvey's letters are laced with endearments and her prose exudes romanticism, even at her most dialectical. Acorn's letters to her have the impersonality of a man whose passion is for his politics and writing. He seems to neglect or evade her affection or to take it for granted. He writes primarily about his poetry and fiction, the Montreal socialist groups with which they were involved, and his "capitalist" family (his farmer sister and brother-in-law, the Hoopers, are exempted from that epithet). The correspondence shows that she loved and admired Acorn, and offered him support and encouragement. His letters are almost entirely about his own struggles and achievements.

"Louise," he writes from Charlottetown on 14 May 1955, after an apparent rupture in their bond,

The period of February and early March was a storm of creativity for me. I wrote a complete radio play GIDEON'S ARMY, another longer poem, as well as went on with my work on A GIRL'S DREAM ... the poem which I worked on all winter.... I haven't destroyed the letters you sent me. I couldn't. I've reread them often, and seen what a great benefit they've been to me, how they've braced me up and strengthened me to triumph over my difficulties.... At the risk of being repetitive I'd like to say this again. The dominating passion of my life has been to write. Many years ago, when I was fresh home from overseas, I debated seriously on the whole question of what my life should be. I remember hearing the parable of the talents repeated in church and then my course seemed clear. I would write, and guide my life in such paths as would enrich my writing. I did this, inasmuch as I was capable. Looking back, I can see many good decisions. The most important was to throw in my lot with the working class. I left my job and learned a trade. After that I wavered sometimes, became infected by ruling-class ideology and because of that, more than anything else, I had my nervous break-down.... Whatever you think of me, Louise, remember that I'm no hero, but only a human being grappling with his conditions of life.

The correspondence provides no direct evidence of why their relationship faltered. Harvey continued writing to Acorn about mutual literary and political concerns and with tender affection. Acorn replied with self-absorbed polemics. The reference to "nervous breakdown" suggests the onset, during the early 1950s, of more serious difficulties in his ability to cope with his inner "contradictions" and to sustain relationships in the social world, including an amorous one with a woman.

But there was always his mother. In fact, Helen "set up an apartment in Montreal with Milton for a few months, after he'd been in the hospital for his nerves," says Mary, alluding delicately to one of his periods of hospitalization for psychiatric care. According to Robert, Helen shared an apartment in Montreal with Milton on two separate occasions.

Reflecting on these visits and on his failed relationship with Louise, it is not unreasonable to wonder whether his attachment to his mother hampered Acorn's ability to form a mature sexual and emotional bond with a woman. It is also possible that Acorn treated Harvey as a substitute for Helen, that is, a woman who would nurture his talent, provide an audience for his political and literary discourses, strengthen his self-image, and offer the emotional comforting he required.

During the second visit, says Robert, "He was having trouble making a living. They started looking into a disability pension. With the help of his mother, and Mrs. Dougan, Harold Dougan's mother, he applied successfully for a war-related disability pension." This development, in fact, seems to have unfolded slowly during 1955-57, and Helen's second visit may have been later than 1956.

Acorn did not seriously consider applying for a disability pension until after a lengthy stay back on the Island during 1954-55. He wrote Harvey from Charlottetown on 29 November 1954, telling her, "I'm working again for—a Montreal company! Anglin-Norcross Ltd.! We're building a new federal building for Charlottetown. It's bitter work in the cold. I'm getting $1.05 an hour—just!" His growing frustration with such jobs helped persuade him to seek and accept a disability pension.

Other letters to Harvey place Acorn in Charlottetown in January, April, May, July, August, and September of 1955. He was in the cast of the Little Theatre's February 1955 production. On July 6 he wrote to advise Harvey about her forthcoming visit to the Island. They rented a cottage near the Cavendish Shore, but their reunion resulted in mixed reviews. After her return to Montreal, Harvey was upset by a hostile letter from Acorn: she thought their time together had been lovely, and was astonished by his hurtful and rejecting tone. Nonetheless, she sent him a love poem, "A Walk on the Island" (13 August 1955). Subsequently, they resolved to be no more than friends.

Louise Harvey may have been Acorn's first "girlfriend" and lover. His next significant relationship is veiled in mystery. "Letter to My Redheaded Son," published in his 1960 chapbook *Against a League of Liars*, alludes to and obliquely deals with the most secretive, and an exceptionally painful, chapter in his life:

> Young maple leaves, copper with a delicate flush,
> are taut and hardly bent by the limb-twist breeze,
> and I'm penetrated by the delight that made you
> and makes fool poets call the spring green.
>
> A poet against a league of liars, I know
> you'll learn love and honesty from her
> who wouldn't learn scorn and left me.
> You'll learn, boy, to be as bitter as me
> against the men with counterfeit eyes,
> their graft and their words: "nigger";
> "people not like us"...and "bastard."
>
> Fool poets call the spring green, but I
> a poet, know I can't give you to yourself
> —only what I know of myself: that
> nothing I've done, no poem, stand,
> thought or act of love, hasn't called for
> another, stronger deed, or I've lost it.
> (*I've Tasted My Blood* 47)

One of his most evocative, heartfelt, and masterfully controlled poems, "Letter to My Redheaded Son" displays the tension between Acorn's indignation and tenderness, hope and disappointment. His impassioned public convictions, his sublime wonder in the presence of nature, and his most intimate pain and longing are complementary. Manifest, too, is his grasp of the seamlessness of nature, individual lives, and social humanity.

The "son" of the title is his own child. Acorn returned to Montreal in late 1955, and was working in the CNR express office in early 1956. He developed a relationship with a woman from the Maritimes, and they had a child who was given up for adoption. Robert is certain the child was born in 1956, and that "Milton did see his son and lived with him and the mother for awhile. It just didn't work out. He didn't have a means of supporting a family, and that may have been a reason." Another factor may have been Acorn's psychological instability, which certainly impeded the formation of long-term sexual relationships throughout his life. As well, his increasingly intense focus on a literary career and left-wing political activism, with negligible financial prospects, may have helped discourage a long-term parenting partnership. In any case, the relationship was short lived, and not long after his son's birth, Acorn lost forever his only child.

Several years after Acorn's death, his son visited the Island, made the acquaintance of Mary Hooper and Hilda Woolnough, and learned about his father. Outside that small circle, however, the identities of Acorn's "Redheaded Son" and the mother remain unknown, a family secret, and we are left with this poem's distillation of Acorn's fatherly pride, sorrow, and defiant wisdom, as well as the knowledge that Acorn "looked for his son throughout his life and imagined several times that he saw him" (D. Hooper). The existence and loss of his son may have haunted Acorn throughout his adult life, and perhaps underlay some of his more virulent and controversial tirades against abortion and homosexuality in later years.

Whatever distress Acorn felt over the loss of his son and the end of relationships with his son's mother and Louise Harvey was absorbed into his poetic quest and political obsessions. In 1956 he began meeting poets who would leave their mark on him—Irving Layton, Al Purdy, and Leonard Cohen in Montreal, and Frank Ledwell in Charlottetown.

A native Islander, Frank Ledwell was a professor of English at St. Dunstan's University, and later the University of Prince Edward Island.[18] He remembers meeting Acorn in Charlottetown in 1956. Ledwell was beginning a career that saw him become one of the most influential and valued teachers of creative writing through several decades on PEI, and that has continued Acorn's legacy of writing poetically about the Island. "He had come home for a short visit," remembers Ledwell,

presumably to see his family, and during the course of his visit he dropped out to the university to see Adrien Arsenault and meet me. It was in the summertime, and we were sitting out on the verandah of the main building. We had a pleasant evening together. But several days later we were visited by the RCMP, who wanted to know what we were talking about. We found this most untoward and strange. But in the context of McCarthyism and the Gouzenko declaration in Canada, there was a lot of paranoia about finding Reds under every stone. And Milton, of course, was quite a vocal socialist in those days, as he was later, so his name must have been on some list. We assured the Mounties that there was absolutely nothing untoward in our discussions—we were talking about the creative arts, and not about politics.

Indeed, the conversations were guided by Acorn's, Ledwell's, and Father Arsenault's devotion to literature, and Arsenault's expertise in the fine arts and knowledge of European culture.

It was around this time that David Hooper first discovered his uncle's existence:

I have two very early memories of Milton. At first I didn't know him at all, other than he was this supposedly famous uncle, who was always talked about by Grandma Helen in a good light, although several other members would make comments under their breath while Grandma was saying this. One Christmas a big present was under the tree for me. It had arrived by mail. It was this humungous toy truck. I'm his godson. This was my first introduction that there was someone anywhere by the name of Uncle Mickey, as we knew him. I don't think I ever got another present, but I sure remember this one.

The other time is when we were sitting in Hillsboro Street in Charlottetown, and he was home from Montreal and reading something. It was 1955 or 56. I was five or so, sitting there playing some kind of game. Uncle Milton says, "Goddamned Capitalist Bastards!" And Grandma says, "Don't say that in front of the kids." And he says, "Why not? They're gonna hear it anyway."

I recall another night we were all staying in town, I believe it was the wintertime, us four kids and my mother, and Uncle Robert. And Uncle Milton was home. He slept on the living room couch in front of the fireplace. Somebody came to the door early in the morning and he jumped out of bed into the fireplace. He took some getting used to. He'd be there eating dinner, and all of a sudden something would hit him, like he'd see a bird, and he'd jump up and run out and no explanations. After a few times that got to be normal and you didn't notice it.

David's memory of Milton and birds is early testimony to Acorn's now-familiar veneration of birds, especially the crow and raven—a devotion which was ornithologically rigorous, and spiritual as well as artistic. "When he was on something he was really on track," says David. "He'd get on sparrows' or crows' or ravens' nests. He'd expound on the murderousness of sparrows. He was always interested in ravens because that's my grandmother [Helen], as far as I'm concerned. She was always very progressive in her thoughts, and in tune with the world. She appreciated nature. I always think of her spirit as the spirit of the raven."

The administrative quest for Milton's disability pension appears to have begun in 1956, back in Montreal, before his mother's "second visit." He wrote to Helen on 21 October 1956, "Everything has happened.... Everything! Besides my book, I went to see Dr. Bowes about a month ago. After a long conversation he asked if I was getting a pension. 'Well ... you should be,' he said, and instructed me to put in a claim forthwith. He would back it with every means in his power.... I applied a month ago." Acorn had trouble convincing the pensions board and "an old bureaucrat who seemed to have a fit of temper every time I criticized the government's handling of the case. He wrote out a form setting me as applying for a pension on the grounds of 'nervousness and ear trouble,' probably because he could see that I could hear perfectly. You know that, with modern drugs, my ear is no problem" (Letter to Helen, 21 October 1956). If his mother and Mrs. Dougan helped him to obtain his disability pension, it had to be after this date. His application was successful, and by 1958 and perhaps earlier, his pension cheques were being sent to his mother's address in Charlottetown, where Helen helped manage his finances. Acorn now could rely on a steady and permanent, if modest, income to support himself as a developing writer.

It is safe to say that 1956 was the pivotal year in Acorn's transformation from an aspiring writer and semi-employed worker to a promising writer with an entrance into the influential literary world of Montreal and a small guaranteed income on the way. His much-mythologized apprenticeship and career as a carpenter was, in fact, quite spotty. But his apprenticeship as a writer had been one of extraordinary effort and attention to craft. He had a small but noticeable publication record, and he was establishing friendships with several poets who would, along with Acorn, be heralded as major writers of their era and ensconced in an emerging Canadian literary canon.

Acorn needed a poetic environment in which to grow beyond convention, clumsiness, didacticism, and raw energy. He picked the right place. Montreal had been *the* poetry capital of Canada for years, starting with F.R. Scott, A.M. Klein, A.J.M. Smith, Leo Kennedy, and Leon Edel, then with later poets such as P.K. Page, Louis Dudek, and Irving Layton. It had also attracted fiction writer and essayist Hugh MacLennan from Nova Scotia. Acorn encountered and associated with some of the major figures in the development of modern Canadian poetry: Scott, Layton, Dudek, the Toronto-based Raymond Souster, Al Purdy, Leonard Cohen, Miriam Waddington, Ron Everson, and others.

When Helen MacDonald asked Acorn in 1969, "What influences do you feel have developed you as a poet?" he answered, "It's the Canadian poets since 1920. I mention F.R. Scott, Dorothy Livesay, and A.J.M. Smith." His acknowledgment of Scott and Livesay is not surprising because of their left-wing affinities, their poetic attention to socio-economic issues and the masses, and their use of innovative techniques, such as colloquial diction and documentary discourse. The inclusion of Smith is more intriguing, since Smith was closely associated with "academic" and "establishment" poetry, and was already under attack from poets such as Layton for his alleged conservatism. Smith, however, was an exceptional craftsman, an erudite practitioner. Moreover, he had been prominently responsible as a poet, editor, anthologist, and professor for the development of modernism in Canadian poetry. In fact, he had been a chief modernizer and advocate of Canadian poetry. Layton and other younger poets were aware of the debt they owed to Smith, even while they claimed the mantle of the next avant-garde. As for Acorn, he knew enough to learn from a master, and not be overly conscious of artistic fashion.

James Deahl stresses the impact of Livesay's poetry on Acorn's:

As a young man he was influenced by the poetry of Isabella Valency Crawford, Archibald Lampman, Dorothy Livesay, and Anne Marriott[19].... Two salient features of this poetry are that it is Canadian and that it is concerned with restructuring society to provide for a more equitable sharing of our material and cultural wealth.... I would say that the first truly Canadian poet to focus attention on Canadian poetry while still alive was Dorothy Livesay. Acorn and Livesay strongly influenced each other.... In fact, it was Dorothy Livesay who introduced Acorn "to Canadian poetry as Canadian poetry." (*In Memoriam* 3, 8)

Leaving aside the vagueness of the phrases "Canadian poetry" and "truly Canadian poet" in Deahl's essay and his claim that Livesay was "the first," we can appreciate the impact of her poetry on Acorn. He was drawn to her socially conscious, socialist, and nationalistic poetry, to her use of social realism, and to the colloquial, documentary, and narrative techniques as well as the lyric traditions in her work. Later, in 1969, when his best poetry from 15 years was gathered in *I've Tasted My Blood* and earned him accolades and lionization, Livesay made another contribution to his career by writing "Search For a Style: The Poetry of Milton Acorn," a major tribute and one of the few serious analyses of his work in print. Her article includes a prosodic examination of his Island classics "Charlottetown Harbour," "Old Property," and "Islanders." He repaid the compliment in a 1974 letter to her: "Why did you walk out without a word from my meeting at Vic. U? Is it possible you misunderstood what I said of you? I said you had been my inspiration, you who made me desire to write poetry for the people. I did refer to another poet who gave me encouragement in exactly the opposite way you did. With you I was filled with a desire to write that well. With the other poet [Joe Wallace] I was encouraged because I knew I could do better than him. Is it possible you mixed up the two?" (21 March).

Yet Livesay was hardly Acorn's only strong influence. In Montreal he became familiar with the achievements of modernist Canadian poets—such as Klein, F.R. Scott, Smith, Dudek, and Page—and with the importance of modernism in the development of serious, innovative poetry in Canada. A few accomplished Maritime poets in the 1950s were acquainted with and influenced by modernism, for example, Alfred G. Bailey and Elizabeth Brewster in Fredericton, Kay Smith in Saint John, and Alden Nowlan. But the lyric-Romantic, late-Victorian realist, and social realist traditions were still strong in Maritime poetry. The east coast modernist movement, most prominent in Fredericton, was not comparable in magnitude or achievement to the modernist movements in Toronto and, especially, Montreal.

According to *The Oxford Companion to Canadian Literature*, "Much of the [poetic] work of the fifties originated in the academic community and displayed some of the effects of the continuing power of high modernism in the influence of Yeats, Auden, and Eliot" (Hosek 661). Modernism is described in *The Concise Oxford Dictionary of Literary Terms* as "a general term applied retrospectively to the wide range of experimental and *avant-garde* trends in the literature (and other arts) of the early 20th century.... Modernist writers tended to see themselves as an *avant-garde* disengaged from bourgeois values, and disturbed their readers by adopting complex and difficult new forms and styles.... Modernist writing is predominantly cosmopolitan, and often expresses a sense of urban dislocation, along with an awareness of new anthropological and psychological theories" (Baldick 140).

The impetus for modernism included: the impact of the second industrial revolution (chemical and electrical); the expansion of democracy, which promoted both greater freedom and greater uncertainty and instability; the devastating impact of the First World War on belief systems, as well as on human life and property; the heady and disturbing effects of European imperialism; the revolutions in scientific thought, psychology, and the social sciences, and the corresponding upheavals in philosophy; and the rapid changes propelled by technology and urbanization. Modernism reflected and responded to a profound sense of loss and the possibility of creating *new* forms, designs, paradigms, and strategies of belief.

Some literary critics believe that modernism ended in the mid-1930s or with the onset of the Second World War. Others maintain that modernism became "high modernism," the accepted tradition and manner of writing for the literary establishment in the 1940s and 50s. Some scholars even insist that contemporary "postmodernism"—which purports to reject, "deconstruct," "interrogate," and supplant modernism—is simply its latest incarnation. Certainly modernism developed in Canada later than in Europe. And its powerful influence, with dictums such as "make it new!" (American poet Ezra Pound's slogan for modernism), was manifest in the work of Montreal and other Canadian poets during the 1950s and afterward.

The modernist influence arrived in Canada's metropolitan centres before reaching its rural regions not only for the obvious reason that new cultural phenomena tend to find more ready acceptance in the cosmopolitan cities, with their diverse populations and intellectual resources. More critically, modernism itself—related to the larger process of modernity, which has come to characterize and dominate much of the history of the twentieth century—involves a dislocation from the recent past and its traditions. Modernism entails a fascination with change and upheaval and demands a constant reevaluation of artistic form and aesthetic goals, and often of society's structures and aims. Modernism's disconnection with the past and devotion to the production of "new" cultural works had relevance for a city such as Montreal sooner than for the Maritime provinces. As well, the referential complexity and experimental difficulty of much modernist literature could seem élitist, intentionally inaccessible, and irrelevant to readers who did not associate closely with the cosmopolitan intellectual élite or avante-garde.

While modernist poetry had become the mainstream in Montreal (and Toronto) during the 1950s, the next wave of talented poets and poetry lovers was already challenging the modernist and academic establishment—the literary rubrics and newly canonized tastes—and building a wave of poetic innovation that was both multinational and distinctively, proudly, Canadian.

It is essential to stress, again, that the development of Canadian poetry before, during, and after the 1950s has been a regional phenomenon as much as, if not more than, a national one. In the 1880s and 90s, Bliss Carman and Charles G.D. Roberts were associated with New Brunswick, Archibald Lampman with the Ottawa area, and Isabella Crawford with central Canada and the Rockies. In the transition between the nineteenth century and the modernist poets, there was E.J. Pratt's Newfoundland. Yes, Montreal was *the* centre of Canadian poetry in the 1950s. But the poets living there often reflected their home region in their writing, for example, Purdy's southern Ontario and Acorn's PEI. Even Klein's and Layton's poetic treatment of Montreal, or Souster's of Toronto, had a regional focus.

These poetic influences—Livesay, the modernists, the new wave, regionalism cohering as nationalism—greatly enhanced Acorn's awareness of twentieth-century poetic theory, form, content, and practice. The modernists and their challenger-successors fed his own desire to "make it new," to confront "bourgeois values," to be an innovator, an original voice. As well, Canadian modernism and its immediate successors were not so pervasively urban as their European counterparts, and concentrated more often on the landscape and its ethos. Thus Acorn could establish a connection with a city-bred poet such as Layton and explore with him the consequences of modernism, yet also share with him an interest in the natural world, and maintain his poetic allegiance to the pastoral and small-town motifs of his Island home.

By 1956 Acorn had made the acquaintance of Irving Layton, the most notable figure in the new poetic wave. By the mid-1950s, Layton had become a powerful force as a poet, as an advocate for poetry and its revitalization in the postwar era, and as a charismatic presence. Their association is not surprising. Acorn found a Montreal Jewish counterpart in Layton's working-class background, passion for poetry, demonstrative views, vitality, extensive knowledge of literary tradition, and drive to revolutionize sensibility and lambaste the evils of humanity. There were differences, of course, such as Layton's confident eloquence and Acorn's mixture of fumbling shyness, bluster, and bursts of brilliance. But they recognized each other's talent. And perhaps Acorn was encouraged by meeting another poet who had started writing and publishing later in life: Acorn was 33 in 1956 when he self-published his first chapbook, a mimeographed pamphlet, *In Love and Anger*; Layton began publishing in small magazines at age 30, and published his first chapbook in 1945 at 33.

Through Layton Acorn also met Al Purdy, his most important friend among poets until the 1970s. Purdy was steeping himself in twentieth-century poetry and poetics, as well as the old masters, and hanging out in the big city. But he came from rural Canada, from small-town life, and that background must have appealed more essentially to Acorn than Layton's immigrant, urban, working-class heritage. Speaking of Acorn's development, Jewinski writes, "The complex mixture of outspoken man and successfully controlled poet of lyricism begins with Acorn's efforts in the 1950s in Montreal, when he first met Layton and Purdy" (38). Acorn later said of Purdy's poetry that "Al Purdy of Ontario is astonishing, absolutely astonishing" (quoted in Burrill 7). Acorn was drawn to Purdy's use of the colloquial. As Acorn later said, "you should be using language as you would use words in ordinary conversation," and this speech should be from "the locality where you were brought up" (Pearce 99). Acorn was also impressed by Purdy's blend of the colloquial and anecdotal with an erudite knowledge of literature and history, and his disciplined devotion to poetic craft. Purdy and Acorn were both "uneducated in any advanced academic sense" (Purdy *Whiskey Jack* 6); instead, they devoured books and tirelessly debated what they read. Acorn also found a fellow-spirit in Purdy's strong sense of Canadian history and place, regionalism, nationalism, and left-leaning politics, and in Purdy's working-class identity. Acorn and Purdy were gruff guys with their hearts on their sleeves.

A lively essayist and one of Canada's greatest poets, Purdy has written three of the most illuminating pieces on Acorn, and is worth hearing at length:

It was thirty years ago in Montreal. Irving Layton had told Acorn I would give him some hints about writing plays. Milton came to my apartment on Linton Street, and stayed till midnight. During those three or four hours we became friends. ("In love" 16)

We talked poems until early morning, disagreeing violently about almost everything, but seemed to get along well anyway.... For the next few years I saw quite a bit of Milton Acorn. He was a carpenter by trade, but had decided to give it up and be a writer, just like that. I went along when he sold his expensive-looking tools at a shop on St. Antoine St. Talk about burning your bridges! But Milton had made up his mind to sell those tools, and couldn't be convinced to wait until he made some money writing. And as it turns out, I think he was right. ("Introduction," *I've Tasted My Blood* vii)

When Milton decided to sell his carpenter tools ... I was appalled. "Why Milt," I said, "even a great writer like me can't make a living at it." Milton eyed me speculatively. "Maybe you should buy the tools." (*Whiskey Jack* 5) When I first met him, Milton lived in a furnished room on St. Urbain Street where he hammered an old typewriter mercilessly, producing both poems and stories for magazines. I don't know if he sold any stories ... but he showed me a letter from Whit Burnett, editor of *Story Magazine*, complimenting him on his prose. I had a low opinion of Milton's poems at that time. He published a small book of them, *In Love and Anger*, in 1956. It had all the worst faults of a beginner, and I felt very superior. But only a couple of years after that, reading an Acorn poem about his home province of Prince Edward Island—"The Island"—I reluctantly decided that he was a much better poet than Purdy. ("In love" 16)

In the manuscript of *In Love and Anger* there are several drafts of a preface not included in the chapbook. It begins with the heading, "IN LOVE AND ANGER: A selection from the works of Milton Acorn, carpenter, communist, poet," and continues:

How could a person feel love today without feeling anger? Love is indivisible. It embraces all except those who have, by their consistent actions, made themselves forever unworthy of it. To honestly love one person you must love human beings as such. And how could you love human beings without feeling the most bitter anger at what is being done to them? Without at least wanting to do something about it? Love of human beings, anger at their day-to-day violation under the jungle-rule of capitalism, these two emotions have shaped most of my adult life and are the basic themes of my poetry.

This apprentice manifesto has a succinct lucidity and appealing directness that some of his later polemical declarations as the People's Poet lacked.
    This is how a friendly critic later described Acorn's first chapbook: "In 1956, in November of that year, there appeared under private imprint, a book of essentially faulted poetry which had only a kind of genuine roughness to recommend it to the interested reader.... The book excited no interest and received only one review of any significance" (Gnarowski 119). That review was by Louis Dudek, a Montreal poet, editor, and professor prominent in the poetic ferment of the era: "And if the latter [Acorn] can discover a personal frame for his anger and revolt, he too will make his mark."
    Acorn said about that period in his poetic development, "I was writing when I had the time and personally found I had a reputation far better than I deserved as a poet" (Martin *In Love*), and "Somebody said, 'You've got a damn good title, there, boy,' and that's all he said. As a matter of fact, I looked over *In Love and Anger*. I then decided I had to publish another book to show I could really write poems, because it was a very disappointing book as far as I was concerned" (MacDonald).
    His constructive discontent and insistence on improvement and innovation appear in a letter to Purdy: "Utterly dissatisfied with my poetry of late, including 'I Shout Love' which I sent you and another which I didn't. The alienation from my previous poetic experience which cost me all my unwritten epics, progressed to all my store of imagery. I think I'm in a new land and must let my poems grow around me" (Undated 'A' c. 1958). In another letter to Purdy he wrote, "I look them [new poems] over and rather than satisfaction, I feel discontent. My thought is fragmentary, eclectic.... It will do me no good to wonder whether the fact is I'm something like Picasso, constantly discovering (a bit of a jump into the future there) and exhausting forms, or just an anarchist dabbler. The point is that I am, slowly and painfully, discovering myself" (Undated 'B' c. 1958).

Without a doubt, *In Love and Anger* was an apprentice offering. Acorn's limitations are obvious, for instance, in the sentimentality, clichés, and comical rhythms of "This Is the Heart": "This is the heart that since the dawn of time / has missed no beat, that struggled out of slime" (6). Yet his lyrical and prosodic gifts make an early appearance in "My Love, A Fierce Altruist," and the "personal frame" is definitely present in "I Will Not Love You too Much": "When will I write you a letter / Old man, / And have that letter returned?" (16). His 1956 chapbook was a debut he could confidently build on. His growth and promise as a poet, in a surprisingly short time, from the rough, derivative, bombastic, and energetic prosody of "Grey Girl's Gallop" is remarkably demonstrated in a poem to his youngest sister, Helen, who was "very musical, played instruments and sang, and was Grandaddy [Robert Sr.] Acorn's favourite" (D. Hooper), and who died of cancer the same year Acorn died.

"To My Little Sister About Her Illness" shows a great deal more poetic maturity and control than "Grey Girl's Gallop." Its lyricism bears early evidence of what critic Zailig Pollock calls "a poetry of opposites, of delicacy and toughness, which comes together in a single dialectical vision: the delicate beauty that Acorn celebrates in man and nature must be defended through tough-minded unrelenting struggle":

> My little sister, you were the youngest.
> Till you were ten we used to call you 'Baby,'
>   * * * * *
> Yet you were always determined
> to sip life's sweetest, most ephemeral juices...
> to sip them lightly, and with no abandon:
> so until now you've lived
> like a silver water-bug
> skating over the sun-blue lake of your youth.
>
> Know then, my little sister:
> that where black seas crash against riven rock
> their roaring drowns out neither life nor thought;
> that in the stronghold of endurance
> the coins of life are counted one by one;
> and sometimes in the pauses of the storm,
> when the sun strikes many-coloured on the battlements
> of new clouds rolling westward on their thunders

a glory can strike you
greater than a lightning bolt. (5)

The tone and technique of this poem are largely modern, with less of the archaic texture of "Grey Girl's Gallop." The diction and phrasing are much more subtle, the rhythm more supple. Acorn's use of imagery and analogy allows the reader to focus on the sister and the poet's regard for her, rather than obliging the reader—as "Grey Girl's Gallop" tries to do—to concentrate on the poet's manipulation of words and story and his insistence on the poem's significance. It may be the strongest poem in his first chapbook, and one of its few poems of lasting merit.

During this eventful year, Acorn also left the Communist Party (LPP). Joyce Wayne says, "He joined the Communist Party only to leave it after the Soviet invasion of Hungary in 1956" (14). This is too simplistic. More to the point is Purdy's 1969 assessment: "But the most important fact about him—and this he would tell you without being asked—is that he is a Marxist poet, a Communist.... But it is a paradox that Acorn has quarrelled violently with every socialist organization he ever had anything to do with, and is a member in good standing of none. In short, Milton Acorn is a red-necked maverick, both in politics and poetry" ("Introduction" x). In his 1986 memorial tribute, Purdy writes, "When I say Milton was a Communist, there needs to be a qualification. Not as to feeling and commitment, but because he eventually joined all the party's offshoots and splinter groups, like the Trotskyites. He argued with everybody. There was something ferocious about Milton's humanism, and humanism is supposed to be gentle. His was militant" ("In love" 16). This complements Acorn's overview in the 1980s of his political involvements: "I joined just about every radical organization I could find, but inevitably found them interested in opposing each other, and eventually organizing against me" (Martin *In Love*).

Purdy stresses that

Acorn was also a Communist with strong humanistic beliefs, and this belief gave his poems a strength and certainty which my own did not possess. Not that his work had any extraordinary excellence at that time: it didn't. But there was something, a directness, naïveté if you like, a warmth especially. And I learned from it.... Whereas I doubt if Acorn ever learned anything from me, not about writing either plays or poems; if he had, it might have been harmful to the sort of instinctual ability of the man. Looking back, I was plastic man; in some ways, Acorn has never changed." (*Whiskey Jack* 6)

Many readers have preferred to minimize, and even ignore, Milton's political nature: not just the Marxism, communism, and socialism, but his political "feeling and commitment." Quite understandably, some people are uncomfortable with, and embarrassed or threatened by, a poet whose critical thinking, "humanism," and passionate intensity are focused on the inadequacies and failures of our society. Some readers have concluded that Acorn's political concerns are tangents, not the real business of his poetry. Even some literary scholars have asked: Isn't it true that Acorn's "political poems" aren't as good as his best poems, and aren't his poems about the Island, nature, work, and people much better?

Invariably, it turns out these people have read little if any of Acorn's poetry. These questions also reveal an egregious assumption: that poems about nature, the home place, family, work, sexual relations, and love are not and cannot be, among other things, political. The problem with the political nature of Acorn's poetry, then, is with the people who want "the real business of poetry" to exclude interrogations of the structures of our communities and society, of our economic and political behaviour. The only legitimate question is whether a poem does its job and does it well, and while many of Acorn's political poems do not succeed artistically or translate well to our era's political sensibilities, in many Acorn poems the political elements contribute to their lasting significance and artistic strength. Acorn puts it well in a letter to Al Purdy, attacking "this social poetry of the kind Dudek tries to write. He fails because he knows fuck-all about it (it's not social poetry that jars, Al, but *bad* social poetry ...)" (Undated 'A' c. 1958).

Acorn was every inch and brain-cell a poetic *and* political being. The collapse of communist regimes, the mutation of socialist command structures into hybrid economies, and the current hegemony of corporate capitalism should not lull us into dismissing Acorn's socially conscious poetry as passé or naïve. In his poetry and his prose articles he frequently assailed three conditions which are no less prevalent now than during his years as a writer: economic inequality, political injustice rooted in economic privilege and disadvantage, and the suffering inflicted and violence unleashed by inequality and injustice. As a longstanding critic of capitalism, Acorn would agree, were he alive today, that the burden of proof is now on "the globalization of the capitalist mode of production" (Williams and Chrisman 2) to deal with inequities and conflicts—and the casualties of competitive capitalism—which are generated or aggravated by capitalism. He would also challenge that globalization and insist on the need for a radical transformation of society according to egalitarian principles and respect for regions and nations.

As a socialist, Acorn insisted on the connection between wealth and political power. Capitalists, too, are keenly aware of the connection. The capitalist might speak of "competition" and the socialist of "class struggle," yet both are focusing on the central issues of the distribution of wealth and social privilege and the political power that derives from this distribution. Obviously, there is ongoing and serious conflict over this distribution. Acorn envisioned an economic, political, and social revolution that would reduce this conflict. In his socialist view, capitalism was a problematic stage of social evolution, a deeply flawed system of economic and political arrangements, a nexus of self-interests which are destructive of the common good.[20] The globalization of corporate power in the 1990s tends to support the People's Poet's views.

Whether or not Acorn's revolutionary vision is validated in the future, his political identity is challenging for those in the present who attempt to assess his poetry. Jewinski represents those readers who attempt, inadequately, to divorce the writer's belief-system from the work of art: "What gives conviction to his best poems," maintains Jewinski, "is not theory or political thought, but an unhesitating sense of lyricism, point of view, imagery, and rhythmic subtlety" (36). If Jewinski means that political theory or thought alone cannot make poems convincing, he is unquestionably right; but if he is denying that political experience, knowledge, and values contribute to the "conviction," then he is guilty of reducing effectiveness in literature to "lyricism," "imagery," and "rhythmic subtlety." Dante, Shakespeare, Milton, Shelley, Neruda, Ahkmatova, and Soyinka would find this laughable. Moreover, Acorn's political awareness and values are part of his "point of view." Jewinski does fairly balance the negative and positive critical reactions to "politics" in Acorn's poetry: "The best of his poems have a unity of focus and subject, and the worst become a rambling insistent series of so-called political statements that border on invective" (37). This assessment in fact does not "separate the man from his art," but rather acknowledges that the man—social philosophy, aesthetics, and all—produced splendid poetry and forgettable verse.

In 1959 Acorn apparently found a practical way to merge poetry and politics, with the result that the Communist Party may have unwittingly helped subsidize the renaissance of Canadian poetry: "When he and I started a magazine called *Moment* together at my Linton Street apartment, it was produced on a mimeograph machine that I strongly suspect had been liberated from the Communist Party. It was a subject never discussed between us" (Purdy "*In love*" 16). In light of this anecdote, it is worth remembering that the advent of inexpensive printing machines, including the mimeograph machine and the photocopier, greatly facilitated the production of poetry broadsheets, chapbooks, magazines, and then books, by writers and other small literary publishers. In a sense, Acorn had traded the traditional technology of carpentry for the revolutionizing tools of the literary and publishing trades.

"After the carpenter tools got sold in Mtl.," writes Purdy, "I don't believe he ever worked again at a formal job" (Letter to the author). "When he was broke with no possibility of quick redemption, Milton slept on the floor of our apartment.... He ate enormously and read all my books before I could read them myself" ("In love" 16). In the winter of 1956-57 Acorn and Purdy wrote poems and plays and "did a great deal of talking.... He had a room on St. Antoine St., a place where you had to wade knee-deep thru poems, wastepaper and books" ("Introduction," *I've Tasted My Blood* vii).

In a 1979 interview in *intrinsic*!, Acorn said, "I had to establish the trade of poetry." Commenting on this, Gudgeon writes that "he had to take poetry out of the hands of academics and other bourgeois élitists, and create a framework where an ordinary man or woman could earn their living writing poems. That meant that the future held no cushy university jobs or nine-to-five grinds for Milt: if he was going to do it the right way, he'd have to do it the hard way—through his poems alone" (66). This sentimental version not only misrepresents the development of Canadian poetry and the contexts of Canadian poets, it also detracts from the actual complexity of Acorn's struggle to survive as a full-time poet.

First of all, no one, then or now, could earn a living writing poems. After 1957, Acorn endured with a combination of his disability pension, ongoing support from his family, generous help from numerous friends for three decades, and various grants, royalties, and honoraria. Indeed, much of this support was inspired by his talent, commitment to poetry, and political and cultural activism. But this "hard way" to survive as a poet and activist is more believable and honourable—a middle-class kind of artistic patronage, combined with the ironic fortune of his modest pension—than a simplistic notion that he survived "through his poems alone."

Second, modern Canadian poetry was shaped by a wide variety of academics, other professionals (e.g., school teachers, social workers, and lawyers), and skilled tradespeople and labourers; it was produced by poets with haute bourgeois, middle-class, and working-class backgrounds. When Acorn was helping "to establish the trade of poetry," its other influential practitioners in the 1950s included Earle Birney, Dorothy Livesay, Irving Layton, F.R. Scott, Ralph Gustafson, and P.K. Page, and in the 1960s, Leonard Cohen, Alden Nowlan, Red Lane, and Margaret Atwood. The variety of their backgrounds and poetic contributions speaks for itself. Acorn and his friend Purdy were more unusual in their determination to avoid "nine-to-five grinds" and to maintain poetry as their primary occupation. Even Purdy, though, was more able and willing to work as a first-rate feature journalist and literary editor, and in later years as a writer-in-residence in universities. Acorn was unable to take advantage of these options for a free-lance writer. Often dependent on family and friends, pensioned in his mid-thirties, Acorn was not exactly "an ordinary man or woman." And he was again fortunate, at the onset of his literary career, to find his soul-mate in Al Purdy: a working-class, full-time poet with sound judgment and practical savvy to match his extraordinary talent and intelligence, and with an emotional stability that helped steady the volatile Acorn.

Purdy and his wife moved to Roblin Lake, Ontario, in 1957 and began building a cottage. Returning to Montreal in 1959 to earn more money, Purdy found Acorn still there, "living on Sanguinet and later on St. Urbain St. I don't know what he was doing for money; most of the time he didn't have any" ("Introduction" *I've Tasted My Blood* viii). Acorn had been poetically productive and successful during this time, publishing over twenty poems in literary magazines such as *The Canadian Forum* and *The Fiddlehead*, including the first publication of "I've Tasted My Blood" in the April 1958 issue of *Delta*. Several of his finest and most popular pastoral-lyric poems about Prince Edward Island, such as "The Island," "Islanders," and "Charlottetown Harbour," date from the late 1950s. In these poems he became an affectionate, belonging observer, detached from his childhood experience of injustices. The Island's charm adheres, in fruition or decay, to the traditional working-class trades of farming, fishing, and dock-working. The production of these poems and "I've Tasted My Blood" during this period demonstrates that Acorn was already developing both a distinctive perspective on his Island experience and an impressive range of registers in his poetic voice.

It was around this time that Purdy and Acorn "visited Leonard Cohen in the latter's apartment," Purdy wrote in 1969. "If ever two men were the antithesis of each other it's Cohen and Acorn. The first elegant, even in morning disarray, self-possessed and entirely aware, moving within a slight but perceptible aura of decadence—decadence not in the sense of decline, but of standing aside and apart, not being intimately involved. And Acorn: a red fire hydrant wearing blue denims, genuine haltingly [*sic*] articulate, recently emerged from the noble servitude of labour, completely out of his element in that distinguished apartment which bore all the marks of Leonard Cohen's own personality" ("Introduction," *I've Tasted My Blood* x-xi). In spite of differences, there was a respectful recognition of each other's exceptional presence and, to use a favourite phrase of Cohen's friend and mentor, Irving Layton, "poetic fire."

Jewinski, whose long essay on Acorn contains the most extensive published study of his poetry, attempts to encapsulate these four exceptional poetic personae: "Purdy became the garrulous, open-ended talker; Layton, the outspoken iconoclast; Cohen, the 'lover.' Poetry, in a word, went 'public.' Acorn, of course, became the 'political poet'" (28). Jewinski's thumbnail sketches are obviously reductionist: each poet is more than a single attribute such as iconoclast or lover. But these aspects of their personae did advance poetry as a more popular artform: less élitist and rarefied, more public and accessible. And this shift toward a more "public" poetry was closely related to the rise of nationalism and regionalism, that is, of regional and national audiences that wanted their experience, history, and sense of place to be realized and manifested in public forms of discourse, including poetry.

Jewinski writes that "the troublesome, if not bellicose, public self-image Acorn created places him among the late modernists like Purdy and Layton who have, with equal force, attempted to break down the comfortable and neat division of the private man and the public poet," and that "whatever Acorn's place in Canadian literature, he is certainly one of the figures responsible for thrusting literature back into human experience, response, value, and politics" (Jewinski 38, 36).

The role of Acorn, Layton, Purdy, Cohen, and others in establishing a "public" poetry is related to the issue of the literary "canon" and "canonical texts"—that is, to the establishment of a valorized literary tradition, and of texts and authors that are deemed to be "major," "central," "influential," or otherwise considered significant. Robert Lecker, in his "Introduction" to *Canadian Canons*, accurately observes that "Traditions and canons are always in the process of being made and unmade, and whatever has been constructed shares its space with all that has been destroyed. There are no constant or prevailing values, no unadulterated inheritances, and no clear-cut lines of descent; canons thrive in flux" (7).

During the 1950s the Canadian literary tradition or canon was in its early formative stage. A relatively small number of writers, scholars, reviewers, anthologists, editors, and publishers were engaged in the multifarious process of canon formation. Yet, inevitably, there were newer writers and critics attacking the youthful canon and questioning the freshly-granted canonicity of certain texts, authors, modes, and literary movements. Acorn, Layton, and Purdy were in the front line of writers contesting the poetic "establishment." Their challenge, like all critiques of literary tradition and canons, was part of the process of canon-making and unmaking which Lecker describes. The protean canon absorbed Acorn, Purdy, and Layton, changing shape to accommodate their poetic gestures. They in their turn became canonic, part of the "flux" of tradition which the next wave of writers would need to remake.

In 1960 Acorn returned with Purdy to Roblin Lake to help him finish the cottage. Amid all of Acorn's economic adversity in Canada's biggest cities, the Roblin Lake days might have been his only experience of rural hardship: "Freezing weather and snow besieged us in that partly built house. We ran out of firewood quickly, and hauled in truck loads of scrap lumber, courtesy of the CPR in Belleville. But there was only a handsaw to cut the stuff into stove lengths.... And we argued. Milton had read more books than I had. He paraded his knowledge ostentatiously, dazzling me with facts and figures. I got back at him by verbal swashbuckling about things I wasn't very sure of, and had to look up secretly. And we laughed, and we sawed boards, and we hammered nails. And wrote poems" ("In love" 16-17).

Purdy had published two chapbooks with Ryerson Press and knew the editor, the illustrious Lorne Pierce: "So Milton and I got together a selection of his poems and sent them to Ryerson, along with a covering letter from me. But Pierce wouldn't believe there was any such person with the unlikely name of Milton Acorn. He thought it was a Purdy pseudonym, and that I was trying to sneak another chapbook past his editorial eye" ("In love" 17). Eventually persuaded of Milton Acorn's existence, Pierce published the poems in *The Brain's the Target* in 1960.

Of his first book, *In Love and Anger*, Acorn later said that "It was received very kindly, I remember. It did say something about the spirit, but the book ... the book was lousy. I resolved that when I published another it would be better—and it was" (quoted in MacFarlane 4). Jewinski refers to "the strange blend of regionalism, love poem, recounting of anecdotes, and social protest" in *The Brain's the Target*, and feels that this "is a characteristic of almost every book Acorn produced" (43). This "blend" appears in many poets' collections, and is more common than "strange." Whether the poems in a collection should be linked or unified in some way is a matter of shifting opinion and fashion. One of those "blends" earned him the title of "People's Poet of Canada."

Irving Layton once said that a poet could die content if he has written six or seven great poems. The same might be said for a book: that the poet can feel a large measure of satisfaction if a volume contains a half-dozen fine poems of lasting value. *The Brain's the Target* includes several of Acorn's best Island poems: "Charlottetown Harbour," "Old Property," "Islanders," and the celebrated "The Island." There is the delicate reflection on his father's aging, "The Trout Pond," and two of his strongest portraits, "Libertad" and "Belle." "At El Cortijo" is one of Acorn's most memorable poems: muscular, feisty, exhilarant, witty, and self-aware. And "The Fights" potently extends the metaphor of small-time, small-town boxing into a meditation on the struggle to survive— "It's craft and / the body rhythmic and terrible, the game of struggle" —and the price the human brain too often pays.

In 1960 Acorn also published a short collection, *Against a League of Liars*, another title sharply revealing of Acorn's passionate stance and genuine character. The imprint was Hawkshead Press, and the publisher was John Robert Colombo, then a young poet and graduate student. The publication was a broadsheet with 15 poems that had been deleted from the Ryerson publication. There were fewer gems in this broadsheet, but several have endured: the keen-eyed and magical invention of "Picasso's 'Seated Athlete With Child'"; the exquisite observation and descriptive restraint of "Hummingbird"; the explosive, minimalist "Annie's Son" about the psychic and physical aftermath of an abortion; and especially, "Letter to My Redheaded Son." Clearly, anyone who maintains that Acorn did all his best writing in the 1960s and 70s overlooks the dozen poems from the mid- and late-1950s that transcend apprenticeship and, in several cases, exhibit mastery.

By 1960, then, Milton Acorn the poet had emerged. So, too, had Acorn the public figure and promoter of his poetry, demonstratively flapping his wings: "And when it came to selling the books," claims Acorn, "I appointed myself as a dealer. I peddled myself. No other writer would have done it—the financial and literary community are absolutely separate from farmers and workers and toilers. But my God, they would never peddle their own stuff. My red Tory blood boiled and boiled. Think of it, selling from door to door. And I hated selling. I used to go to a tavern and get absolutely stinko, and then go out on the streets with my book of poems. I can't remember how I did it, but I always woke up the next day with the money in my pocket and the books gone" (quoted in MacFarlane 4). How much good this self-dramatization does for the public reception of poetry is debatable, but it did attract some attention and contribute to the Acorn legend.

The same year, Acorn received a CN telegram dated Oct 4/60 from Root McCormich of the CBC: "Broadcasting your poems on Anthology Oct 7th hope you can hear programme."

Purdy also writes about Acorn's trip in the spring of 1960 to a poetry conference at Queen's University. After hitch-hiking to Kingston, he was "too shy to speak to any of the poets," whom he watched from a distance, sleeping on a park bench and eating the few sandwiches he'd taken along ("In love" 17). This was the reticent side of Milton Acorn, which would emerge as late as 1986, just before his death, when he was reluctant to attend the annual meeting of the League of Canadian Poets. "Reticent" or "shy" are polite terms for whatever combination of insecurity, distress, and distaste he felt in larger, more formal gatherings of poets, especially those in academic settings or reputable hotels. His comfort zones were the apartments of poets less cultivated than Leonard Cohen, working-class and bohemian taverns, greasy spoons and coffee houses, and low-rent hotels.

He was also feeling more comfortable with his family home, primarily because of the growing reconciliation with his father. Distance and time were no doubt beneficial, as were Milton's increasing self-esteem as a writer and his father's transformation with sobriety. "Dad began to understand Milton more, in the later years," Mary says (Interview). "They understood each other a lot better as they got older." This shows clearly in "A Worried But Easy Habit," published in 1959 in *The Canadian Forum*:

> The past (for that's the only past
> there is) is wound up inside me,
> Old Man, that's our trouble.
> The past when you used to gargle
> your rage in the morning;
> and I was an enemy, quick
> with the desperate curse of the truth.
>
> But that's my trouble, Old Man;
> a worried but easy habit
> of "Enemy in sight: Open fire!"
> And with you changed, your face
> with a smile washed onto it,
> I go on jabbing, provoking,
> fighting a ghost in a bad cloud.
> That's our trouble, Old Man.
> Forgive me, for today
> and tomorrow start with forgiveness.
> <div align="right">(<i>I've Tasted My Blood</i> 23)</div>

Milton's peacemaking with his father appears more lovingly in "The Trout Pond," which also prefigures his later skill as a poet of the natural world. First published in *The Brain's the Target*, "The Trout Pond" carries the date "1958" and the inscription "For R.F. Acorn, 1897-1968." Acorn lets us gaze upon their relationship by watching father and son in a rowboat on a woodlands pond. It seems Robert Sr. did go fishing with his oldest son. Here are the final two stanzas:

> My father's whiteheaded now,
> but oars whose tug
> used to start my tendons
> pull easily these years.
>
> His line curls, his troutfly drops
> as if on its own wings,
> marks a vee on the mirrored
> ragged spruceheads, and
> a crane flapping past clouds.
> <div align="right">(<i>Selected</i> 56)</div>

With this tone of gentleness entering his relationship with his father, Acorn made at least two other trips to PEI during this period. He stayed at his parents' Charlottetown home in March and April 1959, and in October 1960 he returned to spend several months with his parents, who had moved to an old mansion in the rural community of New Glasgow. His father was commuting on winter roads to his post-retirement job as a commissionaire in Charlottetown. This experiment in country living lasted only a few months. Milton's parents returned to Charlottetown, and Milton went back to central Canada.

With soon-to-be-major Canadian poets providing friendship and support, with the Mounties keeping tabs on his radicalism, and with his father poetically forgiven, Acorn was ready to make his next major move, to the city that would be his adopted home for most of his remaining life.

VI

TORONTO AND MARRIAGE

> But what is it keeps me from folding
> The whole damn basketful of stars
> Into my bosom? Why can't I give
>
> My most personal love, which I've often said
> Was universal, when it's asked? You need
> Such a precise almighty balance with me
> As to what you come on with, and what you hold back.
> — "An Afflicted Man's Excuse"

ACCORDING TO AL PURDY, Acorn "left [Montreal] in '61 or '62." Rosenblatt writes that "Milton was in Toronto at the tail end of the fifties.... He was associated with the Bohemian Embassy, an after hours club which started in the late fifties. So Al was wrong on the dates. He hooked up with Gwendolyn about 1960-61" (Letter). According to Rosemary Sullivan, Gwendolyn MacEwan's biographer, "Almost as soon as the Bohemian Embassy opened [1 June 1960], Milton Acorn marched in and took it over, as if it had been created especially for him" (108).21 Founded by the actor-writer Don Cullen, the Bohemian Embassy was a "social club" on St. Nicholas Street frequented by writers and musicians, student intellectuals from the University of Toronto, and other like-minded patrons. The Embassy offered National Film Board movies, folk music, and poetry readings. Acorn presided as an unofficial poet-in-residence, reading to appreciative audiences—and impatient ones when he read and declaimed too long—and offering editorial critiques and encouragement to young poets such as Margaret Atwood, David Donnell, Joe Rosenblatt, and Gwendolyn MacEwan.

Given Acorn's restless movements, it is not unreasonable to accept both Rosenblatt's and Purdy's accounts: Acorn showing up in Toronto "in the late fifties" and 1960, and returning to Montreal and then Roblin Lake with Purdy later that year, before spending part of the winter in New Glasgow, PEI. He was back in Montreal in 1961, writing his mother on March 17: "I'm busy working, being a social lion in Montreal, and chasing girls. You guessed right on every point. Girl-chasing doesn't consume so much time in Montreal as in Toronto. In fact it would be difficult to imagine how a normal healthy man could avoid becoming involved with them, supposing he wanted to do such a ridiculous thing. So I have some time left for other things, including poems." The libidinous bragging about "girl-chasing" barely conceals the sexual anxiety discernible in the next sentences.

In this letter, he tells his mother about being hired as an extra by the National Film Board: "Perhaps the period of picturesque unemployment is over. I've fitted into a scene where the opportunities to make amounts of money continually recur. As long as the work isn't regular, I'm okay. It doesn't interfere with my writing, and opens up new facets of existence.... The Film Board job was very interesting. In the scene I was in they took the Robert Harris painting 'Fathers of Confederation,' they photographed it, and then panned out to a film of the 'fathers' sitting around the table. That was us. 'The Fathers'.... It's called something like 'The Life of Charles Tupper'.... If you see it I'm the 'father' on the extreme right of the picture, your left, in front.'" His "picturesque unemployment" was hardly over, and the "amounts of money" were small. But his role in this film is wonderfully prophetic of his own mythic destiny: years later, Acorn's portrait would hang in the Confederation Centre Gallery in Charlottetown, not far from the permanent Robert Harris exhibit and Harris's painting of those famous "Fathers."

Meanwhile, this enthusiasm for "opportunities" in Montreal, and his ambivalence about "becoming involved" with "girls," was short-lived. Within a few months he was back in Toronto, in love with Gwendolyn MacEwan, and making his presence felt in the Toronto literary scene. Unlike Montreal, with its history and hotbed of significant poetry, Toronto offered Milton a poetry scene in gestation. He

Milton and Gwendolyn in love.

would be there for much of the decade, an integral part of the eruption of literature in Toronto, and eventually a poetic *cause célèbre* of the burgeoning central Canadian literary community and the nation-wide phenomenon that would be nicknamed "CanLit."

His time in Toronto began gloriously, then brought Milton considerable grief. "I gather that Gwen met Milton by the summer of 1960, casually, in the Bohemian Embassy," says Rosemary Sullivan. MacEwan was a precociously talented poet and novelist born on 1 September 1941, in Toronto. She published her first poems at age 17 in *The Canadian Forum*, and left school at 18 to write. When they met he was 37 and she was 18. "When Milton saw Gwendolyn," writes Sullivan, "he must have been overwhelmed. She was beautiful—small, delicate, and yet there were those kohl-limned sapphire eyes and the dangling cigarette, so that her exotic performance had an element of self-amusement" (111). Acorn proposed marriage to her before the end of the year. MacEwan wrote back on 28 December 1960, that she could not accept the proposal, stating, among other reasons, that she was too young to marry. She was determined to guard her independence, especially in regard to her own artistic journey.

By the spring of 1961, however, they were involved. During that summer, Acorn went to stay with close friends from his Montreal years, the Goldbergs, in their Laurentian home near Montreal; MacEwan was with him for part of the visit and helped him edit *Moment.* Their relationship developed throughout the fall and into the winter. Acorn then travelled to PEI early that winter. "Alone in Toronto with Milton gone," writes Sullivan, "Gwendolyn suddenly felt anchorless. She may have panicked, believing she might never see him again." Sullivan refers to MacEwan's childhood experience of abandonment, and concludes that "when Milton returned, she was ready to marry him" (120). They were married on 8 February 1962, at Toronto's old City Hall, with Al Purdy as best man.

Referring to their literary acquaintances, Sullivan writes, "Everyone was disturbed by the wedding.... Purdy was cynical about the May/December love affair. He thought Gwen was with Milton because Milton was 'getting attention'" (Sullivan 120). Margaret Atwood, MacEwan's friend, "was shocked. It was the archetypal story of Beauty and the Beast" (Sullivan 121). Sullivan herself, focusing on MacEwan's exquisitely imaginative psyche, considers that "Perhaps Gwen's attachment to Milton was humanly simple. He was one of the few people who could touch her in her profound isolation—an arm, a voice. She had selected Milton, almost a parody of physical excess, to pin her to the earth" (Sullivan 121).

There is, too, the possibility that MacEwan was also attracted to the softer aspects of Acorn's personality—the tender, lyrical, wistful, and vulnerable facets which appear in his poetry, with which his family and friends were familiar, and which have sometimes been overlooked by those who cast MacEwan as a gifted aesthetic innocent and Acorn as a barbarian.

As for Acorn, he believed that his poetic talent, intellectual prowess, and manliness had attracted a beautiful, brilliant young writer. They could share poetry and all the elements that were distilled into poetry through the alchemy of living and of the brain. He had a constant companion who would listen to his political discourses. A sexually experienced man, he could teach and savour his less experienced lover.

Acorn's mother responded to the marriage supportively:

> I was very glad to get your letter but sorry you felt on the defensive about your civil marriage. That was a matter for you and Gwen to decide and so long as you are satisfied with it that is all that counts.... I received the snaps and am delighted with them. You certainly have a beautiful wife and she has a sweet look about her.... You know I always maintained a hands off policy on my children's lives especially once they married, so I don't think you are in any danger of me trying to run your life for you. What Dad and I did for you we were glad to do and would have done more if we had been able but that was it. (22 March 1962)

Milton and Gwendolyn lived briefly in a Toronto apartment after they were married, then moved to 10 Second Street on Ward's Island, one of the islands in Toronto Harbour known collectively as Toronto Island, a locale thought to be congenial for artists. Purdy notes that "after he married MacEwan he and she came here [Ameliasburgh] for a couple of weeks that spring" (Letter to the author). Acorn also made a trip back to Charlottetown, without Gwendolyn, two months after their marriage, an unfortunate action so soon after their wedding.

David Hooper remembers meeting Gwendolyn: "He must have brought her to Prince Edward Island shortly after they were married. Dark-complexioned woman, I recall, with dark hair. Very quiet. The only impression I got was that they weren't connected." Mary Hooper, who does not remember Gwen visiting the Island, has a different recollection of the relationship, left over from her mother's visit to Milton and Gwen in Toronto: "Mother went out to visit them before they were married and she was really impressed. She thought he was really happy. They seemed to get along well together, whatever happened." Helen's comments about "snaps" and Gwen's "sweet look" in her March letter raises the question of whether Helen visited and met Gwen before or after the marriage. David's version of Helen's visit differs somewhat, but does stress that Milton and Gwen were connected for a time through their poetry: "She [Milton's mother] didn't get as much attention from Milton as she thought she should've gotten, because Milton or Gwen would run into one room and write a paragraph of poetry and come out and read it to the other, who would then disappear into the other room and come out with a paragraph of poetry. Uncle Milton was really smitten by her. The next thing we heard was that she was going off to Egypt.... And we never heard any more about her" (Interview).

In fact, Gwendolyn left for Israel, not Egypt, on 10 July 1962. This effectively was the end of their short marriage. As Sullivan says, "It is apparent that when she was leaving for Jerusalem she was leaving Milton." While she was away, Acorn had an affair. When MacEwan returned from Jerusalem on 28 August 1962 she told Acorn they were finished, moved from Toronto Island into the city, and soon became involved with another man, perhaps, as Sullivan suggests, to give her the support she needed to confront Acorn. He had told her about his affair when she returned from Israel, but his admission had little bearing on her decision to leave him, which had already been made.

They were incompatible from the start. "Almost as soon as she had married, Gwendolyn recognized that she had made a terrible mistake," writes Sullivan (123). Unfortunately, as Sullivan rightly notes, MacEwan "hadn't anticipated that Milton really wanted a wife. His revolutionary bent was actually deeply conservative and family values were important. He regretted not having a normal family life ... and Gwen seemed the closest he had ever come to that possibility.... In Gwen, fiercely independent, he got more than he bargained for" (123).

Sullivan's judgment arbitrarily privileges MacEwan's "independent" persona over Acorn's "conservative" values, yet accurately points to their deeply incompatible needs as a major reason for the marriage's failure. In Sullivan's view, MacEwan was not meant to be his housewife, and Acorn's didactic and stubborn political views clashed with her dislike of ideological rigidity. As well, "They had made a contract on marriage that each would be allowed other lovers.... The grapevine at The Embassy had it that the first occasion of infidelity arose with Milton" (Sullivan 123-24). In spite of this and the contract, Milton exhibited severe jealousy and possessiveness. This behaviour is evident in a letter written several years later to poet Stephanie Nynych: he blames MacEwan for an affair he had while living with her on Ward's Island, claiming he was only retaliating against, he alleged, Gwen's recent affair (19 February 1969). There was also the matter of his heavy drinking—not so devastating as it would soon become, but still a barrier to intimacy and understanding, and a symptom of the inner turbulence that made Acorn a difficult, and sometimes impossible, companion. MacEwan's trip to Israel was not only a fulfilment of a long-standing desire but also an exit from the untenable situation with Acorn and a return to her own imaginative quest.

"I received your letter," Helen wrote to Acorn at Ward's Island, where he lingered, alone and distraught, "and as you know I am bitterly disappointed. You have both done wrong and you will both suffer. It is not possible to escape the result of our acts. However, if you both love each other you should be able to work it out. Love is a matter of give and take. Real love is of slow growth and the best of it comes I think in after years but it takes work on both sides. My advice to you is to take your time, cut out drinking so much wine and concentrate on your poetry, keeping in touch with Gwen if you can't get back together right away." Helen continues with wise but largely irrelevant advice: "Gwen didn't have to come back just to write her novel. If that was all she could have found somewhere else to write it. She must love you and want you there. According to you, you told me she was faithful while she was away. Did this trouble stem from your telling her you hadn't been faithful while she was away? Some women's reaction to that would be to show that what was sauce for the goose is sauce for the gander, not knowing she would be hurting herself more than she hurt you. Neither one of you can say anything to the other so the best thing to do is forget and forgive and try to save your marriage." Her closing counsel was more pertinent: "Cut out the drinking. I thought you never drank unless you were happy.... Whatever you do don't hurt anyone. Remember your own failings and understand that other people have the same" (4 October 1962).

This is the period in which Acorn's drinking became a destructive behaviour that would continue off and on for over 15 years. His marriage was a failure after only five months. There is the matter of Acorn's infidelity while Gwen was in Israel, and the fact that she became involved with another man soon after her return, leaving Acorn no opportunity "to forget and forgive and try to save" his marriage. Acorn had another breakdown, became suicidal, and was admitted to Sunnybrook Hospital.

His mother wrote to him at Sunnybrook, with a more realistic grasp of his situation: "I was glad to get your letter because I have been wondering and worrying about you. I was afraid this trouble would land you back in hospital, but I guess it is the best thing under the circumstances.... Perhaps after a course of treatment you will be able to take this thing in stride.... When you think of the long way round Dad had to take before he obtained peace of mind—which he has obtained to a remarkable degree—it makes you realize that no situation is hopeless however it may appear" (15 November 1962).

Al Purdy put similar advice more bluntly: "I realize you're a sensitive flower of a poet—but you don't expect me to treat you that way, do you? I never have do you think?... Don't give me that crap about the world being ended and you can't write, and how evil the world is—the world is the only place we have, there's no bloody other—If you give it up for worms you're a fool, and perhaps you are a fool. As you know, I've often thought so. It should also be unnecessary to say, but I would find the world a lesser place myself if you weren't here" (5 December 1962). Sagacity from his mother and shrewd observations from his best friend were not enough. From mid-October 1962 until at least mid-July 1963, Acorn was in and out of Sunnybrook and the psychiatric wing of Westminster Veterans' Hospital in London, Ontario.

He made another trip back to Charlottetown later that summer, returned to Toronto, and decided to leave for Vancouver, where he was living by early October. Eventually, while Acorn was in Vancouver, MacEwan suggested a divorce. He refused, and MacEwan sued, citing adultery as the grounds. The marriage was officially dissolved on 17 June 1966. Ironically, Al Purdy was a witness.

The extensive correspondence between Acorn and MacEwan during the first few years after their separation bristles, at first, with Acorn's aggressive declarations of love and, increasingly, his intemperate bitterness, while MacEwan strives to explain to him and herself the reasons for their separation and the path she has taken as a person and writer. Here is one of Acorn's gentler messages: "God how I loved you! How proud I was that you loved me. Yet I did little writing. I was entirely absorbed in you and what you were doing. I thought I was thru writing, but separation from you opened up entire new areas of experience. It also drove me crazy ... perhaps the two are connected. Lying with you in bed at night I used to talk as I never talked to any one person before or since. You understood me, and I was beginning to understand you more deeply.... Now I suppose you look on my love for people with an amused contempt" (20 August 1965).

And here is what MacEwan wrote to Acorn after her return from Israel in 1962 and Acorn's breakdown that fall: "You are a great artist, you are not smashed. The injustice I dealt you was not in leaving, but in marrying you right off—with an idea of time and permanence I actually believed I could deal with.... Because you were gone that winter—back to the east I was afraid ... believed I would not see you again/believed nothing could bring you back—I married you then out of a certain need for balance and permanence—yet did not then understand what more I needed to experience and expand.... I feel I've dealt you a blow. I have—and I don't lack the guilt for it."

Acorn was willing to let MacEwan shoulder the blame, and rather than embrace her overtures for a compassionate dialogue and camaraderie, he fired volleys of verbal abuse in his letters. "He, who had been so nurturing of her talent, took the first opportunity to attack her work" (Sullivan 144). There was no acknowledgment that he might have harmed their relationship by going back to the Island so soon after their marriage. Nor did he consider that his own infidelity and drinking might have harmed their relationship.

Unable to acknowledge any inadequacy on his part, any self-loathing, any responsibility for the failed marriage, he projected the source of his pain onto MacEwan, shouting his love, rage, resentment, and self-justification. For several years, her letters reached out patiently and sympathetically to him. He preferred his wounds, unwilling to see how much they were self-inflicted, and responded to her with self-pity and vituperation.

In light of this behaviour, and because of his reputation as difficult, distressed, and alcoholic, it is tempting to lay most of the blame for this failed marriage on Acorn. He would no doubt have been a challenge for any woman. Even so, it is obvious that MacEwan was far from the best "choice," and that her own needs and personality were profoundly ill-suited to Acorn's and to any sustained intimacy and partnership with him.

"I think the trouble with her," says Hilda Woolnough, who talked about Gwendolyn with Milton years later, "was that she was too young for him and he knew that, but he was madly in love with her.... He knew it couldn't work. She was young and it was very painful for him. I think he always had a soft spot for her. Milton wouldn't talk too much about that relationship. He was a very honourable man."

This "soft spot," which was still evident during his final years back in Charlottetown in the early 1980s, consisted of more than honour: in it there were a profound sadness, a lingering sense of failure, and a subdued bitterness. For instance, MacEwan's photograph was on the cover of a literary magazine that arrived at Ragweed Press, where Acorn visited almost daily. I was working there part-time as a literary editor and jack-of-all trades. Magazines were left out for Ragweed Press's visitors, and Libby Oughton, the publisher, wondered aloud if we should hide the magazine and MacEwan's picture. No, we decided, not from the author of *Against a League of Liars*, *In Love and Anger*, and *Dig Up My Heart*. Acorn came in that day as usual, walked around, and eventually halted beside the small, low stage where books and magazines were displayed. We watched as he stared down for a long time at the photograph of his ex-wife. Finally, he spoke: "Once there was a brilliant, handsome young poet, who could move everyone with his words and his voice, and he married a brilliant, beautiful young poet. And she found him boring." He then walked out with a measured pace, leaving the Ragweed Press staff stunned and in tears.

If Acorn was, indeed, honourable about MacEwan in later years, it came too long after his abundant harsh denunciations. These continued throughout the 1960s and appeared in his letters to her and in his correspondence and conversations with friends.

Later, Acorn would sometimes blame the separation on Toronto, as he does in this 1981 quotation: "Home-wreckerdom, that's what I call Toronto. They'll denounce you to her and her to you. It's a deadly place. I wonder why I've stayed here so long" (quoted in MacFarlane 4). In the NFB film he muses, "I went to Toronto to do a gig, and ended up staying there on and off throughout the sixties and seventies. Got married, divorced, stayed too long. Sort of a negative, magnetic, negative, positive, drawing, haunting, puzzling quality about Toronto.... There's something about it that continually promises and disappoints, promises and disappoints" (Martin *In Love and Anger*).

Underlying this complaint, besides romantic disappointment, was the Maritimer's awareness of Toronto as a power region, which could be both attractive and aggravating for a person from a less powerful region. As a poet, Acorn had been gaining success within this power region; as an overtly proud Islander and Maritimer, his success helped counterbalance the centralizing tendencies in Canadian literature. He was one of the presences in Toronto who helped mediate between literary centralization and the development of literature in *other* regions. The failure of his marriage diminished his sense of success, his presence, in Toronto. And he characteristically responded by accusing the city.

Indeed, Acorn projected onto Toronto the bitterness he felt toward Gwendolyn and his sense of betrayal about her decision to leave him. One of the talented young poets then in Toronto was Joe Rosenblatt, who won the Governor-General's Award for poetry in 1976, the year after Milton had received this highest honour. Rosenblatt writes that MacEwan "left him for her Egyptian experience at the beginning of the first Allan Garden's episode which started early summer 1962. And the marriage was short-lived to say the least, lasting only about a year, ending when she came back from Egypt in 1963" (Letter).

In 1994 Rosenblatt felt compelled to refute a "splenic ... disservice to Milton Acorn's poetry and to the poet" in Douglas Fetherling's memoirs, *Travel by Night, A Memoir of the Sixties*: "Everyone who had been around the Toronto writing scene at the time seemed to have tales about the incongruous and, I gathered, disastrous marriage of Gwen and Milton Acorn, the foul-smelling poet and self-proclaimed proletarian" (quoted in Rosenblatt "Remembering").

Rosenblatt responds:

The Acorn who[m] Fetherling knew in the late sixties was not the individual who became my poetic mentor (along with Gwendolyn MacEwan) back in 1960 when they ran a mimeograph literary magazine for poets called *Moments*. Acorn was clear-headed and very sane when he and Gwen ran their publication.... It might be of interest ... to know that Gwen, years after their marriage breakup, and despite the bad feeling, mainly on his part, had a deep affection for Milton which she imparted to me on many occasions because she respected his poetry and knew the man was plagued with ill health which toward the end of his life resulted in a complete breakdown of his mental faculties manifested in his rabid Stalinism, homophobia and other facets of dementia.

Rosenblatt himself may be accused—by Acorn's friends on PEI "toward the end of his life"—of doing a disservice by exaggerating Acorn's "dementia" as a "complete breakdown," as if he were a raving lunatic. Rosenblatt, however, more than makes up for this by defending and paying homage to his "mentor."

Ironically, Gwendolyn MacEwan was co-winner of the 1970 Governor-General's Award for poetry, the same year Acorn was eligible for his classic *I've Tasted My Blood*, the book many writers felt should have won the award. In the immediate fallout from the jury's decision and all the years since, disgruntlement and literary legend has focused on the *other* co-winner, Vancouver writer George Bowering, and hardly a mention is made of MacEwan. Reasons were given in print for objecting to Bowering's award, but we are left to surmise why friends of Acorn chose not to attack MacEwan's: her location in central Canada where most of Acorn's supporters lived; her lack of direct association with those "American" elements which in some people's view tainted the selection of Bowering; Acorn's agonized memories of a broken marriage; and perhaps a sexism which pitted one male contender against another, ignoring the female. The principle reason, however, may have been the indisputable excellence of MacEwan's work.

MacEwan's career continued to thrive, with nine volumes of poetry, two novels, one collection of short stories, two children's books, a travel book, several radio plays and documentaries, a verse play, and an adaptation of Euripides' *The Trojan Women*. She won a number of arts grants and literary awards in addition to the Governor-General's Award. She travelled in Israel, Egypt, and Greece, and in 1971 married the Greek singer Nikos Tsingos. Her poetry and fiction are among the most visionary, oracular, and mytho-poetic ever produced in Canada. Her interests were as far ranging as Gnosticism, Egyptian religion and culture, Babylonian astronomical metaphysics, Zoroastrianism, and Kabbalism; and these interests were not just historical and literary, they were profoundly personal explorations and incorporations of the mysteries and belief systems which humans have imagined and constructed. As she insisted, the task was to perceive the mythic, not to create it. Her poetry also reveals an equally powerful awareness of everyday life, and her poems often weave together the sublime and the mundane, the sacred and profane, the esoteric metaphor and the vernacular.

Gwendolyn MacEwan died on 30 November 1987, in her mid-forties. Sullivan writes, "The coroner's report on the autopsy is cryptic: '*Cause of death*: Metabolic Acidosis, resulting from a recent history of binge drinking and no food intake'" (383). Yet "there was no alcohol in her system." Whatever its cause, MacEwan's death was tragically premature. Her last books, *The T.E. Lawrence Poems* and *Afterworlds*, showed her sustaining her earlier brilliance while revealing a powerfully mature style, voice, and vision.

Although Acorn never credited MacEwan or her writing with any positive influence on his own poetry, his relationship with her certainly influenced his love poetry. But there are only faint traces of the malignant anger or bitterness he felt and directed toward her in the poems he published during his lifetime. In fact, those love poems are usually remarkable for their tenderness, wistful longing, or plaintive sadness, which contrasts with the gruffness and bluster more commonly attributed to him. The feeling and imagery often blend delicacy and affable swagger, and there is a respectful regard for the loved one. A stanza from "I, Milton Acorn" illustrates two major aspects of his persona and experience as a lover:

My present lover finds me gentle
So gentle I'll be in my boisterous way.

> Another one was heard to call me noble.
> That didn't stop her from going away.
> (*Selected* 148)

The tender-rowdy lover enjoys present success, yet he is shadowed by the mournful knowledge of his past as a lover scorned in spite of being "noble." The "boisterous" nature of the poet's gentle loving—separated from Acorn's biographical context—can seem endearing, a colourful excessiveness in a rough-hewn male.

Of course, it all depends on whether one reads his love poetry without reference to the biographical context of Acorn's marriage, or with knowledge of that relationship and his behaviour in mind. Both ways of reading have value. We must be cautious about the "biographical fallacy"—reading literature as a direct reflection of the writer's life. We often want to read poems as works of art that have an existence beyond the writer's life, and we should be judicious in making connections between the writer and the text. On the other hand, we cannot ignore the experience and contexts that generate poems, especially when evidence is available. We have to decide whether that evidence tells us anything about the poems—and if the poems offer insights into the poet.

The evidence indicates that Acorn was madly in love with MacEwan, yet failed miserably in his attempt to create a lasting relationship out of that love. He had affairs over the next 20 years, but none of them released the same passions—love or wrath—and none developed, in spite of the odd marriage proposition on his part, into permanent involvements. The published poems, meanwhile, tell us that he could artistically render his tenderness and adoration, longing and disappointment. Several poems in his unpublished manuscripts, a couple of which have been published posthumously, show that he occasionally tried to poeticize his bitterness. For the most part, he had to transmute his experience into a wistful, reverent, and well-wishing longing for or disengagement from the loved one. As well, there are few definitive references to MacEwan; as a result, it is usually difficult to know the extent to which the poet's lover is an imaginative construct—a composite figure—or based fairly specifically on MacEwan.

Joyous in love, Acorn would write "Live with Me on Earth Under the Invisible Daylight Moon," which can hold a candle to any modern love poem in the language:

> Live with me on Earth among red berries and the bluebirds
> And leafy young twigs whispering
> Within such little spaces, between such floors of green, such
>   figures in the clouds
> That two of us could fill our lives with delicate wanting:
>
> Where stars past the spruce copse mingle with fireflies
> Or the dayscape flings a thousand tones of light back at the
>   sun—
> Be any one of the colours of an Earth lover;
> Walk with me and sometimes cover your shadow with mine.
>   (*Selected* 98)

Losing the woman he loves, the tenderness, closeness, and distance become exquisitely painful in "First Wife Sonnet"—"Could I forget an arm, a leg, an eye / Which I had once and then had amputated?"—and in "Parting," which suggests the separation from MacEwan:

> My love's got secrets
> of dreamplace, sounds
> in her ear's core,
> keys my fingers
> have never played.
>
> Deeds are folded
> inside her, some of them
> maybe with me.
>
> She's sorting out
> our library,
> her book, my book,
> and now and again
> we exchange a touch
> for old times.
>   (*Selected* 21)

What refined and resolved itself into the published love poetry for Acorn was not bitterness, melancholy, or recrimination, rather, in "You Growing," a loving and generous benediction for both his ex-lover and himself:

> You growing and your thought threading
> the delicate strength of your focus,
> out of a clamour of voices,
> demanding faces and noises,
> apart from me but vivid
> as when I kissed you and chuckled:
>
> Wherever you are be fearless;
> and wherever I am I hope to know
> you're moving vivid beyond me,
> so I grow by the strength
> of you fighting for your self, many selves,
>   your life, many lives...your people.
>   (*Selected* 82)

Acorn channels passion and disappointment into an act of communion full of grace and, for his readers if not sufficiently for himself, of catharsis.

    A decade after Acorn's brief marriage, Karen Kennedy, a student then at St. Patrick's College of Carleton University, would be deeply moved by the love poems at an Acorn poetry reading. Now a speech therapist in Nova Scotia, Kennedy is one of the countless students and other people who attended Acorn's poetry readings in the 1960s and 1970s: "Of all the poets we studied in English, he was my favourite. Then he read at St. Patrick's, and I couldn't believe that such beautiful love poems could come from a person who seemed so disturbed. His face looked disfigured and he ranted a lot, but his love poems were incredible."

    The appearance of facial disfiguration to which Kennedy refers was the result of Bell's disease, a condition involving partial facial paralysis. It may be one factor behind these lines in his poem "Self-Portrait": "I've got quite a face, thank God / for smiling or scowling" (*Selected* 119). This facial feature could reinforce the opinion of those people who thought he was deranged, and it certainly could heighten any pathos in the way Acorn looked, especially Acorn the love poet.

    Notable events occurred in Acorn's life in Toronto during the early 1960s other than his short-lived marriage to MacEwan. Literary readings and gatherings of artists and other intelligentsia took place at coffee houses, especially the Bohemian Embassy. For instance, one November evening in 1960, Acorn shared the stage at the Bohemian Embassy with Libby Jones, a college-educated vaudeville stripper. Jones was performing at the Lux Burlesque on College Street, and appeared at the Bohemian Embassy to lecture poets on the need to be commercial on occasion. She criticized Beatniks, referring to their "defeatist dogma," and expressed confidence that the Bohemian Embassy's audience wasn't those American Beats. Then she defended her particular art-form, attacking "pygmy moralists." A Toronto reporter notes that she rushed off, leaving the stage "to Milton Acorn, a blunt and sun-beaten poet from Prince Edward Island. Acorn is a gifted nut who refuses to put his talent to the use of pretty images, but prefers in a violent age to make poetry out of shock tactics. His verse would rock Miss Jones' 'pygmy moralists,' but it mostly tells a hard truth" (Ferry).

Acorn was at the centre of a group of Bohemian Embassy poets who, according to Joe Rosenblatt, defied "the wretched park ordinances to have the city council adopt the New York City park bylaws, I believe, that allowed speakers in the park, Ban-the-Bombers, poets et al to spout their works under the gaze of the Robbie Burns statue" ("Remembering"). A newspaper report on 16 July 1962, states that "a hundred and fifty voices shouted a random chorus of 'We want poetry' at Allan Gardens yesterday afternoon when police broke up an outdoor reading session.... The crowd, which had gathered to hear pieces from *Midsummer Night's Dream*, jeered at the police." The report refers to "members of Inter-Poet—Toronto's new open air poetry-reading group," and says, "Insp. Genno and two uniformed constables stepped in just as Milton Acorn had finished a preliminary reading on Toronto as a fallout shelter. Mr. Acorn and poetess Luella Booth, who had spoken earlier, were asked to show their permits. When neither could do so, Insp. Genno suggested that they leave.... Mr. Acorn said Inter-Poet would be back with more poetry next week, with or without a licence" ("Police"). The Allan Gardens demonstration resulted in a change in the city's by-laws, allowing freedom of speech, including performances of poetry and theatre.

The Allan Gardens fight also absorbed a great deal of Acorn's time and energy during his brief marriage—perhaps too much time and energy in light of MacEwan's departure for Israel and their separation. But Acorn was too self-absorbed with his poetic energy and role to notice signs of the impending marital disaster.

Rosenblatt writes, "At the time of the Allan Gardens free-speech fight, Acorn was at the height of his creativity in his poetry" ("Remembering"). Acorn's sense of his own poetics within the context of Canadian poetry had strengthened substantially during his time in Toronto. In 1961 he wrote to Cid Corman, a prominent American poet and literary magazine editor, forcefully rejecting Corman's view of Acorn's work:

> I like language, and have too much respect for it to try to "impress" with it. What I want to do is give the exact connotations of a thing image-wise.... To call me a "combination of Layton and Souster".... Really Mr. Corman! I may not be half as much a poet as either (tho I won't guarantee that) but I bloody well have my own identity.... Mine is an independent development from the basic current of folk-song and folk-poetry on the East Coast, influenced by Scott and Smith along the way.... Nevertheless you can bloody well lump me with Irving in one important category ... that of striving for a thurogoing mastery of the full available technique of English verse, both in their traditional and modern appearances, a meticulous attention to sound, to rhythm, to image in relation to both sensual and intellectual content, plus sound, plus rhythm. (8 February 1961)

Clearly, there is some mythologizing of Acorn's "independent development" from an East Coast folk tradition. His poetic development seems to have owed relatively little to "folk-song and folk-poetry," and a great deal to "English verse," his voracious reading of science fiction and other short stories, socialist poets such as Joe Wallace, and especially to major Canadian poets such as Layton, Souster, Livesay, F.R. Scott, and Purdy. But he was not exaggerating his "striving for a thurogoing mastery" and his "meticulous attention" to the central elements of poetry.

Respect for Acorn's poetry as well as his feistiness and courage was steadily growing. Writing in 1962 about the burgeoning of Canadian poetry in *The Globe Magazine*, poet Joan Finnigan acknowledges "Milton Acorn's courageous publication *Moment*" (14). In 1963 his first book-length collection of poems, *Jawbreakers*, was published by Raymond Souster's Contact Press, which had been founded with the help of Irving Layton. That same year, *The Fiddlehead* (published at the University of New Brunswick since 1945) devoted a special issue to *58 Poems by Milton Acorn*. Fred Cogswell, the editor from 1953 until 1967, is celebrated for his recognition and encouragement of talented new writers, and his focus on Acorn in 1963 was typically prescient.

The year after Acorn's separation from Gwendolyn, however, saw the onset of his "bouts with alcohol," as Rosenblatt calls them. Some of his Island friends, such as Reg Phelan, remember the Milton Acorn of the late 1960s through mid-1970s as a man still lucid, focused, and intact, and not yet showing the ravages of too many bouts with alcohol and too much poverty. Others who knew him in Toronto and Vancouver during the 1960s speak of a man already wrestling with his own and society's demons with too little regard for his physical health, mental clarity, and relationships with others. Rosenblatt, for instance, writes, "After Gwen and Milton split up a combination of circumstance conspired against that man" ("Remembering").

While he continued to write with his usual ardour and tenacity, and while his poetic powers were growing, Acorn did not publish another book for six years; and then, during the drama swirling around *I've Tasted My Blood* and his People's Poet award, Irving Layton said to the press, "This is perhaps the last time we can honour him. He's past his prime. His best writing days are behind. His book is a collection that covers 12 years" (Sypnowich). Indeed, some readers do feel that Acorn's best work was written and published before 1970. Others would dispute or qualify Layton's backhanded compliment. After all, one-third of the 156 poems in *I've Tasted My Blood* were previously unpublished—hardly the work of a poet "past his prime." Moreover, he won the Governor General's Award for a book written and published after 1970, and there are several masterful sonnets in *Captain Neal MacDougal & the Naked Goddess* (1982). Even so, Acorn's inner distress certainly increased from 1962 onward, and with it his vulnerability to alcohol and a low-income existence.

His friend Purdy had gone to British Columbia then returned to Montreal. Acorn decided to head to Vancouver, and in the late summer or early fall of 1963, John Robert Colombo took him to the train station in Toronto. Perhaps he needed to leave the scene of his romantic disappointment. Even more, he was probably driven like countless Canadians to travel the width of the country, to experience Canada coast to coast. And being a Maritimer, he headed for the other ocean and shore.

VII

ANOTHER COAST

> What's a man if not put to good use?
> Nothing's happened I want to forget.
> What's a day without a notable
> Event between sunrise and sunset?
> — "I, Milton Acorn"

> Here's to the bottle I'm drinking
> And here's to all the bottles I've drunk
> — "Here's to the Bottle"

ACORN HAD THE KNACK of arriving in a new city and region at a time of lively poetic beginnings. Far from being a loner who shunned literary circles, Acorn flung himself into the centre of poetic ferment as long as there were freshness, vigorous invention, and a challenge to bourgeois orthodoxies. Jewinski writes, "When viewed in terms of the development of Canadian poetry, Acorn seems, at first, a striking and isolated individual. In fact, he probably best represents the shift in aesthetics, poetry, and culture which dominated Canadian literature from about 1950 to 1980. Acorn consistently upheld the popular causes which, at some points, were crucial for many Canadian poets—indigenous modernist poetry, socialism, urban blight, Canadian nationalism, counterculture journalism, popular culture, and so on" (25-26). Acorn encountered most of these "causes" in

Vancouver, and he also experienced the influence of contemporary literature from south of the border.

Throughout the 1960s, a number of talented writers on the BC coast were impressed by the new wave of American poets and poetics: Beat poets who had sustained their authority, such as Allen Ginsberg and Ed Dorn, Pacific coast poets such as Jack Spicer and Gary Snyder, and especially poets associated with the Black Mountain movement (e.g., Robert Duncan, Robert Creeley, Charles Olson)—a movement and poetics about which Acorn was ambivalent. Olson was noted for his concept of "projective verse" with its assertion that content should precede and determine form in each poem. Acorn noted that "my work since 1960 has been greatly influenced by Olson—not his 'formal' theories, but theories on voice. I do not agree with him that form must always be nothing but an extension of content. I think there is a continuous dialectic interplay between form and content" (Livesay 37).

In 1961 the influential magazine *Tish* was founded in Vancouver by poets Frank Davey, George Bowering, Fred Wah, and others. Writes Davey, "The founding of *Tish* marked the beginning of a distinct but inward-looking west-coast writing community.... Paradoxically, in a national context *Tish* was also the most dramatic evidence of the emergence across the country of a new generation of poets more open to the colloquial and popular than were their forbears" (Davey "Tish" 790). Not all younger poets agreed with the American-influenced poetics advocated by *Tish*. Acorn's reservations were to a large extent based on his antipathy to American influence, and on his anti-academic bias—most of the key figures in the Black Mountain and *Tish* movements were affiliated with universities.

As well, he was suspicious that some "free-verse" strategies lacked aesthetic discipline and a foundation in the long tradition of prosody. Acorn was too rooted in traditional British and modernist Canadian poetry to become a devotee of the new American poetics with their postmodernist leanings. He was unable to see the irony in his advocacy of traditional and modernist poetics, which were part of the literary canon of mainstream academia, and in his quarrel with the academic avant-garde. His reverse snobbery toward academics, an attitude not uncommon among self-taught writers, prevented him from appreciating the variety of poetics within academia and the relationship between academic work and the practice of poetry. Perhaps, too, his Island and Maritime upbringing—the "red Tory" in him—encouraged a certain conservatism, a stronger regard for tradition, and a resistance to changes that seemed to be imposed from "outside," from the big cities, by the experts "from away."

Fortunately, Acorn's eclectic hunger to learn from a wide variety of poetry and his need to be among the innovators allowed him to incorporate some of the Black Mountain and Beat strategies, as he had once learned from the academic A.J.M. Smith. Moreover, the *Tish* poets and their U.S. models were the voices of a new era, many of them critical of the economic and political establishment and intent on reshaping consciousness and society. The *Tish* movement was not political— let alone socialist—enough for Acorn. But it did help generate an avant-garde literary culture and sustain a "counter-culture" of dissent which Acorn valued.

One *Tish* member stands out for his effect, partly inadvertent, on Acorn during the 1960s. George Bowering, now a prominent poet and novelist, was a young poet and graduate student when Acorn arrived in Vancouver. In the December 1961 issue of *Tish*, Bowering had astutely criticized Acorn's broadsheet *Against a League of Liars*, but ignored the superior poems in *The Brain's the Target*. Purdy replied in Acorn's defense. Acorn held his fire until Bowering published a favourable review, in the July 1963 issue of *The Canadian Forum*, of Acorn's poems featured in the special 1963 issue of *The Fiddlehead*. In a letter to *The Canadian Forum*, Acorn blasted Bowering, showing no gratitude, and remembering only the earlier criticism. At the end of the decade, Acorn would have another, more momentous occasion to vent his spleen about Bowering and the "Americanized" *Tish* crowd.

Another important player in the West Coast literary and political scene, and a person sometimes linked to Milton Acorn editorially, was Dan McLeod, who became the general editor of *Tish* after June 1964. He was also a founding editor of *The Georgia Straight*, which, launched in 1967, is Canada's oldest surviving underground newspaper, and now a weekly mainstay of cultural and entertainment news and social issues in Vancouver.

The *Tish* influence and people such as Dan McLeod were part of the heady literary atmosphere that Acorn breathed in Vancouver. The urbane Bill Duthie had opened his first bookstore and hired the colourful Binky Marks as his paperback manager: they quickly established Duthie Books as a quality store supportive of Canadian writers and the local literary community. New groups of social activists were springing up, overlapping and supplanting older liberal and left-wing organizations. Acorn's two passions, poetry and politics, found a temporary home in a city beginning to generate a counterculture which would mature into cosmopolitan artistic and social activist communities.

Acorn had arrived in Vancouver from Toronto during the late summer or early fall of 1963. He was living on East Hastings Street, a downtown stretch of rooming houses, cheap hotels, dingy pubs, greasy spoons, pawnshops, and low-end clothing stores. Feeling very much the seasoned poet from the cosmopolitan centres, he wrote to Al Purdy on October 21, "Now as for the poetry scene in Vancouver, I don't believe it exists to anything like the extent it exists in Mtl and Tor. A certain number of kids scribble 'poetry' but the level of accomplishment is very low." The local "kids" might have found this remark patronizing, pretentious, and astonishing coming from another non-central Canadian writer.

A New Year's Day letter to his mother boasts of his optimism and high spirits:

This is going to be a good year, I'm sure. Last night I won a raffle! There's a bottle of whisky sitting in my window box right now.
More serious I was struck by the thought that here it was my fortieth new year, and I guess I am definitely a man. When I was a boy I dreamed of being a millionaire, a boxing champion (yes! me!) and later when I grew more conscious of the problems of the world, a great revolutionary. But I never dreamed of being anything as great as what I am ... a poet! That was beyond my wildest. Dad, when he wrote to me, seemed to be nourishing useless guilt about the troubles we had when we were younger. One of my greatest assets is my extraordinary confidence in myself as a poet. I can't see any explanation for it except in the fact that in our home all the children were encouraged to develop their individual talents. I remember when I was sitting up in bed, writing the most impossibly bad pseudo-history, and how proud you were of me and sure I was showing signs of literary talent. (I wasn't.) That's not how most budding poets get treated. (1 January 1964)

The letter goes on to claim that he had kept writing during his recent illness and that his new "stuff" is better than anything he had produced earlier. He had already found "a political outfit I can tolerate, so I'm once again an activist." His only complaint is that his psychiatrist is "a bit of a fool." He tells his parents that they look wonderful in a Christmas photo sent as a Christmas gift by his sister Helen: "You look like you had a couple of drinks in you and Dad as if he never drank a drop in his life." He'd earned a couple hundred dollars from CBC. His paranoid streak, or at least his desire to be a combative nonconformist, appears when he says, "An enemy of mine's got a strategic post at CBC" and, "The Canada Council doesn't like me either." He announces that he may have a "real job next year, and close to home." Acorn thought he was back on track, stronger than ever. It was, instead, one of his mood swings.

A few days later he was in Vancouver's Shaughnessy Hospital, writing to Purdy: "What hinders me is pain. My life has been so painful, it spreads like a blot over whole areas of my existence.... And where, what, is this my self. Milton.... Where are you? I love you? Ginsberg said something like this. This awful vacuity and meaninglessness, which is oneself? I swear that without art I would have lost myself completely ... as so many people I'd met, especially in this veterans hospital, are lost." This sense of alienation, this lapse of confidence, was the counterpart to Acorn's self-assertion, and no doubt a primary source of his bull-headed determination and manner on so many occasions. He told Purdy, "One thing is that I've never persuaded anybody of anything. I'm a marvellously indefinite person. I put so much into working with particular people, you, Red, Gwen ... and then something happens: Red dies, Gwen leaves me. You are almost my only definite accomplishment, as I am yours" (11 January 1964). Amidst the self-pity and self-dramatization, Acorn fortunately sustained his reliance on Purdy's tough and wise love, a contact second in importance only to the bond with his mother.

Acorn's mother did lose track of him a year later: "I am writing a note in the hope that it will get to you. I don't know your address or the name of the hospital if you are still there" (7 February 1965). Back in touch, he wrote on July 3, "All along the side streets of Vancouver roses are blooming. It's like I never saw a rose before.... Long ago. I think actually when I was nine years old. I had a thought about beauty. That it was *in me*. Not in the sky, that only inspired it. Strange, or not so strange, I thought this must be the commonest of thoughts, and never mentioned it to anyone. Yet nowhere have I read that expressed in literature. Yet it has remained a principle of my life. Beauty was in me, and therefore in other people. Lately I've been trying to look at things so as to connect with the beauty in me. I went a whole day that way and found myself coming up with the most charitable thoughts." Leaving aside his amusing claim to have never encountered this "principle" in literature—Acorn could suppress his erudition when it suited his posturing—this letter is evidence of his rapture and generosity when his mood was ebullient.

The less pleasant phase, for himself and others, appears one month later, in another letter to Helen: "Just a few lines to tell you I'm all right, tho every day I realize more what a sad and empty city Vancouver is. I've been writing lots of poetry, tho I seldom send it out. Somehow I've got to shake myself out of that apathy.... In fact I'm doing something.... I'm bringing out a book called 'I Want to Tell You Love' with a young poet named Bill Bissett" (16 August 1965). Love-hate relationships with cities are hardly exclusive to people suffering emotional crises and struggling with psychological problems. But Acorn's mood swings about Vancouver did parallel the alternations between euphoria and despair about himself, as well as the unpredictable and disruptive shifts in his behaviour toward other people.

In a 1981 interview, Acorn described "Vancouver as 'a bit of a nervous episode,' a stay filled with poetry, of course, and politics. He met bill bissett [now a poetic legend himself], whom he thought a potentially great poet—'but he wouldn't clean up his act, and neither would I'—and he worked with a group of Trotskyites, supporting their opposition to the Vietnam war. But when Acorn's poet friends were denounced for their loosely defined politics, he took umbrage" (MacFarlane 4).

bissett writes that Acorn "belonged 2 th leeg 4 soshulist acksyun out uv th bk store on granville st ... ther was a hall in th back uv it the LSA [Longshoremen's Association] hall Milton put on poetree reedings ther ... he built a paying job th shelvs 4 th bkstore & organized th readings & othr events studee groups ... th LSA folks were *not* trots ... they wer middul uv th road soshulists ... he was organizing reedings at th advans mattress coffee hous in the ubc distrikt ... Milton was veree courageous & veree organizaysyunal.... he had manee frends all ovr th citee in all distrikts & neighbourhoods" (Letter). Acorn later said that "in those days I was not writing a great deal of poems. I spent more time working with other people's poetry than my own" (Deahl "Acorn" 52). Acorn's friendship with bissett, however, led to poetic collaboration as well as mentoring.

"Milton & i made a book 2gether calld *i want 2 tell yu love* ... it was a colleksyun uv equal amts uv poems from each uv us no wun wud publish it but we lovd workin on it.... i have no knowledg that iuv retaind uv anee girl frends he was almost always sew in 2 poetree n politiks n changing th world promoting equalitee i undrstood that he was fresh from a divors with gwendolyn macewan & that was uv cours painful sew i was veree close with him thr 4 a few year period 64-66 as the countr cultur so calld hippee drug movmnt grew & i became veree much a part uv that i saw less uv him" (Letter). bissett's account highlights Acorn's energetic involvement in the local poetry scene and his impact as a friend and mentor on other poets.

An important part of that scene was the Advance Mattress coffeehouse on 10th Avenue near Alma Street in Vancouver. Named after the former tenant in this warehouse, the coffee-house became Acorn's west coast version of the Bohemian Embassy. He read, hosted readings, and, of course, hung out, tirelessly talking about politics and poetry.

Another literary companion and close friend in Vancouver was Red Lane, one of the most talented young poets in Canada in the early 1960s. Red's younger brother, Patrick Lane, a major Canadian poet since the early 1970s, says, "He really loved my brother, and there was a lot of transference after my brother died [in 1964] and he met me." The Lane brothers' background and poetic development corresponded somewhat to Acorn's. Raised in the interior of British Columbia, they were learning the craft of poetry without extensive academic training and by moving to a large city which had a poetic scene. Moreover, the Lane brothers came from a working-class background, and had known rough-and-ready times as children and young adults. Red had moved around Western Canada, working at a variety of jobs and writing poems. Fifteen years younger than Acorn, Patrick worked at manual and skilled labour jobs. Like Acorn, he suffered the tragic loss of people close to him, including his brother Red. Patrick, however, had a much greater ability to cope with adversity and to carry on with a charming moxie and compassion that complemented his toughness. Acorn might have been a poetic influence on Patrick Lane, but it was Patrick who sheltered and cared for Acorn in Vancouver.

"When my brother died, Milton moved to Seattle, living there clandestinely. And he was living with a woman there, she might have been a black woman. It might not have been sexual. Milton had the capacity to get women to look after him, but I think it was more a mothering relationship than a sexual relationship he had with most women." There is not enough psychological evidence to support categorically Lane's contention about Acorn's need for a "mothering relationship." Given Acorn's intimate bond with his mother, however, and given the observations of friends or the evidence in Acorn's letters about his amorous relationships, such as the one with Louise Harvey, Lane's assessment should be kept in mind. If Acorn did have this need, it could help explain the incompatibility between MacEwan's "independence" and Acorn's patriarchal need to be masterful *and* looked after.

Patrick Lane speaks of Acorn's anger at MacEwan. Lane's experience does not accord with the conviction expressed by Acorn's family that he spoke only kindly about Gwen after the separation: "Of all the things Milton could express anger at—and he could go on about political grievances—it was Gwen that he most fulminated against in those days." Lane also reflects on the damage the separation did to Acorn's sexuality and manhood: "I think the break-up and her going off with another man was destructive to his sense of manhood. I don't think he ever regained his full sexual capacity after that. I think Milton suffered a trauma he never got over."

Not all Acorn's post-separation relationships with women were asexual or "mothering." Lane recalls that "the first time I saw Milton was in the Shaughnessy Hospital and Myra McFarlane was there. They got together in 65. That's when I first ran into Milton, with Myra in the arms of Milton in the hospital. She was a beautiful young poet. She was a real talent for awhile. They were definitely lovers. I remember thinking how ironic it was that she was young and beautiful and dark-haired and built just like Gwen. Myra was very important to him."

Acorn stayed in Lane's apartment on the north shore of Vancouver in 1966: "He was going to stay just overnight because he was going back east. Instead he stayed for a month. My kids got a kick out of him, but he drove my wife nearly crazy." Acorn had been talking for over two years about going back east, and as his personal distress grew, Lane and Joe Rosenblatt, now living in Vancouver, began urging him to go.

In 1967 Acorn went on a binge, and Lane discovered him in his apartment, insensible, covered in filth, and reeking. He probably had not eaten in days. "He was on downers from Shaughnessy Hospital. He was drinking a bottle of Triple Sec." Lane took him home, stripped off his clothes and burned them in the back yard—"My kids loved that"—and bathed him. Acorn stayed with Lane and his family for a week. "Then he disappeared again into his world of Hastings Street."

"In his last days in Vancouver," says Lane, "he was always helping the wreckage of society, the underclass. He always was surrounded by those people. That part of Milton has to be stressed quite strongly.

How he helped those people, bought them lunch and coffee. The trouble was, he was never far from that himself." The question has to be asked why Acorn identified so strongly with these people. It was not just the result of his sympathy for socialism and the working class. Perhaps his own experience as an underdog, beginning with the abuse and ridicule he suffered from neighbourhood bullies as a child and continuing through his rejection as a husband, helped foster his affinity with the lower classes. Rather than strive for normality and membership in the middle class, he sought adoption into the underclass. His socio-economic descent was not, of course, constant, for he was often befriended and housed by his family and his middle-class friends in artistic, academic, and activist circles.

Also, Acorn was hardly the first artist to immerse himself physically and mentally in the company of social and economic outcasts. Toronto historian Modris Eksteins, focusing on modernist artists early in this century, writes, "Despite a fascination among the avant-garde with the lower classes, with social outcasts, prostitutes, criminals, and the insane, the interest usually did not stem from a practical concern with welfare or with a restructuring of society, but from a desire simply to eliminate restrictions on the human personality. The interest in the lower orders was thus more symbolic than practical" (42-43). This was not the case with Acorn. Whatever psychological needs were fulfilled by living among the downtrodden and the derelicts, he had a genuine concern for their welfare and a passionate desire, if not the practical ability, to restructure society for their benefit. Perhaps, too, Acorn felt that Hastings Street was where the real people were, ravaged but not warped by capitalism and bourgeois values. There, he could display "the puddle of mother's milk / that almost floats my heart" ("Self-Portrait" *Selected* 119). He may sometimes have romanticized the underclass and his place among them, but his sympathies and sense of identification were genuine.

In early 1968 he moved into the basement of Pat Lowther's house. Lowther was another important poet and guiding spirit in the Vancouver writing community. Before she was tragically murdered by her husband Roy in 1975, Pat Lowther worked devotedly on behalf of poetry and poets, the New Democratic Party and socialist politics, feminism and women writers. Acorn was one of many poets she befriended, and he was able to stay in her house for two months, feeling that he had found artistic and political shelter. But he was still in bad shape. Lane says that:

Joe Rosenblatt and I talked about Milton. We agreed he had to go back east. Joe and I took Milton downtown and talked to him long and hard. "Milton," I said, "You've got to get out of here." Joe and I went down to Milton's apartment and packed everything up in boxes. I stored his things temporarily at my place, and shipped them later. Joe and I took him down to the train station and put him on the transcontinental.

Throughout, '65, '66, and, '67 I spent a lot of time with him. But I just couldn't keep doing that. He just took over your life, demanding too much, like a child. I believe we carry a few people in our life, three or four people who need to be carried, and that's all we can do. You finally say, that's enough, I can't do it anymore, or, I've got enough people, you'll have to find someone else. I really loved the man, I mean, I really admired him. But he was a really difficult human being.

Lane saw Acorn "here and there" in Toronto in the seventies, but "That was pretty well it for me." He says that Acorn went back to Vancouver a couple of times in the early 70s, perhaps doing readings. "He came back out to Vancouver to stay with Pat Lowther in her basement for maybe an extended visit the year before she died."

Acorn waxed nostalgic about his Vancouver years in a 1968 interview for *The Guardian* newspaper of Charlottetown: "Describing his life in large cities like Montreal and Vancouver, he said, 'Just like being in the home town, when I walked down the sidewalk I always met someone I knew. Poets are not introverts. I have never met one who was not an extrovert.'... When asked how he got along with the hippies and flower people in Vancouver, Mr. Acorn explained, 'I got along ok with them, they used to call me "Uncle Miltie" or sometimes "Square Root—the squarest of the squares"'" (MacIntyre). On this occasion, Acorn managed to repress or ignore his agonized times in Vancouver in favour of a light-hearted recollection that makes him sound jolly and avuncular.

Acorn has occasionally been named a co-founder with Dan McLeod of *The Georgia Straight*: "When the marriage ended within a year, he headed for the west coast to co-found the enormously popular Vancouver newspaper *The Georgia Straight*" (Wayne 15). Acorn might have described himself this way, as a 1969 article in a Charlottetown paper suggests: "He was the co-founder of *Georgia Straight*" ("Native Poet"). In 1986 Acorn explained, "First I worked with the Trotskyites, then I worked with the Maoists. Finally I got sick of the whole thing and I gathered a collection of local hippies together and I said let's start a paper, let's start a peace paper. And let's make it a labour paper: pro-working class" (Deahl "Acorn" 3). In fact, Dan McLeod and poet Pierre Coupey are listed as coordinating editors in the first issue of *The Georgia Straight*, dated 5 May 1967. Acorn's name is among the contributing editors.

Acorn's role in the paper's origins, according to Dan McLeod, was less significant than he later claimed. McLeod refers to Acorn "as one of our founders," and says that "I wasn't really that close to him personally. My fondest memory about him is from the pre-*Straight* days, when sometimes we'd meet on Robson Street accidentally on the way to or from Duthie's. He'd be sucking on his ever-present stogie and we'd just talk about poetry.... My worst memory is of the last time I saw him ... when he walked out of a key organizational meeting and slammed the door so hard that the glass completely shattered. When his stubbornness and orneriness came to the surface in such a disturbing way, I was forced to re-examine any romantic notions I had about his idealism" (Letter).

Acorn's enraged departure occurred when the newspaper's collective divided between those, including McLeod, who saw the need for an ownership structure and others, including Acorn, who wanted to maintain cooperative management. McLeod's faction prevailed. McLeod says, "Had he gotten his way, I am sure the *Straight* would not have survived much longer.... Nobody will ever know if Milton had a workable plan for the future of the *Straight*, but I felt angry and betrayed when he didn't try harder. Political poets may be the conscience of a better society, but I believe that we also need our best poets to be the *architects* of a better society" (Letter). Even if "co-founder" exaggerated Acorn's contribution to *The Georgia Straight*, he took to the paper his usual blend of passion, idealism, cantankerousness, and organizational ineptness. As well, he was among its first significant writers, contributing articles to those early issues.

Joyce Wayne's version of his departure from Vancouver insists that "his deep sentiments about Canadian nationalism and his rejection of the U.S. Black Mountain movement in poetry, which had caught British Columbia by storm, forced his return to Toronto in the late sixties" (15). It is true that his anti-Americanism became more pronounced and, at times, virulent during his Vancouver years. And he had quarrelled with the *Tish* and Black Mountain movement poets. Yet these were political passions and aesthetic debates he thrived on, and hardly seem to be differences that "forced" Acorn back east. Mary

Hooper says he claimed he was run out of town, his life threatened, because he spoke out against drug use.

Wayne's version is typical of Acorn's simplistic self-dramatization, which served his poetic and political image, and which often neglected more personal, painful, embarrassing, and ordinary causes. Hyperbole and a touch of paranoia, not exactly rare in Acorn, appear in his story to Mary. In fact, he was "forced" back east by a combination of his restless energy, his latest fallings-out with political and literary associates, his deteriorating mental and physical health, and his loneliness for family, old friends, and familiar surroundings—his longing for home.

VIII

THE PEOPLE'S POET

> Come ye faithful...Come ye faithless ones
> To see this poet writhing, glad and half-crazy
> Overseas, overland, overhead skyline to skyline....
> — "Aurora Borealis"

ACORN WAS BACK on PEI in June 1968, after a short stay in Toronto. He was in much better shape, "residing at 43 Elm Avenue" (now University Avenue) in Charlottetown, and telling a local reporter, "'Making money at writing poetry is not difficult, but the business is tricky,'" and that "the most money he has ever received from his poetry at any one time was $500.00 for a stack of his original manuscripts.... This man, who guesses that he has written a thousand poems during his 48 years, will soon see his work, or some of his work, published by the Ryerson Press of Toronto. Canadian poet, Alfred W. Purdy, will edit this book of poems" (MacIntyre). Acorn had bounced back a long way from when Patrick Lane found him incapacitated by misery, malnutrition, and alcohol. This resilience, demonstrated at several points in his life, testified to his physical strength and suggested a bipolar personality alternating between extremes of mood and behaviour. It was also the result of the devotion he inspired in the numerous capable and talented people who nursed, cajoled, and hectored him back to the world of the living.

One of those was Reg Phelan, an Island farmer, political activist, and writer, who met Acorn in the summer of 1968 during the federal election. "Milton used to come into the NDP office which was in Charlottetown. A number of us were publishing a small newspaper called *News and Views*. Milton was always interested in getting this kind of work done. Milton used to be back and forth in the office that summer, and was a pretty intense guy, a pretty interesting guy." A close friendship formed, beginning in Charlottetown's period of student radicalism and literary renascence, and continuing in the countryside when Phelan finished college and began farming full time.

During the summer of 1968 Acorn also lived with his mother and father on Confederation Street. On September 29, his father died, and Milton continued to stay there with his mother off and on during his visits home until 28 February 1972, when she was admitted to Garden of the Gulf Nursing Home on North River Road. "Really a horrendous place to send anybody with her active mind," says her grandson David. "She was there a long time, and complained every day." Mary qualifies David's recollection: "Mother came out to the farm on weekends, and she sometimes let off steam about the home, perhaps giving David the sense that she was 'always complaining.' In the home she got along well with staff and residents. Our family's situation made it impossible for her to live with any of her children. She was the one who asked to go into the home, and had forgotten that, I think. Much of the time she liked it there and made the best of it."

Some of Acorn's "thousand poems" may have been thrown away on Confederation Street. Mary explains that "my parents fixed up the garage as an office for Milton. A lot of his material was probably lost out there." When Helen moved into the nursing home, "We started to clean out the garage and I guess the landlord thought we were through, and he cleared everything else out and we didn't get all his books. I'm not sure we even got all the papers." David adds, "That's where a lot of the manuscripts were lost. That's where the trunks were, in the garage, and were never claimed."[22] But Robert says, "I was home about that time and Milton told me there was nothing but junk left in the garage as far as writings were concerned."

During his extended Charlottetown stay in 1968, Acorn phoned Frank Ledwell and read new poems he was writing. "The first time he did it he asked me what I thought of it, and I said, well, I thought it was very good, but there was a line that I thought wasn't quite right, and he took offense at my saying that. So I was extremely careful with what I said to him on the phone after that. I didn't want to offend him."

One evening Ledwell met him downtown. "At that time I was living in Keppoch, and I had my parents with me. My dad had suffered a long stem brain haemorrhage. My mother and I had him with us there, and we led a fairly quiet life. But Milton looked a little hungry, and we were having a pleasant chat, so I said, come over and we'll have a bite to eat. I took him over to Keppoch and my mother had homemade beans and fish cakes. Milton sat in and ate with great gusto. We had a wonderful evening. After I drove him home and came back, my mother said, 'Now that's one of the nicest people that's ever come into this house.' And I said, 'Well, I'm so glad,' because I was a little bit apprehensive about how my mother would react. She was somewhat straight-laced, but not at all 'proper.' We were used to having all kinds of peculiar people visiting us at home, some in their cups, and some half-crazed if not totally, so we were used to people eating with their hands. But Milton didn't do that. He ate very well, thank you, and he loved the homemade beans and fishcakes."

Acorn also joined an affable group on weekend evenings at the home of Jim and Connie Little. "Jim was a curator at the Confederation Centre Gallery, and Connie was a social activist with strong leftist leanings." Ledwell explains:

Adrien Arsenault and I, Henry Purdy [a prominent Island artist, and no relation to Al Purdy] and Gertie Purdy, and the Littles used to get together, and Milton came along. He was always invited. We got to know him better there. He used to hold forth at great length, and that was the first experience I had of him smoking cigars and leaving his droppings all around the chair. This was post-*Georgia Straight*, so he had a big build-up of stuff to talk about.

But in addition to his social commentary, we used to read poems together and recite. The ones he recited were even more lyrical than the published ones, and some of them were quite sentimental. There was one particularly that I thought was an extraordinary emblem of Milton's lyrical side. It had to do with a bird landing on a windowsill in Vancouver. It was such a sensitive piece that I've never forgotten the recitation. The rhythms were perhaps somewhere between John Keats and Robert Frost, perhaps the rhythm of 'La Belle Dame Sans Merci.' He had a special love for it himself, but it was not characteristic of what he was preoccupied with at the time, because he was most preoccupied with social reconstruction.

That was a pleasant number of months, and the friendships were warm, and congenial. Later on, when Milton came back home to live permanently, sometimes he could be a little difficult, probably largely because of his degenerating health. But back in those days he was full of piss and vinegar. He was so vigorous, and so wonderful to spend an evening with.

A year later, when he returned once again to Charlottetown from Toronto to read from that pivotal book, *I've Tasted My Blood*, a local paper referred to his time out west: "Mr. Acorn has travelled extensively in Canada, and considers the Peace River District and life among the Cree Indians 'a second home'" ("Native Poet"). If Acorn experienced life among the Cree, it is news to Al Purdy ("Nor have I ever heard about Peace River and Milton"), Patrick Lane, and Milton's family. Acorn did briefly stay in Dawson Creek, but this visit hardly established the Peace River District as his second home. This was more of his myth-making. Acorn's second home, in practical terms, was Toronto—and it was there in 1970 that he achieved the unique and lasting honour of People's Poet of Canada.

Acorn was back in the thick of the Toronto poetry scene in the spring of 1969. He had become one of the most popular poetry performers in the country, reading to enthusiastic and packed audiences. Once more, the Toronto police were called to disperse a poetry audience, with Acorn and his equally popular pal Al Purdy at the centre of the action: "Poetry reading proved too popular last night—by about 150 people. When a crowd of 200—from the middle-aged to the mods—overflowed from a Colonnade bookstore into the private entrance of the Colonnade apartments to hear Toronto poets Al Purdy and Milton Acorn read, management of the Colonnade ordered the people to leave—and called police to back up the demand. However, Classic Book Store manager Rita Smulders promised to try to rent the Colonnade Theatre for future readings and the poetry patrons left peaceably.... Toronto poet, Gwendolyn MacEwan is scheduled for the next reading" ("Epic").

In the early summer of 1969, Acorn travelled west again, and wrote to poet Raymond Souster from Dawson Creek. He praises the northern landscape and denounces Toronto, and states that he has been in the Peace River District "for three weeks," writing poetry and articles (31 July 1969).

On 7 October 1969, Acorn again packed the house for a poetry reading. This time, however, he was back in Charlottetown to give his first public reading on PEI. He had previously read only privately, to individuals such as Frank Ledwell or Adrien Arsenault. Now, the maverick whose mind had been more fixed on poetry than construction, who had once been ridiculed and beaten up for being "dreamy" and "different," and who had left the Island in the early 1950s because there was virtually no community receptive to a serious writer, especially one concerned about the working classes and critical of the establishment—now, he was back as a distinguished citizen, a prominent Canadian writer. Not yet the People's Poet, a Governor-General's medallist, or Dr. Acorn, he was well on his way to those distinctions. Moreover, a receptive community existed, which turned out in force to hear Milton Acorn, who was in the process of becoming *the Island poet*, author of several important books, including the recently published *I've Tasted My Blood*.

The reading was sponsored by the new University of Prince Edward Island and the Canada Council, and was held in Montgomery Hall, part of the old Prince of Wales College campus in downtown Charlottetown. (The year before, Prince of Wales College had sponsored a reading series through The Canada Council with Al Purdy, F.R. Scott, and Alden Nowlan.) As a local paper noted, he had "spent recent weeks with his family in Charlottetown, during which time he has spoken on Canadian literature to classes at the University of Prince Edward Island" ("Native Poet"). A newspaper photo shows Acorn in a suit and tie, with well-groomed hair, looking positively professorial, while Professor Robert Campbell, a Cape Bretoner, looks over the poet's shoulder at *I've Tasted My Blood*.

Hilda Woolnough, who had recently moved to PEI with her husband, remembers that night as the first time she saw and met Acorn: "The place was absolutely packed and this extraordinary-looking guy finally arrived, went up the middle of the aisle, and took his place. We couldn't believe how fascinating his face was. He had this gargoyle face. When he started reading, he dedicated it to his mother, and every time he shouted his mother would respond, 'Yeah Milton!'"

Frank Ledwell explains that "this hall would have held 250 people, and Milton's reading was a full house, which was really quite something. Bob Campbell was teaching Canadian literature at that time, and he was the designated host. Milton and family arrived a little late, and Bob was quite nervous about their arrival. And when they got there, his mother was in her cups, and Milton himself was flying fairly high. Bob was really nervous and asked me, 'Will you look after the

Helen Acorn at a birthday celebration in the mid-1970s.

family, and I'll take Milton up to the front.' There was still a little space at the back, so I invited them to sit with me."

John Smith, poet and English professor at UPEI, remembers Helen cheering Milton on, and yelling at him to read "I Shout Love." Ledwell recalls, "She was shouting, 'Read the one about your father, Milton,' and he'd wave with his hand like a giant bear clawing the air, trying to dissuade her from interrupting. But she was not to be discouraged. That was one of the highlights of the night. It would've been an embarrassment in many circles, but it was so much a part of Island culture that the mother was giving voice to her cultural pride."

There is one other version of that event. Mary Hooper refers to "the play between mother and son. It was true that she requested several of her favourite poems such as 'I Shout Love.' But it was Dad's sister, Sadie, who asked for the one about 'your father.' Dad was the idolized only son among five girls. There was one boy who died in infancy, whose name was Milton. Aunt Sadie was a very vivacious person and, at times, very excitable. She did the clapping and cheering him on. Mother always knew how to act in public and would not have caused that much commotion."

Acorn and his bond with his mother were satirized in *Chemical Eric*, a novel by Gildas Roberts, published in Newfoundland in 1974. Eric, the main character, organizes "a GREAT FESTIVAL OF LITERATURE CANADA" at "Cenotaph University," and invites "Marvell Chestnut, the Pictou Poet. Marvell from an early age had written poems of little meaning though the sense was strong.... Marvell Chestnut now lived in alcoholic bliss with his aged mother in a squalid street of Pictou, Nova Scotia. He was a happy man" (87). Chestnut's mother "insisted that it be written into the agreement that she accompany her son when he came to BOOK ALIVE CANADA! in St. John's" (93); however, "Marvell Chestnut and his Ma" are late arriving at the festival because they "had drunkenly boarded the wrong plane and had to be redirected back from Boston, Mass" (94). Roberts obviously viewed Acorn and his mother as parochial caricatures rather than figures of "cultural pride."

Early in 1970 Acorn was once more at the centre of an artistic protest. The St. Lawrence Centre in Toronto was opening with a gala performance, and several writers, including Acorn, had been asked to share the stage with other performers. Acorn was outraged when he learned that some of the performers, including poets, would be paid little or nothing. The multi-million dollar showcase for upscale theatre and concerts, which may well have lavished money on other expenses that night, was taking advantage of writers, according to Acorn, who was vocal about the need for poets and other writers to be justly paid for their work. On this occasion he made his point by marching around and around the centre during the gala, and placing a curse upon it. Over two decades later an official at the St. Lawrence Centre asked Joan MacLeod, the award-winning playwright, to lift the curse. Recognizing that writers were now better treated in Canada and by the centre, MacLeod did her best to oblige.

Acorn was to read at the gala from *I've Tasted My Blood*, older and new poems selected by Al Purdy. In the introduction, Purdy offers one of the most astute assessments in print of Acorn the poet and man:

Acorn speaks from a personal conception of utopian order, as full citizen of a world that never was and perhaps never will be.... Acorn believes in the perfectibility of people, the infinite capacities and hidden potentials

... inherent and standard equipment with the ordinary person; but not there at all in those who are politically or commercially corrupted.... But politics is only one side of Milton Acorn. He also writes lyrics of nature, sensitive love poems, pieces that see inside the human character like a cardiogram of the intellect. As well, some beautiful evocations of his native Prince Edward Island.... The Acorn-picture I want to convey is of a maverick and outsider, a man who speaks out at the wrong time, asks embarrassing questions of human society, and will not be satisfied by evasions. The fact that the man who asks the questions is humanly fallible and often angrily impulsive makes some kind of answers to his questions no less urgent.... A man who, in a handful of poems, comes somewhere close to greatness. ("Introduction" xii, xiv-xv)

This book advanced and solidified Acorn's reputation as a distinctive and major Canadian poet. Praise and admiration piled up in the reviews. Dennis Lee, poet, critic, and not-yet-children's writer, revised his judgment of Acorn's poetry: "I had a fixed idea about Milton Acorn. He was a gorgeous primitive who stomped across Canada, blurting out things everyone else was too fastidious to say out loud. The result was poetry you could only patronize—it was strong, moving stuff, but it kept getting clumsy or mawkish; it misfired at crucial moments; so you praised the man and the sentiments, but you tried to avoid talking directly about the poems. *I've Tasted My Blood* is Acorn's selected poems. He's 45 now, he's been publishing for 13 years, and was I ever wrong! The poems from these years—the winners, the near misses and the clinkers—make up a testament, a book that is also a man. That doesn't happen very often and it's cause for celebration" (Lee).23

Robert Weaver, one of the most influential figures in modern Canadian literature as an editor, critic, and broadcaster, writes that "the poems in *I've Tasted My Blood* are angry, uptight, ambitious, sprawling, unexpectedly quiet, sometimes generous, committed for better or worse.... It's a tribute to Ryerson Press, with its church affiliations, that it is the publisher of a book as rawly painful as Milton Acorn's *I've Tasted My Blood*" (Weaver). A review in *The Montreal Star* asserts, "I agree, unreservedly, with Purdy that Acorn is a highly moral poet.... His poems take a stand, not a stance. He is a throwback to the times when men believed they could distinguish between good and evil using the simple, powerful criteria of 'nature's mother-wit'" (Richmond "Milton").

And it is ironic that George Bowering, who later figured so prominently in the circumstances that led to the People's Poet award, also applauds Acorn's achievement as an inspired *and* skilful artist, referring to him as a "romantic radical" and a man "resolved to make his lines true, to make the words render their finest possibilities lying in, for instance, juncture and stress, all the joints fitted by a careful craftsman.... In fact, having so many Acorn poems together (about 150, plus two stories) convinces me that he is not only honest and exciting, as no one has ever doubted, but also very much accomplished as an 'artist,' not so much the 'natural,' as he has often been pictured" (Bowering).

I've Tasted My Blood appealed to those who admired a "maverick and outsider," a "romantic radical"; it also convinced those who respected accomplished craft and artistry. Acorn's innumerable hours of poetic study and practice, as well as his life as a dissident visionary, had borne fruit in the judgment of his peers. Many of them fully expected that his book would receive the Governor-General's Award for poetry, the highest formal honour for a poet in the land. Instead, Gwendolyn MacEwan and George Bowering shared the award.

The outrage that followed tended to ignore MacEwan and focused on two grievances. First, the jury had shunned a poet whose recent and major book, combined with his long devotion to poetry and role as a social critic, had earned a great deal of respect. The second grievance has been simplistically misrepresented, over the years, as disapproval of the selection of George Bowering's two books[24] for the award. Acorn fed that disapproval, but not during the months leading up to the award. For instance, in a Charlottetown interview published in the April 1970 issue of the *Cadre*, UPEI's first student newspaper, Jim Hornby, the editor, asked, "Who are some of the Canadian poets you like?" Acorn answered, "Well, Bowering, MacEwan, 'Red' Lane ... and Pat Lane, his brother, Bill Bissett.... Oh, yes, Alden Nowlan, he's a genius" (8). Hornby also asked, "What do you get if you get the Governor General's Award?" After mentioning the cash amount, Acorn added generously, "Actually I think that there's a list of seven names of poets in the list of candidates, and everyone they considered deserving of getting an award should get an award" (9).

After the winners were announced, Acorn added to the censure of the jury's choice with comments like this, in a telephone interview from Charlottetown: "'I say Bowering's book was good but mine was much better. Yup. Yup. That's all I have to say'" (Sypnowich). Some agreed: "'There's more poetry in the dirty little fingernail of Milton Acorn than there is in all the collected poetry of George Bowering,' [Irving] Layton said." Others were more circumspect, such as poet and professor Eli Mandel, who "emphasized that he was casting no reflections on the award winners. But like many others he was dismayed by the omission of Acorn" (Sypnowich).

In fact, the protest had far more to do with the composition of the jury and the surge of cultural nationalism in the 1960s than with the quality of Bowering's books. The jury consisted of Robert Weaver of the CBC, Philip Stratford of the University of Montreal, and—the sore point—Warren Tallman of the University of British Columbia. Weaver was spared criticism, most likely for several compelling reasons: he was an affable, well-liked friend and advocate of many poets; in his influential capacity as producer of CBC Radio's *Anthology*, and publisher and editor of the prestigious *Tamarack Review*, he supported new voices and styles of writing as well as older writers and forms; and he was clearly pro-Canadian, though not anti-cosmopolitan.

As for the scapegoated villain: "But Tallman, in spite of 14 years residence in Canada, is an American citizen. Moreover, George Bowering was a student of his, and in a sense, his ... protégé. In the opinion of some protestors, while Tallman's integrity could not be questioned, there was little doubt that an American would, naturally, plump for a poet who, disregarding the mainstream of Canadian poetic tradition, wrote in an American idiom. They [those who protested Bowering's award] said in essence: Canadian sovereignty over Canadian literary awards is as important as Canadian sovereignty over Arctic waters" (Richmond "Laureate"). Thus, nationalistic defense of "the Canadian tradition" and a "Canadian idiom" in poetry, and hostility to the influence of "American styles and concerns," figured prominently in the protest of the award. It is easy in hindsight to see that Tallman and Bowering were actually part of the richly varied development of Canadian poetic "tradition" and that Acorn's poetry was hardly without its American influences. Bowering's and Acorn's poetry represented two kinds of innovation, and the battle lines that were drawn between them conflated political and aesthetic concerns.

Decades later, it may take some effort not to dismiss this as overprotective Canadianism, knee-jerk anti-Americanism, or literary provincialism. Now, we have the confidence of an amazingly large, talented, and diverse literary community; we eagerly absorb older traditions and newer idioms, concerns, and theories from many countries; we include in our ranks an ever-growing multicultural tableau of writers. Canadian writing influences writers in other lands and makes the best-seller lists at home and abroad. It is easy to forget the struggle of writers in the 1940s and 1950s, such as Hugh MacLennan, to overcome an anglophilia which said that most things British were superior and most things Canadian inferior; and easy to forget MacLennan's warning in *Barometer Rising* (1941) that as Canadians were giving birth to an indigenous culture, consciousness, and identity, we would already be infiltrated by the growing American influence.

The Canadian literary renaissance of the 1960s was part of a larger consolidation of cultural, political, and economic sovereignty, with the United States as the obvious threat. Fear of "Americans heading our English departments, editing our literary magazines, anthologizing our young poets, and even passing judgment on the excellence of our own poets for our national awards" (Richmond "Laureate") now seems exaggerated and misdirected. The real threat to Canadian culture and sovereignty, it has turned out, is from the megapower of American corporations and the U.S. and Canadian governments which serve their interests, not from a landed immigrant on a literary jury. Even so, the nationalistic urge of the 1960s was an essential force in stimulating the growth and maturation of the literary production we now enjoy, and the protest against Tallman was a by-product.

Of course, Acorn's own intense nationalism and rejection of American cultural, economic, and political imperialism were among the reasons attracting supporters to his cause. An editorial in a Montreal literary magazine, *Ingluvin*, written by Seymour Mayne and Kenneth Hertz, advances two other explanations:

Either because of literary politicking or a gross ignorance of Canadian poetry on the part of the Canada Council jury, Milton Acorn has been denied the Governor General's award that he truly has earned. Milton Acorn has been an individual and productive figure in Canadian poetry for over fifteen years. Over those years he has built up a solid body of work characterized by excellence and by social and political concerns largely absent in most Canadian writing. He was certainly never a literary careerist gathering up his collection of approving pats from the poetic and academic bureaucracy. He maintained his independence and forged one of the few true voices in Canadian poetry. (quoted in Richmond "Laureate")

This explanation certainly fed into the image of a ground-breaking maverick, an independent original—genuine characteristics Acorn had learned to cultivate and exploit.

On a more personal—and somewhat illogical—note, Layton says he has "'a much higher regard' for the poetry of Gwendolyn MacEwan, who used to be married to Milton Acorn, but giving her an award served 'to rub salt in the wound.' 'It's a great blow to the man. He's suffered in mental health, physical health and poverty. That kind of courage should be recognized. Here is a genuine poet, one who hasn't gone through the academic mill'" (Sypnowich). Layton's bluntness about Acorn's tribulations is poignant, but personal suffering is not the most persuasive criterion for artistic awards. Moreover, Layton's comment ignores any suffering on MacEwan's part. As well, the inference that Acorn was a "genuine poet" because he avoided the "academic mill" was typical of Layton—who downplayed his lifelong academic affiliations in favour of his mask as an anti-establishment, romantic individualist.

An irony is that if Acorn had been given the Governor-General's award that year, there might never have been a People's Poet award and legend. "Nationalist irascibility and outraged Canadian sensibility were translated into North American pragmatism when Irving Layton and Eli Mandel sent a circular to a number of Canadian men-of-letters asking them to contribute to a Canadian Poets' Award Fund, honouring the author of '*I've Tasted My Blood*'" (Richmond "Laureate").

The event took place on the evening of 16 May 1970, at Grossman's Tavern on Spadina Avenue in Toronto. Grossman's was Acorn's favourite Toronto tavern during these years. Once catering to a Jewish clientele in the old garment district, in 1970 it was patronized by "ethnics and blacks, students and sanguine bohemians en route to literary or artistic success.... Here the pantry-nostalgia of the shtetl, the black ghetto, and Southern Italy rub bellies amicably" (quoted in Richmond "Laureate"). On that evening, more than a hundred friends and admirers crowded into Grossman's, with a remarkable crosssection of Canada's literary talent, including Irving Layton, Eli Mandel, Margaret Atwood, Dorothy Livesay, Al Purdy, Joe Rosenblatt, Doug Fetherling, Ron Everson, Graeme Gibson, and Abe Rotstein. One delegation had arrived by train, on the "Poets Rapido" from Montreal's Central Station.

Layton and Mandel had raised $800—a substantial sum in those days (the Governor-General's Award was $2,500)—and the cheques bore the names of writers listed above and others such as Leonard Cohen, Earle Birney, and John Glassco. But their goal was the round and "grand" sum of $1,000. "So, I picked up the telephone, in a moment of auspicious craziness," explained Layton, "and rang the premier of Prince Edward Island. I was unable to get through to that very busy man. But, speaking to his assistant, I put forward the case for the Island recognizing one of its famous sons. Fifteen minutes later, I had a promise from the government of the right little, bright little, and not tight little island of $200. This is a remarkable tribute from a far from wealthy community to Milton Acorn. Generous and warm, the gesture goes to prove, that islands have their attractive mystiques" (quoted in Richmond "Laureate").

This donation, along with a local misunderstanding, was duly noted by the Charlottetown press: "The office of Premier Alex Campbell reports that the contribution of $200 as part of $1,000 fund to establish an award for Island poet Milton Acorn was made by the PEI Grants Committee and not by the premier himself.... A letter to the editor of this paper, signed by Robert Beum, associate professor of English at UPEI, indicated that Mr. Beum got the impression from press reports that $200 of the $1,000 fund was contributed by Premier Campbell and drawn from the provincial treasury" ("Contribution").

The actual name of the award was "The Canadian Poets' Award." The $1,000 cheque was accompanied by a silver-grey medallion inscribed, on one side, "Canadian Poets' Award 1970, I've Tasted My Blood," and, on the other side, with a misplaced apostrophe, "Milton Acorn, the Peoples' Poet." Irving Layton told the audience, "This is a memorable occasion. It is the first time in the history of this country that a poet has been honoured by his fellow poets.... Poetry, at last, has become as exciting as politics. In honouring Acorn we honour a man who has kept his integrity at a time when it has never been more profitable to lose it or to trade it in. This event is heartening to all of us who value courage and individuality" (Richmond "Laureate").

According to one report, Acorn accepted the award by saying, "I have written ... a 43-page poem for the occasion.... I shall not recite it all.... Only these lines: 'You cannot buy my truth, but you can buy my scorn'" (quoted in Richmond "Laureate"). In fact, he read a twenty-minute poem, "On Shaving Off His Beard," and then an expanded version of his long poem, "I Shout Love." He also spoke about his Canadian nationalism and poetry: "I'm not anti-American, as some people claim. I'm only against American imperialism.... For my

Milton at Grossman's Tavern in Toronto the night he received the Canadian Poets' Award and his People's Poet medal, with Joe Rosenblatt (left) and Luella Booth (right).

country, Canada, I want to see real independence.... After all, Canada is now cosmopolitan, and Canadians have taken over the position of cosmopolitans that was once held by the Americans. So too is our poetry the more cosmopolitan. It can be read by more people, more easily than any other" (Dzeguze).

Numerous apocryphal stories about Milton Acorn accompany the seemingly endless verifiable stories. One of the former is that Acorn returned to his room in the Waverly Hotel, "his complexion reflecting the joyous hours of drinking that evening substances other than his blood" (Dzeguze), without the $1,000 cheque. The medal was safely draped around his neck, but the cheque was lost. According to the story, an employee at Grossman's, sweeping up after hours, found the cheque and helped return it to Acorn.

Hilda Woolnough says of Milton and the medal, when he returned to Charlottetown later that year, "he was totally involved with the People's Poet medal because it was obvious that Milton should have won the Governor-General's Award. The sort of poetry he was writing was the best in Canada ... so when he got the People's Poet award he was absolutely thrilled ... and he wore the medal tucked under his shirt." John Smith remembers Milton wearing the medal in Charlottetown, and it was around his neck whenever he visited Hilda and her husband Réshard Gool at their house on University Avenue, which was a primary gathering place throughout the 1970s for the Island's artists, intellectuals, and political activists.

After his triumph at Grossman's Tavern, Acorn enjoyed the financial fruits of both his award and a Canada Council Short-term Grant for the period of June, July, and August 1970. He divided his time that summer among Charlottetown, Toronto, and Stratford, Ontario. In Charlottetown, Acorn asked Gool and Woolnough to put him up. Throughout the 1970s and into the 80s they often provided him with shelter, food, and companionship. On this occasion, however, "Réshard got him into the Charlottetown Hotel because he was having problems; he was difficult because he was so untrained. He had the medal under his pillow and he wore it at all times under his shirt," says Woolnough. "He swears it was stolen at the Charlottetown Hotel. Réshard went down and searched the whole place inside out but couldn't find it anywhere. He might have lost it on the beach wandering around. He was totally upset."

He stayed on the Island for several months before going away. Brent MacLaine, an Islander, poet, and English professor at UPEI, was an undergraduate at the time, and in September 1971 rented a room in a house where Acorn had recently been a tenant for a number of months. The landlady, Gloria "Sally" Large, told MacLaine about Acorn, and that the People's Poet had been staying in the Charlottetown Hotel just before renting a room in her house. Acorn had been quite distraught when he moved into Large's house because, he claimed, his People's Poet medal had been stolen from him at the Charlottetown Hotel. He blamed it on a hotel employee or manager (MacLaine).

The medal disappeared, then, within a year of the Grossman's Tavern celebration. But Acorn recovered it somehow. Patrick Lane says, "He lost it at least three or four times. He wore it around his neck all the time and once the ribbon rotted off. Three times the medal was returned to him." Joseph Sherman is among those who have "heard the story several times that it was lost on the beach. He set it down on a rock and lost it." In 1986 Acorn maintained that "I was swimming and the medal was on a log. [Rob] McLeod became worried because there were some fellows hanging around his car. I said those are locals, they can't get away with anything and they know it. But McLeod got into a panic and led me back to the car and we drove off. The medal was left on the log. The tide came in and the medal was lost" (Deahl "Acorn" 52). We are left to imagine the medal buried under the sand of an Island beach or in a junk box in someone's home. The date of its final disappearance is uncertain, but has to be after he received the Governor-General's Award in 1976. Kent Martin's film includes CBC footage of an interview with Acorn in Ottawa, en route with his mother in a limousine to the Governor-General's Awards. When the interviewer asks what he will say to the Governor-General, Acorn pulls a silver medal out of his pocket and refers to it as the Canadian Poetry Award.

During this period, 1969-71, Acorn re-established his connection with the Island through the extended visits that continued until his permanent relocation to PEI in 1981. There are several reasons for this renewed contact. Well into middle age and without a wife and children of his own, Acorn needed closer communication with his family. As well, like many Islanders who move away yet remain devoted to the Island, he was drawn back as he grew older.

One of Acorn's close friends at this time was Andy Wells, chief advisor to Premier Alexander Campbell (1966-78). Wells speaks of the familiar pattern of Islanders' out-migration and subsequent longing to return home: "I know of Islanders who have left here and they hated the place, and found it small and unrewarding ... and they'll stay away. But then there are the others who come back almost every summer if possible, who do look forward to retiring here, and who have that almost mystical attachment to the province.... Milton certainly had that latter point of view."

Another reason was Acorn's new stature as a prominent Canadian writer—he could return as a proud member of that select group of Islanders who had achieved recognition on the mainland and nationally. On Acorn's off-Island validation, Wells says:

We tend to view ourselves as Islanders as others see us from outside the Island, because either instinctively or knowingly we understand that we are somewhat parochial and Island-like in much of what we do and say. At the same time we understand that there is a more sophisticated world out there, which we may not want to be part of, but at the same time when that sophisticated world recognizes us it somehow makes our self-image a little better, and Milton was not unlike that. Because of the expression of interest, concern, love, whatever came out of the People's

Poet Award, Milton began to carry himself a little higher and brighter than perhaps he had before.

Also responsible for Acorn's extended visits to PEI were the profound political, economic, social, and cultural transformations there from the late 1960s onward. Wells speaks of the late-1960s through mid-1970s on PEI: "The ferment going on then was remarkable. The university was created, out of turmoil [resistance to the merging of the two older, private institutions into a public university], but still it was established. The Development Plan, the causeway, land questions, all these things were boiling in the same pot. People like Milton Acorn felt that they had something to contribute in that debate, and that may be partly why Milton tended to drift back to the Island."

David Milne, a political scientist at UPEI, describes that period in "Politics in a Beleaguered Garden," and summarizes the mythohistorical context of the changes, tensions, and conflicts that intensified in the late-1960s: "For at the centre of the question of identity—of the 'Island way of life'—has rested a garden myth, which organized for Islanders an ideal picture of themselves as an independent agricultural people protected from the world in an unspoiled pastoral setting. Some elements of this idyllic metaphor ... were always strong enough to make the garden myth compelling and realistic, even if history always threatened to dislodge the gratifying self-image by introducing incompatible elements and rude contradictions" (40) While the garden myth, according to Milne, "has provided Islanders with a lens through which they could see themselves, it has also restricted their ability to see beyond it and grapple with their problems successfully" (41).

Milne's assessment can be applied to Acorn's own view of the Island, espoused in poetry and prose, in public interviews and private discussions. To a considerable extent, Acorn believed in and promulgated the Island's garden myth. He was certainly more able than most Islanders, during the 1950s and 60s, to acknowledge the "problems" presented by "history" and to identify the "contradictions" in "the Island way of life." His temperament, poetic vision, and critical ideology allowed him to recognize the blight in the garden. But he made very little effort, if any, to reconcile his Marxist and socialist position—with its heavy emphasis on industrial development and soviet-model agriculture—with his devotion to the Island's rural economy and lifestyle and to its individualistic small farmers, fishers, tradespeople, and entrepreneurs. It is no wonder, then, that Acorn's responses to the

Campbell government's Development Plan and the construction of a causeway were ambiguous and ambivalent.

"The cornerstone of Campbell's administration," writes Milne, "was surely the Development Plan, a fifteen-year federal-provincial agreement intended to restructure and rationalize the Island economy and society" (48). The plan included centralization of the provincial bureaucracy, a more aggressive industrial policy to increase manufacturing and product marketing, a commitment to small-scale businesses not dependent on the Island's natural resources, the encouragement of tourism, and consolidation of farmland into larger farms with fewer marginal farmers. Farming and fishing would no longer rule the Island economy and define the way of life; they would be important sectors of a diversifying economy and valuable features of the Island's modernizing social landscape.

There was, understandably, resistance to the Development Plan. Milne writes, "Although many attributed this blatant attack on Island values to insensitive federal planners and politicians, it would be a mistake to write off the policy as a nefarious plot 'from away.' For Islanders, that would be altogether too easy and typical. Instead, a new Island élite had come of age, which cared less about the past but had interests and ideas of its own" (49). The Campbell government moderated its policies, or at least its public stance, in the mid-1970s. "Campbell rapidly discovered that, with legislative representation heavily in favour of rural areas, no one could so flout the charter of myths" (Milne 50).

The older Federation of Agriculture and the newly formed National Farmers Union were determined to defend the family farm and the role of agriculture in the province. Rural communities feared for their future. And other factors forced a mitigation of the Development Plan and change of rhetoric: the energy crisis and economic recession of the early and mid-1970s; the growth of environmental consciousness; and the re-emergence on the Island—among native Islanders and immigrants—of the preservationist ethic concerning both the land and Island culture: "the Island way of life." Local interest in protecting and renewing tradition merged with the floodtide of "counter-cultural," ecological, and roots-oriented ideas "from away" washing over the Island. While the new Island élite incorporated business, bureaucratic, and technological ideas "from away," critics of the Development Plan and the proposed causeway to the mainland were drawing on other influences which challenged the ethic of unrestrained development and rampant modernization. In self-defense, the Campbell government borrowed for its new slogan the title of E.F. Schumacher's best-selling book, *Small Is Beautiful.*

Among the critics were the Brothers and Sisters of Cornelius Howatt, "a group of sympathizers of the nineteenth-century foe of Confederation for whom they named their society, spearheaded by historians David Weale and Harry Baglole. In several satirical sallies during the Island's 1973 Centennial festivities, they warned Islanders of government threats to the family farm heritage and eulogized the past as the Island's golden age. With wit and humour, they prepared the ideological ground for a decade-long battle with the plan" (Milne 50).[25] The Brothers and Sisters questioned the growing dependence on tourism and the purchase of farmland by developers, especially nonresidents.

Premier Campbell referred to these critics in a speech on 28 May 1973, in which he tried to balance the need for both preservation and change: "If the Brothers and Sisters of Cornelius Howatt are simply saying that we should return to the ways of our forefathers one hundred years or more ago, I would have to violently disagree with them. But I don't believe this is the message they are giving to us. I have considered and advocated for some time that we in Prince Edward Island must carefully examine change so that we are able to weed out those aspects which would be detrimental to our way of life, and, at the same time, take advantage of those aspects of change which will enhance and improve our quality of life" (Baglole and Weale 112). This speech was applauded by Réshard Gool, whose expertise spanned the worlds of politics and the arts, and who combined a love of the Island's traditional virtues with a passion for beneficial modernization. No doubt Gool and Acorn spent long hours debating the possibility of achieving the balance between preservation and modernity and the risks of imbalance.

This excerpt from Premier Campbell's speech and Gool's reply were published in 1974 in *Cornelius Howatt: Superstar!*. This book is a "collection of articles and letters to the editor which the Brothers and Sisters wrote, as well as a brief resumé of some of the activities in which the organization was involved" (Baglole and Weale 7). Among those activities were opposition to the causeway, a project begun and abandoned during this period. The book is dedicated to "Milton Acorn, Island poet," and prefaced by his poem "The Island."

While Acorn acknowledged some advantages of the Development Plan, he tended to be more critical. "There were various elements of the Development Plan," says Andy Wells, that bothered Milton, and we would argue about the merits and demerits of certain aspects. I think in many respects the Development Plan played an unconscious part in promoting a lot of the intellectual and artistic fervour in that period, if for no other reason than it was a foil for people to respond to. I think there were a number of socially useful activities that came out of it, and that, I think, in hindsight, Milton would have accepted as useful. But he would disagree with the bigness of it, the centralization features, and the bureaucracy that was required to set it up and run it ... and the potential impact affecting his somewhat romanticized idea of what the Island should be and could be.

Again, Acorn's opposition to "centralization" and "bureaucracy" was inconsistent with his communist views, yet consistent with his view of *his* Island.

Part of Wells's responsibility as Premier Campbell's advisor was "to try to understand what was going on at various levels of society and with interest groups in the province, and make sure that Campbell was informed and up-to-date. I found Milton useful in that sense because of his involvement with certain groups and because of his very hard-held opinions, and I think he found me useful in that I was a sounding board." Having served under five Island premiers, Wells believes that "Alex Campbell had the ability to open his mind to other points of view, much more so than any of those others. The Gools and the Acorns and others certainly were a community for him to listen to." Wells is certain that Premier Campbell, who was supportive of the off-Island attempt to honour the People's Poet, met Acorn, though Wells can't recall where or when. Campbell "certainly accepted Milton's position in the fabric of the Island and the contribution he made to it."

It is fascinating to imagine a conversation between the premier and the People's Poet about what the Island should and could be. The premier maintained that the Island needed to adapt to a modern era in order to preserve its distinctive character, and his government's Development Plan set in motion the ongoing argument over the nature and extent of adaptations, as well as over dearly held concepts of "tradition" and "the Island way of life." The People's Poet saw his Island as an embattled haven, troubled within by corruption and class distinctions, and besieged from without by capitalism and neocolonialism—but a haven nonetheless, set apart from the urban, industrial, and ideological maelstroms in which he spent most of his adult life.

"He saw the Island very much in terms of Milton Acorn," says Wells:

Milton didn't demand much in the sense of the niceties of life. He didn't demand a wardrobe most Islanders looked to. He didn't demand shelter and transportation and, I presume, nourishment, to the extent that others did. He was quite happy to walk around Charlottetown and observe the passing scene and write about it. With that as a base, and looking out on the rest of the Island, he saw the 'advancements' being proposed by the Development Plan as being able to demean the goodness of the Island and what he felt the Island should be. Where I seemed to find myself at the greatest odds with Milton was with the belief that there were compromises that were acceptable, that there were things that could change and that wouldn't destroy, and Milton tended to hold a counter view.

The Campbell government's Development Plan gave way in the late-1970s to Conservative Premier Angus MacLean's call for a "rural renaissance," led by, among others, MacLean's principal secretary and speechwriter, David Weale. Historian Ian Ross Robertson notes that "both Baglole and Weale were leading propagandists of the Conservative party in the provincial elections of 1978 and 1979, which first shook and then overthrew the Liberal government.... A model of effective political writing, the Conservative campaign literature focused on the Brothers' and Sisters' misgivings about a changing Island society losing touch with its traditions, losing its distinctive identity, and losing its autonomy" ("Historical" 158). As Milne wryly observes, "Some of the most eloquent spokesmen of the bucolic ideal are precisely the new professionals. Prince Edward Island's pastoral ideal of a land of independent yeomen is, through them, more consciously and conspicuously defined than ever. But even as the mythology of independence is advanced, an increased dependency on federal transfers and outside markets reminds the Islander of his actual distance from the garden myth" (67).

Milne's essay was published in 1982, and since then the tension between the garden myth—so exquisitely embodied in Acorn's "The Island"—and development and modernization has heightened. The pastoral ideal is advertised more loudly than ever—to a greatly increased tourist trade. Family farms remain—many of them pumping potatoes from chemically-dependent and eroding soil for the fast-food factories of the Irvings and McCains. A bridge links the Island to the mainland, while many Islanders strive to link themselves to the information highway and global economy. Yet the landscape is still luxuriant, and the tourists flock to concerts of traditional music and performances of *Anne of Green Gables*. And most Islanders still desire to preserve the Island's pastoral beauty and to maintain enough of those qualities and traditions that have made Prince Edward Island distinctive, not just another outpost of the corporate empire—a place to which Milton Acorn would want to return.

Along with the political, economic, and social developments of the 1970s, there were cultural developments that enriched the Island and that greatly helped to shape and define the changing identity of Islanders and their province, and to attract Milton Acorn home.

Among those developments were the small literary publishing ventures of Gool and Woolnough and Elaine Harrison. Harry Baglole founded Ragweed Press as an occasional publisher of Island historical and cultural works. Island Community Theatre (renamed Theatre Prince Edward Island in 1987) was established by Ron Irving—who became its long-term artistic director—Baglole, and others. The PEI Heritage Foundation (now the PEI Museum and Heritage Foundation) matured into a major cultural and scholarly force, and began publishing *The Island Magazine* in November 1976. The Charlottetown Festival at the Confederation Centre of the Arts was inspiring, then, with its commitment to develop and mount new Canadian musicals. The new university attracted writer-scholars such as John Smith, and the new wave of "immigrants" brought other talented writers such as Deirdre Kessler, who became an important cultural force in heritage, publishing, children's literature, and arts funding. And along with the emergence of writers, there was a blossoming of the music scene, from traditional "roots" music to rock, country, and blues. Returning from Vancouver and Toronto to this enlivened milieu, Acorn must have marvelled, occasionally, at the changes. One of the major changes was the high regard in which he was held by so many people—Islanders who now considered him a valued companion.

During this period, 1969-71, Acorn made a number of close friends on the Island—people who were able to engage with his temperament and mind: young Islanders attending university or beginning their careers, professors native to the Island or recently arrived to join UPEI's faculty, the principal secretary to the premier of Prince Edward Island, older Islanders such as the landlady Gloria Large, and artists and back-to-the-landers "from away" who enriched the cultural life of the Island.

Foremost among these friends were Woolnough and Gool, who befriended Acorn more than anyone on the Island, apart from Mary and Garth Hooper, from 1970 until his death. Acorn's major publication, *Dig Up My Heart: Selected Poems 1952-83*, is dedicated "To the just Neruda, Nobel laureate, spitefully murdered; and for Jim Deahl, Réshard Gool, and Hilda Woolnough plus to the drivers and staff of City Cabs, Charlottetown." Pablo Neruda was the great Chilean poet who died of heart failure during the CIA-supported military coup which murdered the democratically elected socialist President Salvadore Allende. Jim Deahl and Acorn entered each other's lives in 1972 in Toronto. Woolnough and Gool are PEI legends in their own right.

Gool, who died in 1989, arrived on the Island in 1962, and taught in the Political Studies Department at UPEI. Born in London, England, with a multi-racial background, Gool was raised in a family that had a history of political resistance to racial and economic oppression. He was not only a political scientist. With Woolnough he founded Square Deal Press to publish Island writers; he wrote fiction, poetry, and countless articles on politics and literature; he corresponded prolifically with hundreds of artists and intellectuals; and he spent over two decades on the Island arguing for the arts and social justice.

Originally from England, Woolnough is one of the most accomplished visual artists in Atlantic Canada. A tireless advocate and organizer for the arts, nationally and regionally, she was coordinator of the artist-run Great George Street Gallery during the early 1980s. Located on the historic boulevard walked by the Fathers of Confederation from the harbour to Province House, "The George" was the main Island venue for literary readings as well as for the province's visual, performance, and video artists. There, Woolnough could marry her two great passions—for visual arts and literature, especially poetry. Woolnough and Gool were major catalysts for the Charlottetown art scene for two decades, and hosted readings by a great many of Canada's writers, wining and dining them lavishly at home afterward. This was a couple to whom Acorn gravitated whenever he was on the Island.

"He thought electrically," says Woolnough, "and since I tend to think that way myself we could converse with each other. People would say to me, 'How is it you can talk to Milton for hours and hours every day?' and I'd say, 'Actually, we enjoy each other's company and we understand the form of thought we go through.' Milton would take off on a tack and then he would come around and then he might see a

"I've got quite a face, thank God / for smiling or scowling." ("Self-Portrait"). *The working-class poet with his King cigars.*

connection that you hadn't seen before, rather than a predictable conversation, step-ladder form."

Throughout the 1970s Woolnough and Gool lived in a rambling old house on University Avenue. "The house was open to Milton," says Hilda. "In fact, he and Cedric Smith were the people who called our house 'the Consulate.' They came over one night with a bottle of Drambuie." John Smith, a frequent visitor, remembers Acorn's infatuation with Drambuie as "the drink of the oppressed, the Scots, and all." Woolnough says:

They decided to call it the Consulate because, they said, eventually everybody found their way there. The first time Acorn came was with Al Purdy, who was absolutely roaring drunk, so drunk you could not understand a word he was saying. We sat in the greening room in the front and were having drinks. They had a fight and wouldn't talk for awhile, but that was their relationship.

Often Milton would sleep in a chair. And sometimes he would come very early ... and the way you could tell how long he'd been there was how many cigar butts were left all over the house. And he couldn't do anything, he didn't even know how to boil water. He'd say, "And where were you?" when we came down. I said, "Why didn't you make yourself a coffee, you know where it is?" "Oh, I was waiting for you."

When the Drambuie ran out at the Consulate, Acorn would head for Andy Wells's house on Upper Prince. "When things dried up at the Gools'," Wells says, "some of us would walk around the corner to my place, and frequently Milton was one of the drop-ins. We'd stay up till all hours, with others drifting off either physically or mentally, and Milton and I frequently would end up long hours over the kitchen table and a bottle, arguing vigorously and vociferously about matters that neither of us knew anything about." Milton considered himself an expert on "anything from carpentry to politics of the day. In those areas where I did have some knowledge I found that Milton's facts and figures were purely invented, whatever was useful at times." In order to be a conversationalist with Milton, according to Wells:

The first thing you had to do was not put him down. You couldn't say to him, "Milton, you're full of bullshit, get out of my house." That would be the end of Milton as far as you were concerned. You had to engage him on the same ground ... and when you've got a bottle of whisky there with you it's not unpleasant. As long as you knew it was an exercise in discussion and rhetoric, you were all right. I've seen other people get so infuriated with Milton because they couldn't get him to see their point of view or to get him to argue on the same grounds, and walk away in total annoyance or frustration. That was not useful to anybody, because no matter how the discussion might not be particularly valid in terms of truths and wisdom, with Milton you always got something out of it.

Another person apparently able to converse with Acorn was a Toronto woman who showed up at the Consulate. According to

Woolnough she was "one of his ex-girlfriends"—the same "Mrs. Booth" who read with Acorn at Toronto's Allan Gardens in 1962.

She was a Noh poet and very beautiful. She did a performance at UPEI and knocked everybody off their seats. Very riveting. Luella was staying with us and the first night she was upstairs getting herself ready for dinner. She must have been between 50 and 55, and had this longish dark hair with dark copper highlights. We were waiting for her to come downstairs. Milton was supposed to come but he hadn't turned up. She came down the stairs and was wearing a black body suit and around her waist she had wrapped a pinkish-red towel from the bathroom. Over her hair she'd sprinkled geranium petals and she looked absolutely fantastic. She was a really sexy woman. And this was a woman who had lived with Milton. You can imagine their relationship. It must have been really something. And impossible because they both had this great fantastic energy. She was almost like a female Milton with her power. But there was precision. Everything was just right, physically, materially. Almost like the poles meeting, their opposite ends.

Rosenblatt remembers Luella, but not a relationship:

Booth was her husband's name in the sixties. Apparently the man was a dentist, and Luella was quite a respectable lady, and it took courage to get tied in with the protesters at Allan Gardens. She was a raging red head, a gorgeous woman, and one who certainly made an impression on me and Milton. She wrote a poem in his honour. A very talented lady. She could write. She was a very loyal friend. Now who knows if she was Milton's ex-girlfriend. I honestly wish they had had an affair. She called herself Luella Kerr in the eighties and died with that name (Letter).

Lane says, "Milton probably never got it on with Luella Booth. He wanted young women." Deahl states that "she was an important woman from Milt's Toronto days. Her best collection [*Dance In the Cage of My Bones*] was published by Ekstasis Editions in 1992 the day after she died of cancer" (Letter 12 November 1994).

The Woolnough-Gool house was the main hangout for Charlottetown's small but vigorous circle of artists and intelligentsia and for the Al Purdys and Luella Booths who now wanted readings and performances on the Island. Every night a crowd gathered for Hilda's gourmet cooking. Here, among people from England, Ontario, and the U.S., as well as PEI, Acorn ironically found a community to which he could belong in his home town. At the same time, he was also spending time with another circle, a new generation of native Islanders—the UPEI undergraduates living in or visiting the "Bear House."

The Bear House was a student house located near the old Prince of Wales College campus. "The university was really hopping with intelligent people, and a lot of these students lived there. They were unbelievably outrageous," says Woolnough. A group of exceptional people with the right social dynamics and creative energy came together at the Bear House. They were influenced by the beginning of the Trudeau era and the social changes of the 1960s, including the exposure of PEI's more rural and insular society to cosmopolitan forces. Some of the Bear House crowd wrote poetry. "They were quite big on literature," says Frank Ledwell. And the political opinions of this younger generation of Islanders were more attractive to Acorn than what he remembered from his youth. "Of course Milton loved all this," says Woolnough.

"There is a very large, fine crop of poets on Prince Edward Island," Acorn told Helen MacDonald in 1969, "some of whom are actually good, politically and culturally. In my boyhood Prince Edward Island was dead. The old folk culture had died out almost completely and nothing had come in its place.... I had to leave. I'm not so sure a person has to leave now."

Reg Phelan, then a UPEI student, was part of the Bear House:

Milton used to come down and spend quite a bit of time with us. Sometimes he'd be there for 10 or 12 hours talking. He was always pretty intense politically. He had an incredible background knowledge of what was going on worldwide. No end to it in terms of conversation with Milton. We'd have a few drinks sometimes and the next day I couldn't remember where we'd finished off, but Milton would come back and could remember just where this conversation had stopped. He had an incredible memory. Some people found Milton kind of disjointed. If you weren't familiar with him or his train of thought, it would be easy to get lost.

Phelan was one of those—like Woolnough, Gool, Ledwell, and Cedric Smith—who was comfortably familiar with Acorn's conversational style. Phelan, too, had known him long enough to see him at his best and watch the deterioration. He remembers Southern Comfort, not Drambuie, as Acorn's "favourite drink for awhile in the 1970s."

He would get drunk now and then, Phelan recalls, but would not be hungover in the morning. Out on the farm, Acorn occasionally stayed up until four or five in the morning, talking and "finishing a quart of Southern Comfort" with Phelan, then was up after a few hours of sleep, sober and working at his writing.

"Back then he was much more together. Later, he was getting pretty burned out. It's a pretty intense life to have to live like that, so many years. I think that gradually builds up in a person, if you don't take care of yourself physically, and the mental stress of that. People talk about the binges and blame it on the booze. But I don't think it was the booze. It was how intensely he worked, and he gradually burned himself out." Phelan also believes the heavier drinking occurred in Vancouver and Toronto, not on the Island. "He spent a lot of time on picket lines in Vancouver and other places. In some ways he'd come down here to get away from it. He'd get pretty strung out on it, I gather, up there with political groups. Because Milton had his own ideas and concepts. He'd never mind saying it. He wasn't too diplomatic about it. You were going to know about it and hear about it."

Obviously, Acorn did not leave politics behind entirely when he was on the Island. But the left-wing political scene on PEI was now more congenial. He was initially involved in one of Charlottetown's two alternative newspapers of the early 1970s. The *Broad-Axe* was named after a PEI paper associated with the land struggle, first published in 1871, and produced collectively by the Tenants' Union and Inverness Organization for Community Development. The reborn paper appeared in August 1971, published by Woolnough and Gool. That same month Acorn joined the famous "tractor demonstration"—farmers blocking the Trans-Canada Highway and Borden ferry with their equipment. Also, "He used to claim he was part Native," says Phelan, "and had a pretty strong attachment to how the natives made use of the land. We'd talk at length about the land issue and tenants' revolt. Milton did a lot of library research on that, which was a basis of *The Island Means Minago*."

During this time, Acorn was always welcome to live at his mother's place on Confederation Street and he could stay overnight with Woolnough and Gool, but sometimes he wanted a place by himself. Various people have wondered why he chose to rent rooms in rundown apartment buildings when he could stay with family and friends. The answers are fairly obvious. At times he needed more privacy to write and to read, or his psyche needed its own space. Sometimes he rented a room before he wore out his welcome—or after, when, as Woolnough says, he was "too difficult." Then, too, he seemed to require periodic immersion into the underclass and proletarian life of the tenements. Finally, his material needs were basic and few. As Phelan says, "All Milton would need would be a room. There'd be a mattress in it. He'd get so intense with his writing." Acorn did, however, have a threshold of comfort higher than Charlottetown's worst slum dwellings. Mary Hooper remembers "trying to get some old apartment on University Avenue clean for him. It was so black we had to use pails of water and you couldn't get the darn place clean. Then the toilet wouldn't work. The rain came in. He wasn't there very long. He seemed to be always moving."

Woolnough recalls, "He would ring up Réshard any time of night or day and say, 'I've got to get another place,' and Réshard would say, 'Well, okay, will it wait until tomorrow? I'll see what I can do.' One time Réshard found a place for him where he stayed awhile. It was a beautiful old house down in the centre of Charlottetown and he was very happy there for a long time, because the lady who ran it had been in the air force, and he felt he had a spiritual buddy." The house is on West Street, a short street with stately trees and elegant homes along the harbour near the entrance to Victoria Park. With a beautiful porch facing the harbour and park and a lawn stretching to the water's edge, the house afforded Acorn a modestly luxurious residence.

Gloria Kathleen "Sally" Large was an early woman aviator. Her father, Heber Large, was a First World War pilot with the Royal Flying Corps and then a transport pilot with American Airlines in California. Historian Don B. Smith writes that Heber returned to Charlottetown "to establish a coal import and distribution company. He continued with his flying and became a stirring example to his daughter, Gloria, who was quick to capture an enthusiasm for flying that rapidly grew into a lifelong passion" (9). With her father's support, she enrolled in the Coast Flying School in Anaheim, California—"the only woman learning to fly at Coast during that period" (Smith 10)—and then trained at the Hamilton Flying School in Ontario, "where she was again the only woman pilot." According to Smith, she "served briefly as a pilot with the Air Transport Auxillary in 1942 and was the only Islander and one of a very few Canadian women to be accepted for service with the ATA for service in Britain during the Second World War" (6).

When Acorn moved into Large's home, remembers Hilda Woolnough, "they got along like a house on fire for ages. Spiritual buddies. And he wrote a lot of poetry there. It was a good place for him to work.... She was good to him, left him alone, but was there paying attention when he needed it." Brent MacLaine recalls what Large told him after the relationship between Acorn and Large went sour and Acorn moved out: "When Milton was there she mothered him, and he was a real problem for her. He wouldn't bathe or wash his clothes, until one day she said, 'Give me those pants,' meaning 'right here, right now.'" Woolnough says that the spiritual buddies "had a huge fight and that was it, and about three o'clock in the morning Milt came up and said, 'I've got to get out of there. I can't stand this woman.' Too bad that blew up, because I'd hoped he would enjoy staying there for longer than that." Their camaraderie was no doubt largely based on their similar histories as forerunners, iconoclasts, and wilfully focused individualists who had triumphed over considerable odds. Those same attributes probably contributed to their falling out.

Acorn left Large's house before September 1971. He may have spent a bit more time with his mother on Confederation Street before Helen entered the nursing home in February 1972. He came and went too often from the "Consulate" for Woolnough to remember if he was there between his blow up with Large and late 1972, when he was definitely back in Toronto.

Milton's love of nature and the Island landscape prompted him to spend time in the countryside as well as in Charlottetown during visits home. He rented a cottage from Joe Flynn at Nine Mile Creek, on PEI's South Shore west of Charlottetown, for two to four weeks during the summers of 1971 and 1972. A letter dated June 28, 1971, to the other alternative newspaper, *Square Deal*, gives his address as "Lem Gorveatte's Shore." Gorveatt is a family name in Nine Mile Creek.

Phelan speaks of Milton living in a cottage on the South Shore during 1971, and writing "a fair bit" of *The Island Means Minago* there: "I remember that summer, I used to be out quite a bit to his cottage there. He was living with a woman from Sweden that summer, her and a couple of kids. The first I'd seen of Milton living with somebody during the summer. She might've been an immigrant."

Regarding that woman, Acorn wrote to Irving Layton seven years later:

Once in Toronto I met a Swedish girl. I invited her down to the Island with me. All went well til someone addressed her as Mrs. Acorn. She said, "I'm not Mrs. Acorn." Things went from one to another til she was asked who was taking care of the children....

"My husband," she said. This conversation got repeated back to me by my mother, as you might imagine, within a day ... word for word! I was taken aback myself (since she'd acted single, I'd presumed she wanted it presumed she was), but said, "But what's all this mother? Every second couple on this Island is living in sin; and otherwise the switching is incredible." "Yes," said my mother, "but you shouldn't say it." "You shouldn't say it" sums up Canada in a nutshell, but the country's endangered now, and our secret weapon had better be unzipped. (16 December 1978)

Acorn was showing off his anti-puritanism to Layton, the self-declared apostle of liberation from Canadian sexual repression and hypocrisy. He was also vaunting his defiance of Island mores, which were hardly inviolate, as Acorn exaggeratedly declares, and which were not yet, in 1971, besieged by the sexual revolution.

Several letters Acorn wrote from Nine Mile Creek in the summer of 1971 show that his ill-temper had not entirely deserted him during his idyllic days on the Island. Since at least 1969, when he wrote to Helen about "some very dark relatives," he had been badgering his mother about their heritage, hoping to find native Indian lineage and even "any 'Jew' in our ancestry" (17 January 1969). Apparently his mother's replies were not satisfactory, and they disagreed, with Acorn writing, "You are not my mother" (August 1971).

Another letter was sent to the League of Canadian Poets: "I do not wish any longer to be considered a member of the League of Canadian Poets. Reasons (1) Too many bad poets (2) Too many BAD MOUNTAIN POETS (3) Attempts to drive down rates for poetry!!!!!!!! In other words the leadership is a dirty bunch of scabs (+) Unpatriotic.... I find the membership as a whole incredibly stupid and trivial people" (26 August 1971). Acorn and his mother quickly repaired their relationship. His involvement with the national organization of poets continued, predictably, to be stormy. Meanwhile, Island locales such as Nine Mile Creek afforded Acorn the temporary pastoral retreat he needed from the metropolitan tensions—especially of literature and politics—without which he could not exist for long.

Later in the 1970s Acorn rented a cottage at Rustico on the North Shore, an area with a strong Acadian identity. Even when he stayed in Charlottetown, he needed to visit his favourite shores and rural friends, such as Reg Phelan, and being a non-driver, he relied on friends to serve as chauffeurs and companions.

After Phelan moved back to the farm, and whenever he was on the Island throughout the 1970s, Acorn would phone from Charlottetown. Reg would drive in and pick him up. Sometimes they'd have a few beers first in a hotel, then go out to the farm. Acorn would wake up before dawn, go downstairs, and be so absorbed in his writing he wouldn't notice that Phelan was up and getting ready for work.

Acorn enjoyed walking around the farm, going back into the woods:

He enjoyed meeting some people here. You see, Milton found it hard to meet others here, although he would really desire to do that. Probably the rough side of him having been in some of the bigger cities for quite awhile and some of the political struggles there, and at times, I think, people weren't too personal in terms of how they did some of their work. So he had to have someone as a go-between. If you introduced him to someone they'd get on. He could take off in their conversation, and remember what people had said. I saw in some poems later on what a certain person had said. But he'd really stand out in a crowd. We used to go to ballgames in Morell. He really liked to watch the ball. But he'd never make up to any of the others there and start conversation easily. (Phelan)

Elaine Harrison and Eleanor Wheler offer an unflattering view of Acorn during one of his visits to the Island countryside in the mid-1970s. A distinguished Islander, Harrison is a retired English teacher, prolific visual artist, poet, and former poetry publisher. Wheler had been a pioneer nurse in northern Ontario. Their summer house sits on a bluff, among wind-sculptured spruce trees, overlooking the sea in Fernwood. Devoted readers of poetry and politically progressive, they believed they would enjoy Acorn's company, especially since they had a high regard for Acorn's poems and shared many of his political views. Moreover, Elaine had been one of Milton's early champions on the Island, advocating recognition of his poetic achievements and respect for his social vision.

One day novelist Adele Wiseman was visiting their summer home, Harrison recalls, and "Milton was staying at Libby Oughton's Cape Traverse house. We went down to see him. We invited him down to the shore. But he wanted us to stop in Borden and get him a case of beer and in Summerside for a certain kind of cigar." Finally, they arrived at their home. "We had remembered all his wonderful poems about spruce trees and the sea," says Wheler, "but he just sat there like a brick wall." Harrison adds, "He didn't look at the sea at all. He didn't speak to us. He just sat there. Maybe he wasn't well." Acorn dropped and broke several beer bottles in the car. "He just got out and walked away," says Harrison. "It was Adele who cleaned up the mess." Clearly, Acorn was in one of his depressed moods, and while he was not gracious or communicative, at least he was not combative.

Author Frank Turgeon, who was an aspiring young Island poet in the 1970s, has fond memories of driving Acorn around the Island:

For years I was his chauffeur service on the Island. During the summer on his visits, I would find him walking the streets of Charlottetown, honk my horn, pull over in the summer traffic, and open my passenger's door for him. Though not always, he frequently had an itinerary in mind: usually a jaunt to the north shore, possibly a quick visit with relatives, and often a visit to friends he hadn't seen in some time.

The excursion I remember best was the time we went to Panmure Island [on the Island's eastern end] to visit Glen and Gertrude Partridge.... Milton's deal was that he was to put some gas in the car and buy the rum and I was to provide the vehicle and do the driving.... Like most of our excursions, there were many stops en route. And much heated discussion regarding the merits and demerits of certain poets, or politicians, or people of power and means, or people of no means whatsoever who were going nowhere but possibly could or maybe would if Milt had a say in enacting some of his poems or backfence political philosophy upon not only the decadent Island imposters, but the entire collection of political vermin infesting the arena of Canadian politics, with concessions, possibly, to the NDP.

I remember this one occasion for different reasons. Milton didn't confide in many people that he was precognitive. I guess it's not something you spread around out of your circle of close friends if, indeed, he ever confided that aspect of his being to others at all.... Nonetheless, Milt chose me on this particular occasion to be the one that he would, as the fine poet he was, enlighten in the fine art of precognition. It took place on the north shore where we frequently went to view the beauty of the dunes and the water. (Letter)

Acorn's belief in his precognition has its antecedents in the "psychic powers" and "psychic dreams" of both grandmothers, Mary Fairclough and Kate Carbonell, in "the Celtic tradition of female powers" to which David Hooper alludes, and in Milton's mother's claims of prescience:

"Prescience, I suppose you would call it, the ability to see what's coming before through dreams, that's what they claimed. They claimed to be able to communicate with one another through numbers. Helen, Grandma Acorn, did that all the time, and some of her relatives claimed to be able to do it. I don't know if it was a parlour trick or what. They used to demonstrate: one go in one room, one in another, and read the numbers on a dollar bill. Take it or leave it" (D. Hooper). With claims of psychic powers on both sides of his family, Acorn seems to have taken it upon himself, too, though confiding it to very few people.

On Panmure Island he found a fellow spirit in Glen Partridge. "They knew each other in Montreal," says Gertrude Partridge.

We were from Prince Edward Island. Glen was in the Second World War overseas, a chaplain, Presbyterian. He became a teacher after the war. He taught English literature in Ottawa and Hawksbury, Ontario. He went to Presbyterian College in Montreal. Glen was president of the Montreal Civil Liberties Union. It was the time of the Padlock Act,[26] and he helped get it declared *ultra vires* [beyond one's legal power or authority].... Milton and Glen used to go down to a coffee house in Montreal and talk. I stayed home with the children.

We retired back here. Milton used to come out here to visit my husband. He'd stay a couple of hours. They were good buddies, and my husband thought Milton was very brilliant and knew so much about history. They talked mainly about history, I think. Maybe some poetry, but mainly history. My husband was very much interested in modern European history. He enjoyed talking with him. He had patience with him.

Gertrude was a long-time social activist, running for office with the Labour Progressive Party, and working with progressive movements on PEI. But "I found it hard to understand him. He spoke so quickly. His mind was so quick. I used to see Milton at Pat's Rose and Grey Room [in Charlottetown], and sometimes we sat together and talked."

Even with a supportive community of Island friends, a surge of poetic activity in Charlottetown, the pleasures of the Island landscape and seashore, and his new public stature as an honoured Canadian poet, Acorn returned to Toronto. Reasons can be offered: his restlessness; the fact that PEI, for all its charm and intimacy, was still too small and old-fashioned for his energy and purpose; and his need to be in a major centre of artistic ferment, especially since "CanLit" was coming of age with himself as a pivotal and exemplary figure. As well, his need for political forums could not be satisfied on the Island, even though his poetic attention would soon focus on its political and economic history.

IX

THE FIGURE IN THE LANDSCAPE

> If you're stronghearted put your ear to the ground
> to hear the lilt and cut of soft voices
> discussing enemy moves without fear.
> — "If You're Stronghearted"

ON 25 NOVEMBER 1972, Acorn, Cedric Smith, and poet Stephanie Nynych performed at the "Revive the Spirit of '37 Festival," organized by the Canadian Liberation Movement. A photograph of Acorn and Smith from this performance is on the front cover of Acorn's *The Island Means Minago*. The note for that cover photo reads, "The Festival is a celebration of the brave Canadians who fought in the Revolution in Upper and Lower Canada, 1837-39." That book contains the vision poem "William Lyon Mackenzie" and a dramatic dialogue, "Hypothetical Meeting between William Cooper and William Lyon Mackenzie"—Cooper being the salient leader of the PEI tenants' revolt in the 1830s.

That Cedric Smith is on the cover of Acorn's Governor-General's Award-winning book is apt, for Acorn and Cedric Smith—the multi-talented actor, musician, singer, and song-writer—were developing a fast friendship and artistic partnership, including their collaboration on the play *The Road To Charlottetown*. As well, Smith was a member of Perth County Conspiracy (Does Not Exist), a seminal folk-rock band out of Ontario in the late 1960s and 70s, which performed and recorded Smith's musical interpretations of Acorn's poems and the pair's collaborations. Their album *Tune Up* contains a version of Acorn's "I Shout Love" and two songs by Acorn and Smith, "Hurray for the Farmer" and "Pasture of Plenty." On the band's 1971 double album, *Perth County Conspiracy Alive,* is "I spun you out," co-written by Acorn and Smith. Next to the lyrics on the cover is a photo of "Milton Acorn the People's Poet," bare-chested, bemedalled, and scanning the horizon, probably for "History's greatest change."

During the intermission of that festival, Acorn met James Deahl, a young Toronto poet originally from the United States, and one of the next generation of writers Acorn would influence. "I do not know when Milton joined the Canadian Liberation Movement (CLM). He for sure was a big time member when I met him on November 25, 1972. And he kept his membership right to the bitter (and it was extremely bitter) end in 1976" (Letter, 16 August 1992). Here is Joyce Wayne's unsympathetic view of the CLM: "Impoverished and in ill health, Acorn managed to hook up with the Canadian Liberation Movement, a left-nationalist group of Stalinesque drum-rollers and majorettes" (15). She then credits Acorn for preserving the "integrity of his poetry" from their "dogma," even though "For seven years he stuck with CLM" (15).

More Poems for People was published in 1972 by NC Press, "the Canadian Liberation publisher," as was *The Island Means Minago.* In the back of the latter, there is an ad for the CLM: "*The Canadian Liberation Movement* is devoted to building an independent, socialist Canada. Join the fight for independent rank-and-file controlled Canadian unions. Participate actively in the struggle to free Canadians from U.S. imperialist control." These objectives appealed to some recent ex-Americans, as well as to Canadian-born nationalists, and by February 1973 Acorn had talked his new friend Deahl into joining the CLM. For the next two years Deahl "worked with Acorn on various political projects.... An example of the joint work of Acorn and Deahl was the strike of Local 101 of the Canadian Union of Operating Engineers against A.E. LePage. This strike ran for seven weeks ... at the OHIP buildings in Toronto. Acorn and Deahl served as support pickets, and as picket line representatives of the National Committee for Independent Canadian Unions (a CLM front)" (Deahl *Chronology*).

"The real foundation of our friendship was politics and poetry. We agreed largely on poetry and disagreed largely on politics. Nonetheless, we worked very closely on political matters for two years at the very start of our friendship." In 1975 Deahl "was gone from the CLM and its various fronts" because "the Canadian Liberation Movement took up the slogan 'Yankee Go Home!' and began to purge its ranks of U.S. citizens" (*Chronology*). Acorn's nationalistic anti-Americanism was political and economic, and did not indict the individual American. Deahl was a prime example. "Acorn's likes and dislikes were always large likes and dislikes. I mean, it would be the Americans, not a particular American. He never singled out people whom he disliked. It was always the group" (Woolnough). In fact, he held Canadians just as responsible as Americans for Canada's neocolonial submission to the United States. While he interrogates American neo-imperialism in "Our True/False National Anthem"—"Canada, the cruel north stripped stark bare"—he also illustrates the passive-aggressive posture of Canadians: "We masters of the Canadian bow / Backs turned and arse up to the U.S.A." (*Selected* 183).

As for the poetry part of Acorn's and Deahl's friendship, Acorn presented the first of Deahl's LINK Poetry Work-shops on 6 March 1973 in Toronto: "Milton Acorn Discusses his Working Class Poetry." Deahl writes, "It was the first of many things he did for LINK over the next eight years." Such "things" were indicative of his enhanced public role: "Once Acorn had received the title of 'People's Poet,' he constantly referred to it. Along with the title, he took upon himself the responsibility of being the 'people's voice,' the people's BARD. He constantly proclaimed himself a SOCIAL POET, a poet with a public role and duty, and all his later writings reveal the shift toward public and political poems" (Jewinski 52).

Some critics, such as Zailig Pollock, feel that "Acorn's increasingly public stance in this period seemed to lead him away from the personal experience that nourished his best work" (5). Jewinski moderates this view, maintaining with a curious logic that "on the whole, *More Poems for People* is tremendously uneven, yet its unevenness is really the essence of its vitality" (58). In fact, the unevenness results, not in "vitality," but in a weaker collection than *I've Tasted My Blood*, with fewer masterful and memorable poems, and more writing that lacks impressive weight, finesse, or discernment. Jewinski does regret Acorn's "comprehensive, bardic political statements" (58) and wishes that Acorn had more often "turned to depicting the state of human wretchedness and exhaustion of spirit and hope" (59). In other words, why did he not write more about the people he encountered in Toronto, in the hotel where he lived, and generalize less about the human condition? Acorn had borrowed the title for this volume from Dorothy Livesay's 1947 collection *Poems for People*.

Just as Livesay's weaker political poems suffered from an excess of ideological principle and abstract sentiment, *More Poems for People* is too often hampered by Acorn's anti-capitalist and anti-imperialist content, tone, and rhetoric and his laboured effort to uplift ordinary Canadians. Meanwhile, there is too little evocation of the individual lives of those Canadians with whom he associated every day.

Acorn's main residence in Toronto throughout the decade was the Waverly Hotel at the corner of College and Spadina, just south of the University of Toronto. Adjectives used to describe the Waverly would depend on one's expectations in accommodation. To some, it might have seemed one step up from a flophouse. To others it might have been a respectable place for people of modest means. According to Acorn, "The Waverly Hotel was full of character and characters. It was a place for all sorts of strange but true types. People who were down but not out" (Martin *In Love*). The Waverly was certainly a suitable home for Acorn, and it became identified with him—the place where the People's Poet always kept a room, even during the two years he lived with Deahl on Palmerston Avenue. Another apocryphal story is that the Waverly's manager occasionally suggested that Acorn stop renting the room at the daily rate, and instead rent by the month or week. The savings would be substantial. But Acorn insisted on paying the higher daily rate.

At this point in his life and career, he sent Al Purdy a semi-confessional progress report—on both of them:

People criticize you and say you made too much of yourself, and a romantic picture of me, in *I've Tasted My Blood*. Fact is you understated your responsibility for me. I sold my tools because I was too sick to work as a carpenter. Tho still capable of manual labour. It was you who dragged me out of that room on Saint Antoine and down to your house to write poetry.... Later we hammered out a two-man new school of poetry between us, never admitting we were a school. If that didn't show the country it should uv. I think the results are still to come. If Canada had only you and me to justify her, she'd still be justified. (4 May 1974)

Few if any would deny Purdy's immense contribution to the "justified" substance of Canada—as a voice of Canadian history and experience, and as a maker of Canadian self-awareness. Acorn's poetic achievements now seem less than Purdy's; hence, Acorn's self-assessment seems inflated. Yet Acorn had, by 1974, made a powerful impact on

Canadian poetry and Canada's maturing cultural identity. "We're progenitors," he wrote Purdy, and they were, both of them.

Here was Acorn, then, living in the heart of Toronto, the paradoxically appropriate place for the next major phase in his art: the completion of *The Island Means Minago* and the writing, in collaboration with Cedric Smith during 1975 and 1976, of *The Road To Charlottetown*. Living in the central Canadian city he loved to denounce, he focused poetically on PEI, the essence and locus of his Canada.

The book which finally won him the Governor-General's Award began, however, on the Island. Phelan describes an important stage in that process and the oral history, as well as library research, which underlies this book:

Conversations I've had with my grandfather—When I was a young kid we used to go down and spend hours talking to him on the doorstep. He'd be sitting there in the rocking chair, telling stories, and you'd get the feeling of the history that had taken place. The same with other older guys around. But when you started to drag out your history books, it just didn't match. They didn't mention anything about the struggles of the tenants and the landlords, and yet you heard about colourful incidents. So I'd bring that up with Milton and he'd get pretty fascinated. Milton did a lot of library research on that, on the tales about particular incidents, and some of that would make its way into some of Milton's poems, things that happened in the countryside here.

The Island Means Minago combines several techniques: historical narrative and imagined dialogue; satirical and didactic prose; regional description; and lyrical, political, historical, and satirical poetry. A profound awareness of regionalism, of the Island and Maritime experience, bonds these diverse techniques into a coherent work. Refined political indignation unites convincingly with a mythic construction that is part historiography, part nostalgia and wishful thinking, part ideology, and part inspired perception. The book is sometimes unreliable in terms of historical fact; yet as with all eminent literature, the liberties it takes are justified by the "truths"—including the regional significances—it presents, and by the substance it discerns and reveals in this region's history and the lives of its inhabitants.

In *The Island Means Minago* Acorn reprinted a dozen "Island" poems such as "Charlottetown Harbour," "Offshore Breeze," "Old

Property," "Islanders," "The Schooner," and "the one about your father"—"The Trout Pond." With succinct eloquence, these poems celebrate the natural beauty and social character of the Island, as do new poems strongly evoking the landscape and working lives of Islanders, such as "Dragging for Traps" and the philosophically vigorous "The Squall." There are old and new poems not specifically "Island": "Hotel Fire," "On Speaking Ojibway," "The Fighting Cape Bretoners," "The Newfie Bullet." And something new appears: an absorption in PEI history, particularly the famous land struggle and tenants' revolt, and the ambivalent entrance of the province into Confederation. Growing out of this, too, are allusions to "a new still-just-brooding / Struggle for the land." The result won Acorn the 1975 Governor-General's Award for poetry—the honour he had been denied for *I've Tasted My Blood*.

More important for readers today, and especially for PEI and Islanders, this book incarnates the struggle of the Island's tenant farmers and many merchants and artisans for autonomy, justice, and an equitable return on their labour and investment. Acorn also trains our sights (to borrow his imagery) on the people he perceived as oppressors and exploiters: absentee British landlords who failed to live up to their responsibilities, and their rent-collecting agents; local merchants, capitalists, and officials who collaborated with and profited from colonialist exploitation; the local Tories who opposed responsible government; and the alliance of certain local entrepreneurs and officials who, when negotiating Confederation, in Acorn's view, sold out to central Canadians and compromised the Island's best interests to feather their nests.

Island historians, even those who value this book and sympathize with Acorn's political and economic views, can point out that Acorn adjusted history to suit his poetic purposes and political interpretations. Moreover, he was not the first writer to address these issues. For instance, David Weale and Harry Baglole wrote and published in 1973 *The Island and Confederation*, which Ian Ross Robertson, another historian specializing in Island history, describes as "a somewhat romantic interpretation of Island history from the 1760s until entry into Confederation. It proved to be the most significant book on Island history published between the 1950s and the 1980s, and sold 3,000 copies before going out of print in 1979" ("Historical" 158). One "somewhat romantic" statement sounds compatible with Acorn's pastoral poems about PEI: "Thus was gradually shaped, almost as if by a faithful and unconscious adherence to some Divine plan, the symmetrical pastoral beauty of the Island countryside" (Weale and Baglole 43-44). Indeed, the writings of Weale and Baglole in the 1970s may have informed and influenced Acorn's rendering of Island history in *The Island Means Minago*.

Even if Acorn's version of Island history was partly derived from other writers—of necessity, since he was a poet and not a specialist in Island history—and even though his interpretation is more slanted in favour of the tenant farmers than the historical record may allow, the general outline of Acorn's poems about absentee landlords and leasehold tenure, the tenants' revolt, and the struggle for land ownership and responsible government is sound enough. Moreover, as artistic versions of the historical conflicts that helped define the Island's identity and that operate powerfully in contemporary Island society, Acorn's poems about "the struggle for the land" in *The Island Means Minago* are valuable in several respects.

First, they reassert the significance of a huge part of Island history, including its unique political and economic development, and of certain characteristics of the culture and people. Acorn reminds readers that PEI, too, had a rich history of exploitation and rebellion, of rivalry among vested interests, of political maneuvering and economic struggle. The history was not a romantic, simplistic case of farmers, fishers, merchants, and tradespeople struggling against the elements and building communities. That kind of pseudo-historical portrait is a reductionist discourse which thins Island and Maritime history to a quaint, nostalgic, and grossly superficial past. Acorn legitimately asserts that the Island's history consists of many of the same complex issues and conflicts found in European and U.S. history. He insists that Islanders must know about it, take pride in it, and learn from its lessons.

The reclaiming and declaiming of this part of Island history is directed as much to central Canada as it is to the Island and the Maritimes. "There's always the problem for the hinterland, in bourgeois nations, of the centre," says Acorn. "Always the centre thinks it is it. Isn't it ridiculous?" (Burrill 5). *The Island Means Minago* speaks from what postcolonial literary, economic, and political theory calls the "margin" or "periphery" and "marginalized" people, or the "Other." Postcolonial theory explains how the geopolitical centres and élites devalue the other "regions" (the inferior "others" out in the boondocks) in order to justify their exploitation and manipulation of the "regions."[27] The centres and élites impose their world-view as a "totalizing discourse" on the periphery.

In response to this, *The Island Means Minago* speaks to its own people, Islanders and other Maritimers: you are not marginal (i.e., unimportant), even though you were marginalized by the geopolitical centres, by colonialism and imperialism, by corporate capitalism and its media-entertainment vehicles. Acorn says: you, your history, society, and culture are just as vital and rich as those of the cosmopolitan centres. Acorn's poems send the message to the centre—Toronto, Ottawa, central Canada—that the Island and the Maritimes are not marginal, not an inferior hinterland, and are equally worthy of respect and attention.

One term for this position is "resistive regionalism"—a recovery and assertion of regional importance which resists the centralizing power of metropolitan élites, of the central regions. Acorn's poems in *The Island Means Minago* about the Island's historical conflicts and its contemporary political and economic situation are certainly examples of resistive regionalism. As well, Acorn' poetic career and political identity may be partly defined by the concept of resistive regionalism: the poet from a marginalized region, who succeeds in the metropolitan centres and nationally *as an artist from and of that region*; the political voice of the Island and Maritimes in resistance to the centre, and of Canada in resistance to U.S. neo-imperialism. It is also vital to note that Acorn's writing was not marginalized as a token voice from the boondocks. Rather, his work emerged in the supportive context of numerous resistive regionalisms in Canada and throughout the postcolonial world.

The literary and cultural critic Edward W. Said points out that "the power to narrate, or to block other narratives from forming or emerging, is very important to culture and imperialism, and constitutes one of the main connections between them. Most important, the grand narratives of emancipation and enlightenment mobilized people in the colonial world to rise up and throw off imperial subjection" (xiii). The power to narrate is equally important in the postcolonial or neocolonial world, in which a narrative such as *The Island Means Minago* must compete with the narratives provided by *The Globe and Mail*, CNN, and the business empires of Irving, Disney, and Conrad Black. With *The Island Means Minago*, Acorn provides a narrative written by and from the periphery. It works as an alternative to the dominant or "master" narratives imposed by the centres on the regions—narratives which are "exclusivist discourses," that is, excluding the historical reality, and even the existence, of the regions.

The Island Means Minago, then, is also valuable as a postcolonial text, and may be grouped with a great deal of literature from Ireland, Africa, Australia, India, and other regions which were colonized, marginalized, and exploited by the "centres." "We live in a sub-colony," said Acorn, "a double sub-colony—a colony both of the south [U.S.] and the centre [central Canada]. Islands have particular troubles with monopolies. But try to explain that to those buggers up-along! They think it's the same all over, that exploitation is the same all over. Bullshit it is. It's more intense on islands. You look at the great islands of the world. How many of them are empty! They've lost the struggle with monopoly, and the monopolies, by over-exploitation, have just wiped the people out" (quoted in Burrill 5). Replace the dated term "monopoly" with the fashionable "economies of scale," "competitive environment," or "globalization" and Acorn has described the ongoing dilemma of PEI and countless other "marginalized" places "too small" or "too remote" to "compete in the global marketplace." The powerful élite in the centres, through their totalizing and exclusivist discourse, would have us believe this is inevitable. Acorn wants us to analyze and challenge the self-serving assumptions and master narratives of the central élite.

The Island Means Minago portrays Island history not just as a picturesque tableau, but even more as a dynamic process of politics and vested economic interests: class structures and conflicts; colonial and imperial power; rivalries among traders, merchants, and manufacturers with conflicting allegiances to autonomy or subservience to the geopolitical centres. There were, for instance, merchants and traders who profited from colonial rule and the absentee landlord-tenant farmer system, and others who would profit from self-government. In other words, the Island is a real place with a real history, not a sanitized haven with an idyllic past for tourist nostalgia.

This leads to a third value of *The Island Means Minago*: the past as a metaphor for the present. Acorn had not turned into a poet preoccupied with the past. Indeed, he was proud of his Island's history. But he also wanted to show, through historical precedent, the political and economic reality of the present, and the challenges Islanders must embrace. These poems and *The Road To Charlottetown* were as much about the present as the past.

One other value is inherent in this book's pointed title: island "is a translation of the aboriginal name" Minago—meaning "The Island." More respectfully: *The Island Means Minago*. Acorn was at least a decade ahead of most other Euro-Canadians (including most writers) in acknowledging the "precedence" of "the senior race." This is not primarily because he believed he had aboriginal ancestry. The reverse is most likely true: Acorn insisted on aboriginal descent because he was in the vanguard of Euro-Canadians beginning to respect the history and presence of aboriginal peoples—not as a construct of European myth and prejudice which justified exploitation and repression, and which generated images of romantic primitives or pathetic victims—but as the indigenous First Peoples of the hemisphere, who were reclaiming their heritage.

The fact that Acorn was saying all this in a literary form, especially poetry, had another value, in this case for Island culture and society. Acorn's subject matter has been central to the literatures of older nations. Before him, however, Island poetry was largely devoid of the great themes of literature associated with our economic and political existence—not to mention the revolt of the underclass against the ruling élite or the margin, the "hinterland," standing up for itself instead of bowing down to the centre. In the same decade, UPEI bestowed honorary doctorates on Milton Acorn and the Nigerian Chinua Achebe, the first great Black African novelist of our era, who has written tirelessly of his people's struggle against colonialism, marginalization, internalized inferiority, economic and cultural domination by geopolitical centres, and the Black African élite who have replaced colonial rulers in the exploitation of the people. Acorn was in good company, not an eccentric in his poetic concerns: he was in the vanguard of what is now the mainstream, and was urging Islanders to stand up for themselves as their ancestors once had.

In the process he published one of his two strongest collections. *The Island Means Minago* may quite possibly be consistently superior to *I've Tasted My Blood*. The latter is a thicker collection, with more minor poems, while the former has some of the best poems from the 1969 book and the memorable new poems about Island history. As Burrill writes, "Despite the fact that he is well-known as a Canadian nationalist, a very good case could be made for an interpretation of Acorn's regional, Island poetry that it is his best. He admits there is a strained quality to some of his national poems.... And there is no better foundation for a radical Island nationalism, certainly, than what is arguably Acorn's best book, *The Island Means Minago*" (5).

Here is Acorn's Island nationalism in the book's prose introduction: "The official story is that Canadian history is brief and boring. The

Island is supposed to be distinguished by having no history at all, except the Charlottetown Conference where Confederation was conceived though not born.... Long before the Canadian Revolution of 1837-39, a fierce people's struggle against landlords, many of them absentees, raged on the Island" (9). Acorn's synopsis is certainly spirited, and the poems which follow provide a dramatic mytho-historic reply to any assertion that the Island has a boring history. Indeed, Acorn's treatment of the nineteenth-century land struggle in *The Island Means Minago* is central to his mytho-poetic and ideological vision of the Island. It is worthwhile, therefore, to examine the perspective of Island historians on this crucial aspect of the Island's history and development. The scholarly perspective is required, not so much to challenge or correct Acorn's treatment, but to provide a complementary historiographic context for his version of Island history.

With measured restraint, Ian Ross Robertson writes, "The distinguishing characteristic of the history of Prince Edward Island as a colony within British North America was the controversy over leasehold tenure known as the land question" ("Introduction" xi). Other historians, such as Lorne C. Callbeck in *The Cradle of Confederation*, emphasize and censure the role of absentee landholders in the leasehold tenure system: "When the lots of St. John Island were lotteried off in 1767 the scandalous system of tenure which had been so aptly called 'absentee proprietorship' was foisted upon the young colony to throttle its progress for over an hundred years" (171). According to Weale and Baglole, "The Island Land Question was that century-long social and political conflict which resulted when this strong desire of the individual settler to possess a farm of his own found itself opposed and thwarted by a stubborn system of absentee proprietorship. The problem was aggravated, moreover, by the fact that it was unique in British North America. Island settlers were generally aware that it was relatively easy to obtain freehold Grants in the neighbouring colonies, and thus they felt themselves to be in an especially disadvantaged condition" (51-52). In fact, in Nova Scotia over one million acres of land had been confiscated from absentee proprietors in the 1780s and given without charge to loyalist settlers.

In his article "Drawing Lots," Baglole notes that "the mould of land ownership ... was set on a single day, July 23, 1767" (1298). Four years after the brutal expulsion of Acadians and French from Ile St-Jean by the English conquerors, and three years after Captain Samuel Holland surveyed and divided the Island into 67 townships of twenty-thousand acres each, "A group of influential men, or their agents, assembled in London to dole out among themselves the property of St. John's Island" ("Drawing" 1298). A lottery distributed the twenty-thousand acre parcels, which came to be known as "lots." Baglole argues, with a perspective not dissimilar to Acorn's, that "from the outset, landlords and settlers were at loggerheads, dwelling apart in spirit and fact. Few proprietors ever took up residence on the Island. The ancient animosities of class which emigrants carried with them across the ocean were soon sharpened by the New World expectations and experience" ("Drawing" 1299).

The proprietors had obligations regarding their land. Most owners, however, were more interested in collecting rents from their tenant farmers than meeting their obligations. Robertson observes, "If a landlord who held his land from the crown on condition of performing certain duties failed to meet his obligations, his land was liable to be *escheated*, or returned to the crown" ("Introduction" xv). The principle of *escheat* was, unfortunately, never applied by the colonial government on the Island. As Baglole points out, the settlers' high expectations turned into bitter disappointment: "No sooner had a crude dwelling been built and a bit of land cleared than the agent would appear at the door: Sign this lease, pay your rent, or be evicted! The tenants found it difficult to understand why the contracts they had signed should be enforced by the authority of a primitive and often arbitrary colonial law system, while the proprietors could continue to flout with impunity the conditions of their grants" ("Drawing" 1300).

Robertson is more charitable toward the proprietors. In an overview of the work of another Island historian, J.M. Bumsted, he values "Bumsted's rehabilitation of the historical reputation of the early proprietors" ("Historical" 170). According to this view, certain early settlers, such as the Highlanders who came with the 5th Earl of Selkirk, "were not demoralized victims.... They went to Prince Edward Island with him [Selkirk] because that was the best way open to them to fulfil plans they had already made on the basis of rational assessment of their own interests" ("Historical" 169). Apparently there were mutually profitable relationships between several Scottish proprietors and their settlers. As well, many Loyalist settlers from the U.S.—including Acorn's own ancestor, John Eichorn—were rewarded by the crown with land. But these positive examples from the early decades of colonial rule are overshadowed by the widespread grievances of most tenants from the 1810s through the 1860s, grievances based on the fact that most proprietors extracted rents from tenants, while utterly failing to honour their obligations.

Referring to the fact that some absentee proprietors did not profit from their land holdings on the Island, Robertson reports that "the evidence led Bumsted to venture the opinion ... that the wise landlords were those who acted as speculators, putting as little money as possible into the Island, and hoping that the efforts of others would cause their lands to appreciate in value and enable them to sell and thereby escape with either a gain or as little loss as possible" ("Historical" 168). Such an observation unintentionally reinforces Acorn's view of the land struggle: hard-working tenants—the figures in the landscape who made the landscape—exploited by absentee landlords who justified their behaviour with the familiar owner-speculators' complaint that they were losing money. The complaint was designed to reduce criticism of leasehold tenure and to shift sympathy from tenants to proprietors. Acorn's sympathy was clearly with the tenant farmers, who by the 1820s were beginning to protest their condition.

The Island Means Minago contains a dramatic dialogue, "The Execution of William Abel, Rent Collector, by a Farmer Named Pierce," and two poems, "Rent Collection" and "Incident from the Land Struggle (1767-1873)," based on the tenants' growing discontent with the leasehold tenure system. Baglole recounts the murder of Edward Abell, the local land agent for Lord James Townshend, an absentee English proprietor of twenty-thousand acres in eastern Prince Edward Island: "The time was a summer Saturday, August 1819. The man who killed Abell with a bayonet was Pat Pearce, a poor Irish tenant farmer. At issue was the payment of rent on Pearce's farm. Perhaps the most extraordinary feature of this event is that the people of the community sympathized with Pearce. It is said that they protected him from law officers and helped him escape the Island. To this day, people in that community take pride in telling how their forbears gave Pearce shelter" ("Drawing" 1297-98). Abell's murder and other tales of tenants' refusal to pay rent and their harassment of landlords' agents inspired Acorn's "Incident from the Land Struggle (1767-1873)," in which tenant farmers plan their tactics for dealing with the agent:

> "Well sirs, then we're agreed on the plan.
> Black John here will fire on this Englishman
> And miss (make sure of that, lad

> The battle depends on this)
> One quarter mile on, White John
> Will miss too, but closer, and if that
> Stinking piece of rent-collecting manure
> Who dares call himself a gentleman
> Keeps on, Red John will shoot his horse.
> Old John here will then happen along
> And lend him his horse—the red stallion.
> Once he's on that beast, no more worries
> Except to collect the remains, living or dead
> And carry them back to Charlottetown
> And, of course demand our expenses
> Be very particularly
> > angry
> > about that." (*Minago* 71)

Acorn may have exaggerated the extent to which tenant farmers took armed action against rent collectors, but the sentiment of this poem was no doubt part of the wishful thinking of many tenants. And the voice speaking in "Rent Collection" is certainly a reliable echo of their experience: "The highwayman has come / In the name of the King / If he gets his loot / It will be called rent" (*Minago* 19).

One of Acorn's best-known poems about this period in Island history is "William Cooper" (*Minago* 29-30). The leader of the farmers' Escheat Party, Cooper was a remarkable character from England. Baglole sketches Cooper in *The Dictionary of Canadian Biography*: "According to an account probably based on oral family tradition, he ran away to sea at age eleven, was with the British navy at the battle of Trafalgar, and subsequently sailed the seven seas as a ship's captain" (155). By 1819 he had settled at Fortune Bay, PEI, on a farm named "Sailor's Hope," where he built a grist mill and a 72-ton ship. Cooper's role as a reform leader began ironically, or perhaps fittingly. "On 26 Feb. 1820," writes Baglole, "Lord Townshend appointed Cooper as Abell's successor. Cooper was reputedly one of the more efficient of an apparently negligent and often corrupt class of land agents" (155).

Cooper's career as a reformer began not long after he "was dismissed by Lord Townshend in 1829 for somewhat obscure reasons. In later years his political enemies frequently alleged that Cooper had misappropriated funds, a charge which ... Cooper never seemed quite able to refute convincingly. It was perhaps not entirely coincidental that by 1830 he had apparently undergone a change of heart amounting almost to a religious conversion, and had become the lifelong, implacable foe of the absentee proprietors" (Baglole "William" 156). Elected to the legislature in 1831, Cooper advocated a

> radical and uncompromising position on the land question.... Cooper and his political associates maintained that practically all the land in the Island should be escheated and regranted in small tracts to *bona fide* settlers. This heady doctrine, promising redistribution of virtually all landed property in the colony, proved attractive to a populace comprised largely of small tenant farmers.... During the 1830s Cooper became the founder and leader of an informal Escheat party, and proceeded with considerable energy to polarize Island politics on the single issue of land tenure.... Cooper's agitation contributed to a violent mood among the tenantry, many of whom refused to pay rents and on occasion banded together to threaten rent collectors and sheriffs physically. But Cooper was always careful to keep within the law, and appears not to have been the man to lead an actual armed uprising. (156)

This authoritative account differs somewhat from Acorn's plaintively melodramatic one:

> How many times did he aim his musket
> In threat? How many times did he fire it?
> Always to warn and miss or sometimes to hit?
> Who knows William Cooper? Who gives a damn?
> Who wants to remember that old war?
> How many claim him for ancestor?
> (*Minago* 29)

Acorn and Baglole had a brief discussion about their respective portraits of Cooper. Baglole was excited about his piece, which included new and dramatic material, and he wanted to share it with Acorn. Thus he was surprised by Acorn's response: "You've ruined my poem." It was more a lament than a criticism. Acorn may have momentarily felt deflated, as if his imaginative reach and research had been outstripped by the historian, and his own portrait of Cooper invalidated. Baglole, though, believed that their work would be complementary.

Indeed, Acorn's "William Cooper" does present home truths that stand on their own and complement the historian's perspective:

> William Cooper's part of the history
> Of Prince Edward Island—Canadian history, therefore
> Officially blank; but forbidden history
> Is still history; We react and think
> According to our history
> Even though we may not know it.
> Except our actions are slower, confused
> And since our history's been misused
> Old mistakes are often repeated.
> (*Minago* 29)

Acorn's poetry and the work of Island historians have helped ensure that the region's history is no longer "blank" or "forbidden," though the reminder of class struggle still makes many citizens uncomfortable. Acorn's romanticization of William Cooper aside, the poem reaffirms the historical role of reformers, even ones who seem "radical" in their time and context. Also, the land question and the figure of Cooper become history lessons, a frame of reference for "our actions" and the avoidance of "Old mistakes."

Although Cooper's Escheat Party won 18 of 24 seats in the 1838 election, Cooper was unsuccessful in his presentation of petitions to the colonial secretary, Lord John Russell, who refused Cooper an audience. "Cooper's prestige never fully recovered," writes Baglole ("William" 156). Nonetheless, "the political movement he founded was the undoubted forerunner of the reform-minded Liberal Party, which led the struggle for responsible government in the 1840s" ("William" 158). Even though Acorn lamented that Baglole had "ruined" his poem, Baglole's summation of Cooper's contribution would be music to Acorn's ears: "Cooper remains an enigmatic figure—a visionary, an adventurer, and a pre-Marxist advocate of an ideology to support and justify the cause of an oppressed class, yet a man with evident weaknesses and inconsistencies" ("William" 158). Cooper remained politically active, but his influence had greatly diminished, and he focused more on his interests as a shipowner, merchant trader, and sea captain.

The land question itself was resolved slowly throughout the period of responsible government and during the years immediately following Confederation. As well, many Islanders, including most Charlottetown residents, either had little interest in land reform or had a vested economic, political, and social interest in maintaining British colonial rule, including the leasehold tenure system. The escheat route was never taken. When the British government granted responsible government to the Island, George Coles, a brewer and distiller in Charlottetown and the leader of the reform movement, became the first premier. As Baglole writes, Coles "acknowledged the proprietorial rights of the landlords.... Then his majority Liberal party passed the Land Purchase Act of 1853, empowering the Island government to purchase the estates of obliging proprietors for resale to the tenantry" ("Drawing" 1303). Almost one third of the colony's land—457,260 acres—was purchased under this act between 1853 and 1873. Some absentee proprietors, however, refused to sell, and this resistance contributed to the formation of the Tenant League in 1864 and the disturbances of 1865.

Robertson writes, "On 19 May 1864 ... an Island-wide 'Tenant League' was founded at a meeting in Charlottetown. The formation of the league and its rapid spread throughout most parts of the Island in 1864 and 1865 indicated absolute frustration on the part of many, perhaps most, Island tenants with the conventional political process" ("Introduction" xxv). The league's formation and continued government inaction led to the non-payment of rents, physical resistance to sheriff's officers, and, finally, intervention by soldiers from Halifax.[28]

The leasehold tenure system and absentee proprietorship were doomed by Confederation. According to Baglole, "The dénouement came with Confederation, at which time 383,720 acres remained in the hands of the large proprietors. The Canadian government gave assent to the Island's Compulsory Land Purchase Act of 1875, establishing an absolute limit of 500 acres per landowner" ("Drawing" 1303). The act was denounced as "tyranny" and "Communistic" by one proprietor, Miss Georgina C. Fane. "With the purchase of the final estate from the last proprietor," writes Baglole, "the contradiction of absentee landlord and resident tenant found resolution in the person of the farmer-proprietor, an enduring feature of the Island landscape" ("Drawing" 1303).

In Acorn's view, however, this "resolution" benefited proprietors, as well as the Island's bourgeois élite who dominated local government, at the expense of the tenants. As Acorn fumed, the tenants had to pay thrice for their land: first, in rents to the landlords; second, in taxes the Island government used to buy the land from proprietors; and third, in the purchase of their own land from the Island government. Historical hindsight might deem this solution practical and inevitable in light of British colonial power and British law. But Acorn attacked a legal process established by and for the British and colonial élite, which was practical for the privileged classes, but not for tenant farmers. Acorn's treatment of this "resolution" in *The Island Means Minago* provides an eloquently satirical commentary on the drawn-out compromises that settled the land question on Prince Edward Island.

The Island Means Minago includes other poems about that period in history, a "Scene From: The Road to Charlottetown," and prose pieces in which Acorn presents his interpretations of Island history, the identity of Islanders, and contemporary challenges to Island society. This is Acorn the essayist on the land struggle:

Feudalism was nowhere more extreme than on Prince Edward Island.... Many of the settlers, after the Acadians, were Loyalists. They were promised land, given it briefly, and then, presto-chango, put in the position of tenants. Their resentment was natural, they were experienced in arms, many brought arms with them. They changed rather quickly from counter-revolutionaries to revolutionaries. The other part of the landlords' program to settle people who could pay rent was just crazy. They brought Scotsmen, Highland clansmen and Presbyterians from the Hebrides. These people had been fighting the English for centuries. Still, enough rents were being collected to drain the Island of money. This also had a result unanticipated by the landlords. The Islanders established their own industries, traded by agreement and barter, became quite self-sufficient. All the conditions for a Liberated Area were being set up. (56-57)

Acorn chooses to ignore the varied experience of Loyalists and Highlanders, some of whom did prosper as landowners or tenants. Moreover, the tenants and their merchant allies perhaps would not have shared Acorn's view of them as "revolutionaries." And Islanders were less united and self-sufficient than he claims: there was a strong pro-colonial faction. But Acorn is correct that a large portion of the Island and percentage of Islanders became remarkably self-sufficient, defying the landlords and establishing separate industries and trade links. Acorn was enamoured of the idea that there was a "Liberated Zone," described by Acorn's friend Errol Sharpe in his *A People's History of P.E.I.*: "In the 1840s the Island was divided between the Liberated Area lying north and east of Charlottetown which was controlled by the tenants, and the city and the remaining rural area which was controlled by the landlords" (87). The extent to which the eastern half and North Shore of PEI were "liberated" and "controlled by the tenants" is quite debatable, especially given the evidence of continued rent collection and growing frustration among tenants into the 1860s.

After the 1840s, as Acorn acknowledges, the struggle changed from one of rebellious autonomy to one of compromise—progress or sell-out, depending on one's gain or loss—among vested interests and their political parties. That process of compromise was more disappointing for Acorn, who saw it as the defeat of the self-sufficiency and autonomy embodied in what he referred to as the "tenants' revolt." As well, it meant the hegemony of those Island business interests who would trade one master for another, breaking British shackles only to surrender to central Canada in return for personal gain. Acorn's heroes would not be the Fathers of Confederation—who immediately enacted legislation to benefit their own business investments—but William Cooper, whose ships plied the trade routes that tried to ensure Island autonomy and maximize prosperity for farmers and tradesmen—to New England, the Caribbean, and Europe, not up the St. Lawrence. One hundred years after Confederation, Acorn demonstrated the Maritime suspicion of central Canada, a stance, it should be noted, which did not prevent him from living and enjoying success there.

As for Islanders, "It was said that Islanders were trying to stop progress. Nowadays they are suspicious that the Islanders were not behind the times, but far ahead of them. Nevertheless the accusation of being old-fashioned struck deep into our sensitive souls, paralysed us for decades" (*Minago* 95). Acorn's wit appears in his view of the transformation of PEI from a rural society to a tourist destination:

That's the trouble with the Island ... Sports. Once a bunch of Sports came over and organized Confederation, which we never were against in principle. We did object to the way it was fashioned—that unelected senate for instance—and stayed out as long as we could. Those Sports kept coming, more and more. We didn't object because the Island is a visible sample of Heaven, and this evidence of the truth of religion shouldn't be kept from anybody, as long as they came in reasonable numbers. But then some Sports started calling the tourist trade an industry. Nobody was murdering tourists on the sly and canning them for export ... still those Sports kept calling tourism an industry. They started advertising The Island and now so many Sports come here in summertime it's hard to find an Islander in all that crowd. (*Minago* 98)

Clearly, Acorn had reservations about tourism becoming a major industry, and might be even less happy with the "Land of Anne" boosterism. And yet, in his essay entitled, "Goddam it Prince Edward Island Needs that Causeway," published in 1969 in *Notes for a Native Land*, he writes, "Then the tourists start crowding in on us. Certainly they're welcome, for more than one reason" (116). The ambivalence of this statement is characteristic of Acorn's attitude toward the Island's transformation, and leads one to wonder where he would stand in today's debates about the economic development of Prince Edward Island. Would he defend a traditional rural economy, or could he accept the move to "value-added manufacturing" of food products? How would he feel about high-tech industries and the information economy? What about the development of "cottage industries" in the arts and crafts into "cultural industries"? Would he see tourism as an invasion: Island society conquered by the transnational culture of capitalism? Or would he accept it as a way for Islanders to survive and the Island to become a part of global culture, maintaining its regional uniqueness while gaining trendy cafés, quality bookstores and cinemas, boutiques and galleries, and other features of cosmopolitan culture—no longer "paralysed" and "old-fashioned"? How would he feel about the "fixed link" with the mainland, the Confederation Bridge, which after so many decades of debate and aborted plans, is now a reality?

Most people believe Acorn was adamantly opposed to a bridge to New Brunswick. Therefore, Hilda Woolnough was shocked one day by his response: "I remember the only time that he and I ever had it out was when we were talking about a bridge to the Island, and I told him that if they ever had a link to the Island I'd blow it up. And he got angry. I was very surprised because he was totally on the other side and he got very upset.... He marched up University Avenue.... 'A great link,' I think he told me later." One interpretation of this episode is that Acorn was merely feeling contentious and wanted to quarrel with Hilda. Another interpretation is suggested by his article "Goddam it Prince Edward Island Needs that Causeway." Acorn notes that Cape Breton Island is "out on a corner; but it's got a causeway, which has done it some good" (116). He then reflects on the Island's attempt to survive economically and its social problems, and concludes that "all of this is going on in a community that is dying, all for the want of good communications with the rest of Canada. Canada, it claims, can't afford that causeway" (117). Here his socio-economic reasoning—

influenced by his perception of the Island's economic disadvantages and more in line with his left-wing emphasis on economic development—prompts him to support a fixed link with the mainland. At other times, his devotion to the Island as a pastoral paradise needing protection from the mainland and imperialistic capitalism may have urged him to oppose the link. At any rate, Acorn's conflicting views on a fixed link support Joyce Wayne's remark that "the contradictions in Acorn's life still abound" (18).

Whether Acorn's views on tourism and a fixed link are considered ambivalent or contradictory, they are understandable responses to the predicament of a small island community, long ago prosperous, but marginalized for decades by the relocation of economic power. In *The Island Means Minago* Acorn celebrated the Island's struggle to overcome colonialism and its brief heyday of postcolonial autonomy, which was thwarted by vested interests. That struggle, for Acorn, was also a metaphor for the Island's vulnerability in the latter half of the twentieth century to the neocolonial forces of economic imperialism and cultural domination. Acorn created a narrative in *The Island Means Minago* which situated PEI's contemporary vulnerability and its quest for survival and renewal within the framework of its historical strategy for overcoming colonialism and for resisting the perils, according to Acorn, of Confederation.

As a narrative which asserts the Island's indigenous and vital reality and opposes marginalizing narratives, *The Island Means Minago* metaphorically suggests a way to overcome domination and exploitation and to achieve both autonomy and prosperity. This alternative narrative includes the deconstruction of narratives that glorify the governing class at the expense of workers and smaller entrepreneurs. In this regard, one of Acorn's strongest poems is "The Figure in the Landscape Made the Landscape." It combines his interpretation of the tenants' revolt and land struggle, his conception of Islanders' identity, his awareness of the Island landscape, and his political vision of the Island today. It is much more complex, rich, and challenging than "The Island" and "Charlottetown Harbour." This poem is too long to quote in full, but the first and last stanzas are central to his work as a poet and life as an Islander:

> The figure in the landscape made the landscape
> Like the farmer you see in this painting I've imagined
> Pre-Confederation, pre

> Any moment you might wish to be in or not
> Since the loyalists came, instantized themselves into
> rebels
> Or when they were joined, reinforced by Scottish
> clansmen.
> * * * * * *
> Today the tourists, pawns who don't know they're
> Pawns in a new still-just brooding
> Struggle for the land, skim past
> Or poke around slow wondering
> At the beauty and gentleness
> Of the Island countryside, the Island people
> (those who fight best are kind to each other)
> With every turn in the road a new surprise.
> Few of them think that's the way it was designed.
> "A lovely land," they say, "and peaceful"
> When every part of it was laid out for war. (47-48)

Acorn's framing device is brilliant and terribly true: while a few monied power-brokers had their pictures painted by Robert Harris for "The Fathers of Confederation," all those thousands of women and men who literally made the landscape—who built the Island, who generated its economic and political culture—were left out, shoved aside for a version of history as the work of a few influential men. Acorn's poem and *The Island Means Minago* present a much more accurate version of history, restoring all those who made this landscape to their rightful place. While the 1983 volume *Dig Up My Heart* presents the most famous selection of his poetry, *The Island Means Minago* is Acorn's great rendering of and tribute to Prince Edward Island and generations of Islanders.

Jules Léger presented the Governor-General's Award for poetry to Milton Acorn for *The Island Means Minago* on 29 April 1976. Turning to the Ottawa audience, Acorn quoted from one of his poems: "Stick to your guns. You'll win or fall beside them." He now had the nation's highest literary honour, and could even more confidently tell interviewers, "As a poet I play for keeps and I'm staking my life on this country" (Marchand). He was now a national spokesperson for the Island: "I was brought up in Prince Edward Island and I was constantly irritated by the tourist-board portrayal of the island as a place of eternal calm. Hell, a lot of history has happened on that island" (Marchand).

Milton receiving his honorary doctorate from UPEI in 1977. Left to right: Ron Baker, UPEI President; Preston McIntyre; John Deifenbaker; Milton; Gordon Bennett, UPEI Chancellor.

One popular and indisputable story about Acorn is that he wore running shoes both to the Governor-General's ceremony and, the next year, to receive his honorary doctorate from UPEI. Some people have assumed this was another rebellious or iconoclastic gesture, years before this attire became a trendy fashion statement. "They made a big deal out of those sneakers," says Mary Hooper, "and they always claimed they were the same pair. I've got a trunkload of them upstairs. He bought more sneakers than anybody I ever knew. It wasn't that he wanted to be rough or anything. It was a matter of comfort. He couldn't get his feet to be comfortable in anything else." She also notes that, before the Governor-General's ceremony, Acorn practised walking up to receive his medal: "He wanted to do that right."

Acorn's preoccupation with PEI's historical land struggle and tenants' revolt and his recognition that a new land struggle involving tourism and economic development was underway found another outlet in *The Road to Charlottetown*, a play he wrote in collaboration with Cedric Smith. The bulk of the script was drafted in 1975 and 1976. "I had written some scenes on the history of the Islanders' struggle, but I hadn't completed them. Cedric took the incomplete scenes and linked them with lines from my poems and now it's a finished product"

(Marchand). The play was directed by Smith and ran 1 August through 3 September 1977 at the MacKenzie Theatre in Charlottetown. The cast consisted of Smith, Eric Peterson, Stephen Bush, and Janet Laine Green. A revised form of the play ran from 7 November through 10 December 1978, at Theatre Passe Muraille in Toronto.

The third of Acorn's great honours came in 1977, when the Island's university elected him to the degree of Doctor of Laws, *honoris causa*. John Smith presented him on 15 May 1977 to UPEI's convocation as

Milton James Acorn, a man militant, gentle, and generous, a poet, an Islander, a patriot, a lover, a revolutionary.... His poems are poems of faith in the common people. Poems of wit, and of how wit has enabled the people to survive, and will enable them to prevail. Poems for the liberation of men and women from all forms of oppression. Poems of a tough and tender love. When Milton Acorn writes of the things of this world—of the patchwork countryside of this Island, of manhandled, seabattered lobster traps, of a trout pond or a hummingbird or a man's bristly head on its backbone stalk—those things become more concrete, more material, and also more alive to us. He seems to find the words—rough textured and resilient—that the things themselves would be if natural things could be words. (Citation)

John Smith was in charge of Acorn for this event, and remembers that Acorn went shopping for clothes and "invested fairly heavily in a new rig for this occasion." He wore orange canvas sneakers, which stuck out beneath his grand doctoral gown. Mary Hooper thinks "they had somebody watching Milton all the time to make sure he didn't get up and make a speech." His most memorable remark on the occasion was an aside to Mary about one of the other recipients of an honorary doctorate that day: "Milton and I were sitting together and he looks over. 'Diefenbaker,' he says. 'Diefenbaker. In a hundred years time they will be saying, "Oh yeah, that's the fellow that got his doctorate the same time as Milton Acorn."'"

Smith had to take Acorn to the airport afterward, and arrived at the Charlottetown Hotel with an empty suitcase for Milton. Piled on an antique table in the hotel lobby was a "mountain of wrinkled clothes and other belongings. On the way to the airport he seemed to be quite terrified that we were going to have an accident. I don't know whether earlier in life he'd had a fright or whether he distrusted pro-

Dr. Milton Acorn with his mother and Ron Baker at the UPEI convocation reception.

fessors to be on time to the airport." Smith phoned him later that day at the Waverly Hotel to see if he'd arrived all right: "The desk clerk replied, 'Dr. Acorn is busy right now and can't come to the phone.'"

Armed with his honorary doctorate, "Milton made it quite clear to me," says Smith, "that he would accept a post as writer-in-residence at the university. I didn't encourage him with that hope, because even Réshard Gool argued that Milton wouldn't be the best choice for our first writer-in-residence. He did talk about how hard up he was, and made some of us feel guilty about taking the easy way out and not giving him the means to make a living as a poet."

Now that Acorn had awards and acclaim, some friends thought there was irony in an anti-establishment person enjoying such recognition. There was the example of Leonard Cohen's refusing the Governor-General's Award. But Cohen could afford such a gesture, even in 1968, and it added to his mystique. Acorn needed to accept and treasure these honours on his own behalf as an example of artistic and proletarian struggle, and on behalf of the "People" to whom his life and art were dedicated. "This thing about Milton and praise," says Woolnough. "Most people don't realize that Milton was very shy. He would go on a mile a minute, so much that everybody would move away from the table. But underneath that it was all terribly shy. There was the thing he'd done with Cedric Smith, *The Road to Charlottetown*. We met him outside [the Mackenzie Theatre] and he didn't even want to come in and he stayed way in the back shadows. He was nervous and sort of proud."

Woolnough tells of Milton's behaviour at the Toronto production of *The Road to Charlottetown*. Gool had gone to Toronto and picked Milton up at the Waverly. Woolnough says, "They got in a bit late and had to sit about three-quarters of the way up.... After it was all over everybody started clapping. Suddenly Milton started yelling, 'Author, author!' And then everybody else picked this up, saying 'Author, author.' Finally Milton ran down to the front and took his bows. He probably forgot that he was the author, you know he just really enjoyed the play. That would be possible with him." During that same visit, Gool took Acorn to a bar "where there was a piano and a couple of old guys who could play anything. And Milton would hum and do this drumming thing. He was always into drumming. I had some drums. He bashed the hell out of them because he would get totally carried away."

Actor and playwright Cheryl Cashman was in the Toronto production of *The Road to Charlottetown* and met Acorn during rehearsals. "The *Road* production was good, but it wasn't raw like Milton was. He walked in and it was such a relief for me. He took one look at me and threw up his arms, I threw up my arms and we spent the next month in the Waverly Hotel. My impression of him was of a beautifully crafted ship that had crashed. It took me three weeks after this passionate affair started that I realized how ugly he was, because his soul was so beautiful." They lived together for a month and "carried on passionately for three months. He broke the mold in the way he loved because he had an anarchic heart. It was like being lovers in a foreign country during a war. Because living in Toronto we were both foreigners. I made plays. He drank some, and wrote poetry. But he didn't become a parody of himself. He remained himself through to the end."

She found piles of paperback novels in his one small closet and threw them out in garbage bags. But there were also hundreds of poems on crumpled sheets of paper, which she smoothed out and stacked neatly. But Acorn wanted more than a Toronto companion and helpmate. "It took me a couple of months to realize that fantasies of moving to the Island and having babies were not realistic. With every woman he wanted that dream of everlasting unity. But if a woman spoke up and said, 'That's a dream,' he couldn't take that. It wasn't the same for him again. I basically said, 'I can't live with you. It's a dream to go to PEI and have a child. But the love doesn't change.'

"'I can't see you then. It hurts me too much,' Milton said.

"'Okay, I have to respect that,' I said, 'but it's not what I want.'"

Poet Penn Kemp remembers going with Acorn and Cheryl Cashman to the Horseshoe Tavern to see Sneezy Waters in his show about Hank Snow, *The Show He Never Gave*: "Scarlet with pleasure, Milton hopped up and down on his chair in time with the guitar" (Letter).

As for poetry, Acorn had become absorbed with the sonnet, and published *Jackpine Sonnets* in 1977. James Deahl asked in an interview what "sparked your return to shorter, more sharply focused poems?" Acorn replied, "The reconstruction of my psychological nature, my adjustment to the kind of life I had to live" (Barker et al. 164). Perhaps he meant that he needed a prescribed structure to cohere his poetic process. Such a structure can be both supportive for someone who needs "reconstruction" and "adjustment," and liberating—the form is already given, freeing energy to shape content within its parameters: "The sonnet does not limit me, but gives me a body or skin to my poems," Acorn said (quoted in Marchand). He was also of a generation that still studied traditional poetic forms with some rigour. And one of his models was Archibald Lampman, the late-nineteenth-century Ontario poet who wrote sonnets and, almost alone in his time, attacked capitalist iniquities in his poetry. Perhaps, too, now that Acorn was a distinguished poet, he wanted to show that he could write successfully in the most prestigious traditional form.

There was, of course, an ideological agenda. He wanted to recreate the sonnet for the working classes; more accurately, he wanted to maintain that it *was* a populist form, and no longer an élite form practised by poets of privilege for centuries: "I deliberately called them Jackpines because that tree is synonymous with Canada" (quoted in Marchand). "The sonnet is meant to be heard—by the masses. It is a spoken form. My poetry speaks to the essential question—the cause of the working-class. The rupture between the petit-bourgeoisie and the working-class on the question of poetry is now complete. Workers like music in their language. They don't take to this sour-porridge style at all. A lot of modern poetry sets up a barrier of language between the poet and the people. You will notice that I write for the working-class—my poems are for ordinary people" (quoted in Meyer 132).

A partisan review of *Jackpine Sonnets* states, "This is Acorn at his best, splendid in his passionate defense of his fellow men, lovable even when his contemptuous denunciation of the fake and the second-rate descends to strident rhetoric" (Van Steen). Tom Marshall, a critic and poet, offers a more scholarly assessment: "His individuality is paradoxically and sometimes rather curiously in evidence in his 1977 collection *Jackpine Sonnets* ... it attempts to revitalize the sonnet form.... Acorn himself seems gradually to have moved away from an earlier concreteness of statement and image, partly out of a desire to make larger and more general political and social statements and partly because of the fascination with technique that is apparent in all his work" (108). Marshall is generous. In fact, though Acorn's imagery in *Jackpine Sonnets* shows that he had not significantly lost his sensory imagination, there is a striking decline in poetic control and substance. As for the jackpine sonnet theory, Acorn demonstrates too little facility with the sonnet form to create the rough-hewn variation he desired. Certainly Acorn's argument for the sonnet as a "working-class" form was strained and contributed little to the production of poetry, whether "populist" or "elite."

Jackpine Sonnets was published by Steel Rail Press, a publishing house he helped support: "Acorn consistently donated cash to keep the ever-foundering company afloat. During a financial crisis, when the press's banker requested a private guarantor for a loan, Acorn put on a tie and put up his own savings to negotiate the bank manager's confidence. On occasion, he wrote cheques to support budding writers on the promise that I would not discuss his philanthropy with them" (Wayne 17). He also once hauled a bag of laundry up several flights of stairs and asked a Steel Rail editor to wash it for him. The staff were less compassionate than Sally Large or Mary Hooper when it came to his laundry.

In January 1979 Acorn shared an apartment with James Deahl. Cashman admired Deahl's willingness to live with Acorn: "Not just 'Let's do lunch,' but take him into his life." This arrangement lasted into early 1981. "When he and I met he was living at the Waverly," writes Deahl, "and I understood he had been living there since he returned from Vancouver after the publication of *I've Tasted My Blood*.... He kept his hotel room during the two years he and I lived at 555 Palmerston Avenue.... Milton, you likely know, was always on the road. He went to PEI often ... and he went other places too. Thunder Bay, Ottawa, Kitchener, Guelph. He was restless and, since he never had any sort of job aside from poetry, would just up and go places for weeks at a time" (16 August 1992). A Canada Council grant of $16,348 awarded to Acorn on 13 February 1979 helped him travel and to maintain his Waverly residence while living with Deahl.

Acorn organized for 22 July 1979, his "Isandhlwana Centennial" poetry reading to celebrate the Zulu defeat of a British force in 1879. This victory of indigenous people over colonialist-imperialists became a recurrent theme in Acorn's conversation until his final days. It was as if the Zulus had become for Acorn an exotic counterpart of his nineteenth-century Island tenant farmers and, like the Island rebels, an example for Islanders and Canadians today. Later that year Acorn read twice at Toronto's newly eminent Harbourfront, the second time with many contributors to an anthology, *To Say the Least*. Deahl notes that "Acorn forgot to read his poetry and ranted about Islam and Iran instead. This was his final reading at Harbourfront" (*Chronology*). There were other readings in Toronto during 1979-80, and he gave workshops and a short-lived course entitled "Art of the Jackpine Sonnet."

He decided in December 1980 to return permanently to PEI. Acorn and Deahl read together at the Axle-Tree Coffee House in Toronto—Acorn's "Farewell Reading." He was back on the Island at least by 14 June 1981, when he wrote a letter to Deahl from Charlottetown. "When he came back to the Island," says John Smith, "I remember him saying more than once, 'John, I've come back to die.' I remember my own superficiality in dismissing these thoughts. I think now how straightforward he was and how dishonest I was. I guess when a poet knows he's going to die, he knows it." Acorn was more life-assertive in a 1984 interview: "I'm never going to leave here. I'm never going to leave the Island. I know how to measure up every man that comes toward me. I know where I am here" (Burrill 7).

X
A BIRD IN THE BUILDER'S HAND

> Your many voices speak of much, sir poet...
> Lover of the moment and eternity;
> Universe and atom, bass and treble;
> As sometimes it's my privilege to be.
> — "MacDougal on Deck"

BACK ON THE ISLAND, Acorn shared with John Smith a challenging view of his fellow citizens: "I walk down the streets of Charlottetown and there are people dying. No one notices, but me. I'm the only one who notices there are people dying." Smith added, "We don't look people in the eye, and see their despair, addiction, hopelessness, but Milton noticed this and stood up and said this. It seemed to me he was there performing one of the important functions of the poet, which is to say what is true, and what many people recognize but are afraid or embarrassed to admit, even to themselves."

Acorn's vocal awareness of the darker and sadder side of humanity was an uncomfortable message. It could be particularly disturbing in a place with just as much human malevolence, frailty, and suffering as anywhere—and with the desire to maintain its salubrious image and keep bad news confined to private gossip characteristic of smaller communities. Moreover, a tourist destination wants its poets to praise its charms, not to point out the other "Island way of life"—of its less fortunate citizens.

Acorn was, as well, one of the greatest boosters PEI has ever had. Reading through his poetry and prose, we find ample criticism of the excessively or smugly privileged, and abundant empathy with economic losers. He makes it clear that inequality and corruption have tainted his beloved Island too. But the dominant impression he gives of the Island is a place of great beauty, with a history of worthy deeds and a strong, admirable populace.

It was fitting, then, that his next poetic achievement would commemorate his Island and maritime ancestry: *Captain Neal MacDougal & The Naked Goddess*. He thanked his publisher, Libby Oughton of Ragweed Press in Charlottetown, and Fred Cogswell, the distinguished professor, poet, and editor from New Brunswick, "who turned a rather uncoordinated bunch of sonnets into a coherent story" (*Captain Neal* dedication).

Acorn would have been reassured by Anne Compton's assertion that "the best use to which he put his sonnet was the late collection *Captain Neal MacDougal*" (3). Observing that "an island, however, is not only its landscape, but also the sea that surrounds it" (2), she writes that "oceanic vastness and the vastness of history are both present" in this collection (3).

The story is "a creditable analogue for the Captain Neal MacDougal who was my ancestor and remains a spirit and a legend in Charlottetown. How close that character of the MacDougal of these sonnets is to the MacDougal of life and legend remains speculative, but it's probably very close, for the number of persons who are convinced they have known and conversed with MacDougal, when they would not have done so during his life (he died August 4th, 1914, from angina just saving him from apoplexy) is astounding" (*Captain* 9-10). Mary Hooper adds, "Milton claimed that *Captain Neal MacDougal* had been 'dictated' to him." To quote James Deahl again, Acorn "was an A-1 bull shitter," for there is nary a trace of his grandfather Neil MacDougall in Charlottetown legend and the barest of records in the archives. No matter. Acorn was again crafting myth, and this involved both an invocation of maritime heritage and a transformation of a sea captain and trader into a visionary and prophet who bears a remarkable resemblance to Milton Acorn.

The author's cover photo shows Acorn in an oracular pose on the Island coastline, his head covered with a bardic shawl (which Mary Hooper says was "probably some old towel"). This image corresponds to "poems dealing with a commitment that is both earthly (in fact

Photo: Kent Nason

A bardic, hieratic Milton Acorn. This photo was taken on PEI *in 1982 for the back cover of* Captain Neal MacDougal & the Naked Goddess. *The "shawl" was probably one of Mary's old towels.*

earthy) and spiritual" (*Captain* 11). Indeed, the poems are not only about seafaring ("The Record Run," "MacDougal's Armed Truce with Booze," and "The Smugglers Coast"). The Captain also views the seascape through a poet's imaginative eyes, and his ship becomes a metaphor for our journeys in earthy and spiritual reality. The captain philosophizes: "'Poetry and sainthood ought to be / The aspiration of a man or woman, / Or they should ply some instrument at least'" (19). He muses on politics and history: "'Those who call us "common men" will get their shocks'" (24). He declares the principles of his faith in "Oath," "Creed," and "Parable."

But there is something new in Acorn's poetry: spiritual inquiry and assertion. This was not a complete surprise to those who knew Acorn and his poetry. "He was religious in a different kind of way," says David Hooper. "He had to have been indoctrinated as a young person, and still retained some of it." Acorn was "indoctrinated" as an Anglican. His ancestor Matthias Eichorn had probably been Lutheran, the dominant religion of his native Germany. John Acorn appears to have joined the Church of England after arriving on PEI. John's son George is listed in the 1841 census as Anglican, but as Methodist in the 1861 census. His son Charles was baptized Methodist. Chester, Milton's grandfather, moved to the Anglican church, having married into the Anglican Fairclough family. On his mother's side, Captain MacDougall and his daughter Kate were Presbyterian, while E.T. Carbonell was an Anglican who had trained for the ministry under the influence of the Oxford Movement. Helen and Robert Sr. were both brought up as High Anglicans in Charlottetown's St. Peter's Cathedral; High Anglicanism was the religion of Milton's childhood home.

Milton stopped attending church, according to Mary and Robert, around age 13. In typical fashion, Acorn attributes precocious radical perceptions to his adolescent self: "I left the Church of England because the priest was preaching against the words of Jesus.... Jesus was a proto-Marxian, an early Marxian. Take one of those King James Bibles with the words of Jesus in red, and read through first just the words of Jesus. They put an entirely different aspect on the whole meaning of Jesus, totally different" (Burrill 7). Whether Acorn had such mature thoughts at age 13 or projected them backward much later, he was hardly the first to see in Jesus a proto-communist, a spokesperson and leader of the oppressed, a radical man of the people. As for God, Acorn had straddled agnosticism and a wry belief earlier in "Non-Prayer," published in *I've Tasted My Blood*:

> Dear old God, I'm not at odds with Thee;
> I've got stronger friends
> And more ferocious enemies—
>
> If there's no God there's no atheist god either;
> Nothing commands me to acts of villainy,
> Nothing commands me to hate what doesn't exist....
> And is there a rule against loving It? (134)

There is an ironic apology in "I, Milton Acorn": "I beg pardon, God, for the insult / Saying You lived and were responsible." And one of his most exquisite poems, "What I Know of God Is This," published in *Jackpine Sonnets*, is profoundly spiritual:

> What I know of God is this:
> That He has hands, for He touches me.
> I can testify to nothing else;
> Living among many unseen beings

Like the whippoorwill I'm constantly hearing
But was pointed out to me just once.

Last of our hopes when all hope's past
God, never let me call on Thee
Distracting myself from a last chance
Which goes just as quick as it comes;
And I have doubts of Your omnipotence.
All I ask is...Keep on existing
Keeping Your hands. Continue to touch me.
           (*Selected* 181)

Referring to this poem and to God, Acorn said, "I'm skeptical of the whole concept, but nevertheless can't deny it. I've had too much personal experience with it" (Barker et al. 169). As for experience, Acorn's sea captain testifies to more than touch. He sees and converses with a divinity, and she is female.

"As for the Naked Goddess of some of these poems, she is historical, inasmuch as a deity may be. Thor Heyerdahl mentions and illustrates her as a goddess of ancient seamen.... She was always a Goddess of the poor, having few statues and many amulets. Her massive vulva seemed to illustrate some doctrine like the latter, 'We all come from Allah and return to Him.' In most cases her features are as personalized as those of Jesus. She may have originated in a real being" (*Captain* 10). In this idiosyncratic gloss on his goddess, Acorn loosely interconnects a non-Judaeo-Christian deity, a vague allusion to the Islamic Allah, and Christianity: Acorn will not limit his awareness of "God" to one religious tradition; his God is trans-sectarian, with various manifestations in different societies and historical eras. It is this kind of thinking that made some of Acorn's left-wing friends believe he became "quite mystical there in the last years of his life" (Martin Interview).

Why this upwelling of spirituality? Perhaps it was partly the familiar pattern of a person confronting the spiritual dimension as old age approached, especially a person whose health and strength were faltering after three decades of hard living. Mary Hooper says that "Milton spent many hours of the last couple years of his life in St. Dunstan's Basilica," the impressive Catholic church on Great George Street in Charlottetown.

James Deahl claims:

> Throughout his life Acorn has been, at least from time to time, a
> practising Christian, attending church and receiving communion. There
> is much Christian imagery in his poems.... This has caused problems for
> many of his Marxist supporters. One may wonder what sort of
> Christianity Acorn practises. After all, he is a follower of the Naked
> Goddess (really Isis). The Goddess, it turns out, has a role to play in
> Acorn's Christianity for "There might be a memory of this ancient
> womanworship in the Song of Mary." If Acorn appropriates anything
> from Christianity ... it is the emotional content of the Gnostic tradition.
> The core of Christian Gnosticism is the knowledge that love conquers
> death: a concept expressed in poems like "I shout Love."
> (Deahl "Acorn" 58)

Leaving aside this reductionist treatment of Gnosticism and of Christian elements in Acorn's poetry, it is fair to say that Acorn—like so many poets in our century—drew on and was sometimes drawn back to his Christian heritage, while sustaining his criticism of institutionalized and dogmatic religion and of the church as an instrument of power and wealth.

Acorn's permanent return to PEI, too, was a conscious, avowed completion of the circle, and this obviously included a revisioning of the poet's relationship with the unseen, the divinely revealed. In this case, the unseen takes the form of the symbolic deity, the Naked Goddess, who is muse, protector, and voice of creation. With Captain MacDougal a projection of Acorn, seafaring becomes analogous to the poet's life-journey, and the goddess appears as a reward and helpmate for the master mariner/poet/visionary on his late voyages.

There is also the possibility that Acorn was responding to other upwellings: feminism, including feminist studies in theology, and women's writing.

> So why do I make God a woman? Woman, the seed of life, the creator of
> life. How then do we define the beasts? In the ultimate phyla, we name
> them after the characteristics of the female. And what do you say of any
> impressive phenomenon? The neuter disappears—but it's not he, it's she.
> Oh, the feminists go mad at this—so-called feminists, petit-bourgeois
> feminists.... The greatest thing that's happened in poetry has been the
> liberation of women. Women brought a more remarking eye. They are
> the mothers of images, that is, a *particular* look at the image. It's called
> the feminine sensibility. And it's real. But the point is, the human race is

an intelligent species, and men can learn that feminine sensibility. And the cause for the most improvement of poetry in this century has been the feminine sensibility, which men have learned. (quoted in Burrill 7)

The merits of these statements in terms of feminist discourse or poetic theory are debatable; however, we can value Acorn's positive recognition of women's creative power and "the liberation of women." Some might say this is merely recycled male artistic infatuation with the female muse-figure and fascination with the survival of token goddess-motifs, that Acorn is mouthing patriarchal clichés about woman as "creator of life" and "feminine sensibility." This may be partly true. And such a reading could be supported by the coarser aspects of Acorn's "masculinity": a manner that made some people ask, after *Captain Neal MacDougal & the Naked Goddess* appeared, "But wasn't he a male chauvinist?"

We can also conclude that Acorn was partly synchronized with those feminists investigating and invoking women's creative power, the role and representation of women in religion, and women's poetics. It might be excessive to suggest that he had become a feminist. But the misogynist outbursts that appear in his correspondence of the 1960s and early 1970s, usually associated with bitterness over his failed marriage, had virtually disappeared from his conversation.

Acorn's fixation on the goddess motif may possibly have been connected to his adoration of his mother, his lifelong closest companion, with whom he was now living most of the time. Also, his closest Island friends in the early 1980s included two powerfully feminist personalities, Libby Oughton and Hilda Woolnough, and Réshard Gool was a strong supporter of feminism. It was impossible to hang around Ragweed Press or the Great George Street Gallery, to read Canadian literature or engage with enlightened political thinking without sailing in the currents of women's writing and feminist discourse. We cannot know the extent to which Acorn was influenced by this environment, only that the Naked Goddess appeared off port and starboard in the final collection of new poems published in his lifetime.

The book was launched by Ragweed Press at the old MacKenzie Theatre, which had become a second stage for the Confederation Centre. There was a huge turnout to honour the People's Poet of PEI. John Smith remembers, "He was especially glowing that evening. He was basking in the adulation, in his star status. It was almost as though he didn't have to do anything. He would just stand there and be who he was. He didn't have a well prepared reading. He stood there sometimes in extended moments of silence, with that childlike look on his face he sometimes got. At one point Libby Oughton called out from the back row, 'Are you a feminist Milton?' He replied, 'Of course I'm a feminist. Women are the superior species.'"

Oughton and Acorn were disappointed, though, in the poor sales of the book. Twenty-six copies sold that night, and two years later total sales had not reached three hundred. It seemed inconceivable that a book by the People's Poet, a book steeped in Island lore and published locally, would do so poorly. The poet might be held in a certain esteem, but his poetry was not yet worth a ten dollar bill. Poetry is not a bestseller, but popular books do generate Canadian sales in the range of one to three thousand copies, and Acorn's books had once sold quite well.

Acorn was not deterred, however, by poor sales, and he settled further into the rituals that characterized these final years: writing, reading, walking in town and at the shore, birdwatching, and visiting friends. He had a number of regular haunts in addition to Ragweed Press and the Great George Street Gallery. He often went to the Islander Restaurant in the Islander Motel across from Ragweed Press and was a regular at Linda's Coffee Shoppe downtown—both places frequented by a wide cross section of locals and visitors. He found companions and tables to write at in Pat's Rose and Grey, a fashionable eatery and watering hole across from Confederation Centre. He could also be found at Johnny's Mayfair Tea Room, a lunch counter and newsstand beside City Cab; a long-time institution, Johnny's was a place where men hung out to gossip and argue the issues of the day. He often went by Kent Martin's cutting room on Sydney Street and read new poems aloud.

His political activism had waned, though not his ideological passion. Yet, apart from his regular hang-outs, the Island offered precious few forums for Acorn's political persuasions. He did occasionally join a rally or demonstration, such as the Island Peace Walk of 13-23 October 1983, which covered the length of the Island. Milton made a brief appearance on October 19 at Warren Grove near Charlottetown, arriving and leaving by taxi. Harry Baglole recalls that Acorn was "rather grandly attired," and Libby Oughton felt that Milton had elevated the significance of the march with his brief presence.

Milton's poetic energy, unlike his political activism, had hardly diminished, and filmed by Martin at his Charlottetown apartment he said, "I'm an early riser.... I'm up at four. I start work with the morning star, not the sun. And so I get in about twice as many working hours as your average poet. Is there such a thing as an average poet?... A professional athlete of the tongue and the mind. It's play. Like soccer, it's play. You sometimes have to play soccer very hard, but it's still play. Why should I regret it?... How can I regret? I've got three squares a day most of my life. I've never done a tap of work since age thirty-five. I wish I'd fucked more, but who doesn't?" (Martin *In Love*).

Not everyone admired Acorn's public posture as poet. Elaine Harrison is a critical voice: "He was sort of a poser. I feel he was the kind of poet who believed he had to write a poem a day, no matter what. Not that one should wait for inspiration. But he wrote to be a poet. He did pose, and he loved posing. Walking through the streets of Charlottetown with all those pens in the pocket of his shirt, leaking over his $350 suits. I preferred the man's poetry." The question of whether Acorn was a *poseur* is moot. It depends on one's view of human behaviour, that is, to what extent we all dress and behave—pose—for desired effects. A *poseur* is usually considered to be someone who behaves for effect in an excessive manner. At times, Acorn did seem to be posing in his role as the people's proletarian poet. Mostly, his appearance and manner were the deeply rooted identity he had grown into from his mid-teens onward.

When he first returned to the Island in 1981, Acorn lived with his mother at 86 Cumberland Street, then one of the shabbiest and rowdiest streets in Charlottetown. By that time, "she had been in a nursing home for about ten years," Mary Hooper recalls. "She suddenly decided she was going to leave and she had a hard time trying to persuade us to go along with it. She asked Robert and Robert said no, and she said, 'Well, I'm doing it anyhow,' and wouldn't wait for a decent apartment." As well as hating the nursing home, Helen thought she needed to provide a home for Acorn when he finally returned, and that having an apartment would encourage his homecoming.

Helen moved out of the nursing home on 10 March 1981. Says Mary, "It didn't matter what our finances were like, Mother was always very particular that the places we lived in were respectable. I found it ironic, then, that she rented this little apartment on Cumberland. There was everything going on in that house." When Acorn arrived at home, he moved into this dive with his mother. There were episodes of heavy drinking, a man throwing his girlfriend down the stairs, and hungry children on welfare going to Helen's apartment for food. A lady wrestler lived next door. One day a male friend of the wrestler knocked on Helen's door. Acorn apparently wasn't home at the time. Helen let the man in and he attacked her, first trying to strangle her, then stealing the small amount of money she had. Immediately after this, they moved to a much nicer place at 26 Donwood Drive, in a "respectable" part of town. David Hooper says, "There was the People's Poet at one end of Donwood and the People's Cemetery on the other."

"When he was in the apartment with Mother on Donwood Drive," Mary says, "sometimes you didn't know who was looking after who. Because they both needed looking after. One time Mother couldn't eat a bite, and Milton would bring home a lobster every day. It was the only thing she would eat. She thought she was looking after him and he thought he was looking after her and neither of them would know how much longer they were going to be able to do it." This is how Acorn evoked his mother in "It's All in Mother's Head," which Chris Gudgeon (229) describes as "The last poem Acorn ever wrote, completed weeks before his death":

> It's all in mother's head that she can dance.
> At seventy-nine that's just ridiculous.
> But when the band commences purblind romance,
> Spinning dizzy on a dizzy record,
> Her eyes begin to burn and feet to tap.
> Hands work an invisible accordion,
> Till presently she's up with some assistance,
> Like a tall ship heaving out its sails
> Despite the wallops of the waves and tide
> To convert the elements' resistance.
> (*Uncollected* 45)

Helen was readmitted to the nursing home on 13 January 1984, and died on April 6 of that year. Milton remained in his Donwood Drive apartment until the last year of his life.

Meanwhile, he had begun to spend a great deal of time at Mary and Garth Hooper's farm in Milton. He became one of City Cabs' best customers. "He would come out here several times a week and sometimes even twice in one day," says Mary, "and I used to tell him, 'You can't afford that Milton.' But when he wanted to go, he was something like Mother: when she wanted to go, she wanted to go. We might be going to town in half an hour, but he couldn't wait for us."

The Hoopers' farm is situated on a rise with a lovely view of the countryside. An old lime tree shades the lawn behind the farmhouse.

"He loved to visit our country home," Mary says. "He would pace and talk and sit under the trees and look at the birds. He sat many hours under our huge lime tree, gazed at the beauty around him, and scribbled in his huge journal. This is the picture that comes to mind when I read 'Pastoral.' Here he found refreshment. One might wonder how such a neurotic man could find stability to produce so much. I believe the poem 'Pastoral' provides us with part of the answer. I believe that this pastoral part of creation helped him to carry on, to continue to create":

> That sudden time I heard
> the pulse of song in a thrush throat
> my windy visions fluttered
> like snow-clouds buffeting the moon.
>
> I was born into an ambush
> of preachers, propagandists, grafters,
> ("Fear life and death!" "Hate and pay me!")
> and tho I learned to despise them all
> my dreams were of rubbish and destruction.
>
> But that song, and the drop-notes
> of a brook truckling thru log-breaks and cedars,
> I came to on numb clumsy limbs
> to find outside the beauty inside me.
>   (*Selected* 17)

Mary describes Milton's poetic process in relation to "Charlottetown Harbour" and "Pastoral": "A lot of his poems took years and years to develop. When I saw the first draft of 'Charlottetown Harbour' I thought it was awful. And when you think of what it came to be, I wish I'd kept it. It was in one of the notebooks. The idea for 'Pastoral' was probably born in Milton's mind in the 1940s when he decided to shift from prose to poetry. This poem was completed in 1963."

The "huge journal" was an Acorn trademark. He bought them at Carter's Office Supplies on Queen Street in Charlottetown, and was often seen "scribbling" in Linda's or Pat's Rose and Grey, or on a bench outside the Confederation Centre. Acorn explained in the NFB film why he started carrying these "scribblers": "The muse. The muse is some spiritual being, either imagined or perhaps real, to whom the poet either addresses or dictates his poems to him [*sic*]. I didn't take this too seriously until I was well past 40, then began to realize that some of my poems were being dictated. That's how I got in the habit of carrying scribblers. It was like being a personal secretary" (Martin *In Love*). At the National Archives of Canada in Ottawa, the Acorn papers include 65 boxes of poems, prose, letters—and some of these impressive notebooks containing drafts of published poems, fragments, notes, and unpublished manuscripts-in-progress. And this collection includes neither all the material that may have been mistakenly thrown out on Confederation Street in the early 1970s and otherwise lost or stolen in his various residences and travels nor all the scribblings on café napkins and scraps of paper in friends' homes. A list in *Dig Up My Heart* of Acorn's published books names five manuscripts "in preparation," including *The Bare-Eyed Birdwatcher*, the poetry project which seemed to absorb him most during his final years.

Of this manuscript, Acorn wrote in a draft of the introduction:

In our own times there has been an extension of this insight that the Living Spirit is everywhere in nature, via the suspicion amounting to a certainty that there are other beings of godlike intelligence.... Among them, according to this poet, are the Corbies—crows, ravens etc.... This is an insight which developed during the long matriculation of this "book of beasts ... principally birds".... In '78, for reasons of health, I had to forefend and forego that lovely brew which had previously kept me going. I had had the horrors but think I actually enjoyed them. It was when in a state of sobriety I began to look about me that the true horrors became evident. But also I experienced intensification of wonder: keener appreciation of what the sights of my eyes inferred. Therefore this book. (29 November 1981)

"Milton loved to watch the birds," says Mary Hooper. "He wrote hundreds of poems about them. He called a series *The Bare-Eyed Birdwatcher*. The bird seemed to provide a quiet outlet for his racing mind." John Smith, an excellent amateur naturalist, shared Acorn's interest in birds:

Milton got into the habit of phoning me, and would stay on the phone, sometimes an hour or more. These were long Miltonic monologues on whatever was obsessing him that day. The crows and ravens were an important theme. He'd read up on this stuff pretty well. He'd get me to look up information about crows and ravens in my library, and read it over the phone. His observations about these birds were really quite acute. I have the feeling he felt more in common with them than with any people in Charlottetown. I think he felt they'd been forced into some kind of underclass by the intrusion of people into their environment, and yet they had somehow triumphed, as the underclass was bound to do by the laws of history.

Indeed, the ravens and crows thrive in Charlottetown, especially in Victoria Park where Acorn loved to walk, gaze, and write. A few of his Island acquaintances have ironically noted that the territorial domination of the crows and ravens has driven many of the smaller songbirds away. And more than one person has heard echoes of Acorn in the raucous, assertive vocalizations of his beloved "Corbies."

Speaking of which, John Smith says he "never got in an argument with him. When he got very serious, I would laugh it off, or slip away. During these telephone conversations several themes would come up, such as the Zulus versus the British Empire. He would also claim that Marlowe wrote Shakespeare. Perhaps he thought that, as a teacher of Shakespeare, I would bite. My reply was, 'Yes, and Shakespeare wrote Bacon.' He called during the Falklands War, and read a poem about the sinking of the Belgrano. A mocking poem, not a very good poem, fired off in the heat of the moment. All his rage against the British Empire came roaring out. The big guy picking on the poor little guy, Argentina." As Mary Hooper says, "He did get boring at times. That is a sad thing about Milton. It is not that he wasn't interesting. It was just how long could you stand it. I couldn't listen that long. My head would go around in circles and you have to operate."

Three other obsessive themes during his last years were the female pharaohs of Egypt, abortion, and homosexuality. They could dominate his conversation and correspondence, both of which became more disjointed and meandering. His fascination with female pharaohs emerged from the same part of Acorn that created the Naked Goddess and waxed enthusiastic about the creative power of women, "the superior species." We can also wonder, without dabbling too much in amateur psychology, what function these female figures served in a psyche which had not been blessed with enduring conjugal relationships. If Acorn the man had largely failed as a lover with women, Acorn the iconic poet could identify himself with—vicariously wed himself to—the grand figures of goddesses and female pharaohs, with their powers and sensuous beauty. Perhaps this was a metonymic fulfilment of his need for a female companion, and an unconscious connection with Gwendolyn MacEwan. As well, the female pharaohs may have partly functioned in his psyche as symbolic analogues to maternal authority and care, that is, the role of his mother Helen. Intriguingly, and not surprisingly, Acorn needed to identify with "underdogs" who had asserted their power and triumphed—Zulus over British soldiers, the Naked Goddess within the pantheon of male gods, female pharaohs within the Egyptian patriarchy. But whatever the function of the female pharaohs, this theme in his conversation, like the Zulus, became boring from beloaboured repetition.

His strident opposition to abortion and homosexuality provoked more than ennui. Friends at Ragweed Press and his other Charlottetown hangouts were puzzled by these political positions that seemed, in Acorn, uncharacteristically regressive. "The homophobia," Kent Martin says, "I don't know where that came from.... I can never figure those things out about Milton. The same with his thing about Stalin" (Interview).[29] And his overall support of the liberation of women seemed unreconciled with his anger at abortion. Eventually, some friends concluded that Acorn's homophobia and opposition to abortion grew from his childlessness, and from the loss of his son. Denied children of his own, he could not tolerate others' choice of abortion; he could not accept others' homosexual orientation. A more thorough analysis might take into account his closeness to his own family, including the sanctuary he found at home during his childhood tribulations, his intimate—in fact dependent—relationship with his mother, and his possible anxiety, frustration, or confusion about his own sexuality.

In 1981 Acorn attended the annual meeting of the League of Canadian Poets in Toronto. Not long before, the Metro Toronto Police had raided four gay bath clubs in Toronto. The raids made the national news, and were an event that galvanized the gay community and its supporters. At the poets' meeting, a motion was made in support of gays and lesbians. Acorn rose to denounce homosexuality. He opposed the motion with an inflammatory disapproval that aroused a great deal of outrage. The meeting degenerated into a shouting match, with Acorn at the centre of the storm. Even an old friend such as Rosenblatt felt impelled to tell Acorn to sit down and shut up. Finally, the elder statesman, F.R. Scott, rose to defend the right of a distinguished poet and member such as Milton Acorn to express his views on a controversial subject, to acknowledge the discomfort that such views might cause, and to praise an organization that would embrace discussion and dissent on such a difficult issue.

Island poet Joseph Sherman remembers how explosive and disagreeable the situation was, and how Scott restored the gathering with his graceful eloquence. Scott was able to remind other poets of their respect for Acorn's accomplishments, meanwhile providing Acorn with time to cool down and fall silent with dignity. Calm was restored. But Sherman also remembers how embarrassed Acorn's friends were for him: not that he spoke against homosexuality, but that his manner of speaking drew others' wrath down upon him and left the impression of Acorn as a raving, irrational bigot. Sherman could tell that Acorn had, once again, been wounded. This time it was not a left-wing political group which had turned on him, but the national association of poets. He would be loath to return to their fold.

He quarrelled even with his best friend Al Purdy, who had agreed to select the poems for Acorn's *Dig Up My Heart: Selected Poems 1952-1983*, to be issued by Canada's "flagship" publisher, McClelland & Stewart. This meant reading Acorn's published poems and all the unpublished manuscripts he could gather and send to Purdy. Acorn complained to Dennis Lee, who was overseeing the project for McClelland & Stewart, "I understated my difficulties with Al. He hates me and has done a thing to harm me (deliberately messed up an interview)." Purdy, of course, had done nothing to harm Acorn, and was doing everything to help make *Dig Up My Heart* a monument to Acorn's poetic achievement. Acorn's deteriorating physical and mental health meant that some of his friends and colleagues were increasingly subject to his attacks of paranoia or anger. Fortunately, Acorn dropped this unreasonable attack on Purdy, the selection of poems was made, and their friendship continued.

Back on PEI, Acorn felt more comfortable in the Island's artistic community than he did in Toronto, where his old suspicions and disappointments were never far from the surface. People were accustomed to his views and periodic tirades. His friends also knew he had dealt with one of the problems that had tested his relationships for nearly 20 years: booze. According to everyone who knew him on the Island, he was on the wagon by the time he returned in 1981. "He never drank when he came home," Mary says, and adds that he stopped drinking "quite a long time before, I think." Robert Acorn did find a bottle of hard liquor in Milton's apartment one time, but it was unopened, and

Robert thinks that either Milton no longer drank at all or took only the occasional drink. Shortly after Acorn's death CBC Television in Charlottetown aired a documentary on Acorn, and lamented that he suffered from alcohol abuse, but neglected to mention that he had overcome this problem for at least the last five years of his life.

Acorn returned to the Island a sober man, but one now diagnosed with diabetes. His diabetic condition was probably one factor in his decision to stop drinking. He also reduced his smoking, but certainly did not abandon the Cuban cigar: "He sure did like his cigars. If he was out of cigars you would have to drive him all over the place until he got them. It had to be a certain brand too" (Mary Hooper). He also became a patron of The Root Cellar, Charlottetown's favourite health food store.

Regarding his health, Acorn wrote to Purdy on 24 September 1982, "Anyway I am not just sick but very sick. To top it all a quack at the local hospital sugared me up, with a diabetic tag right on my wrist. Then when he looked at the dials and saw I was a diabetic (which I had forgotten—having controlled it by diet for years) then he tried to sell me some jigg diabetic remedy. When I told him to get that I.V. out of my arm, he did but then some co-crook sugared me up again so that I fled out the fire door, thinking I was being murdered. Now my weight is 212 pounds, my piss smells like atar of roses; but I shall recover."

Picture Milton Acorn in the early 1980s: walking up Charlottetown's Queen Street with his bag of health food, huge black notebook, rows of coloured pens in his shirt pocket, and maybe a Cuban cigar. He also wore fancy sneakers now, Reeboks or Nikes, not the cheap canvas hightops. "Milton was a closet capitalist," David Hooper observes. "He had an account at Henderson and Cudmore [an upscale Charlottetown haberdashery]. The pair of gloves he used to leave lying around here were the very best from Henderson and Cudmore." A former clerk there remembers Acorn wanting to buy a leather jacket. Knowing Acorn and aware that the People's Poet was not always flush, the clerk suggested several moderately priced jackets. Acorn, however, wanted only the best, selected the most expensive leather coat on the rack, and paid cash.

Hilda Woolnough says:

He'd come to the Great George Street Gallery. Of course, he'd won the Governor-General's Award, so he was quite well dressed by Henderson and Cudmore. I love it that he had to go to the most expensive place in town to get clothes. He had this crazy hat that he bought there. A pork-pie hat. He wore it like the Duke of Edinburgh, with his hands clasped behind him, bending slightly forward, listening to Valerie LaPointe going on about the paintings. It was a wonderful sight to see them going by the paintings, one by one, Milton doing this little side step thing, bending like a painter with his hands behind his back with this crazy hat.

These gestures toward elegance barely moderated an appearance that was at best proletarian, often unkempt and unwashed, and sometimes disconcerting for the more fastidious. "Usually he was covered all over with stains of one sort or another," says Woolnough.

It used to be amusing because we'd get these women coming in to do the coffee-clatch gallery tour, and I remember once, four of them came in, eleven in the morning, all dressed to the nines to do the art tour. And Milton was there, sloshing around his coffee, with his cigar. That was his ritual. He'd sit and read his paper and be perfectly happy. Then these ladies came in and for some reason Milton stood up and they took one look at him, the four of them in unison, and they literally ran out of the gallery, totally terrified.

Another time there was this very sophisticated French woman wearing this fur coat, a highly intelligent woman. I was talking to her when Milt came in. He was absolutely fascinated by this rather chic older lady in her sixties who looked smart and beautiful. She was trying to find out places to eat, to live. He came up and circled around with this wonderful grin on his face, a lopsided smile, totally fascinated, being charming. And then he let out this enormous fart. He could fart like a horse. And she, totally sophisticated, totally ignored it, and it was totally wonderful. They spent quite a bit of time together talking.

Acorn could also, according to Woolnough, "piss like a horse." This was most noticeable at literary readings. "He always arrived on time for poetry readings. He'd choose his chair, get his coffee," and sit attentively. If he liked what he heard, he would listen transfixed, sometimes nodding approvingly. Woolnough describes his response if the reader was found wanting:

Usually he was very polite to poets because he understood what they were and where they came from. But if he felt that the poet was really no good, he would get up while the poet was reading and walk carefully right in front between the poet and audience, very slowly, with deliberation, not saying anything, go to the washroom on the other side of the gallery, throw back the toilet seat with a thunderous crash, and piss like a horse. Then he would walk slowly back in front of the poet, and sit down. Can you imagine being a poet and having that happen? I said, "Milt, how could you do such a thing?" "You have to listen, you have to pause," he said. That's why he did it, so they would really hear themselves.

One evening the reader at the George was the young Montreal playwright David Fennario, who had leapt to prominence with his first major play. The first half hour of his presentation was a harangue on the need for socialist activism, for revolutionary action within and outside the theatre. Seated close to Acorn, I watched his reactions. He looked thoughtful and approving. The ideology was certainly in accord with his own, even if the rhetoric was that of a younger generation. By the time Fennario began reading from *Joe Beef*, his work in progress, some of the audience were feeling annoyed by his tone and manner, which seemed condescending, self-righteous, and quite oblivious of his audience. The material he read seemed rough and tedious. Still, at the end of the presentation, Acorn applauded appreciatively.

Afterward, two dozen people from the audience, including Acorn, accompanied Fennario back to the home of artist Ben Kinder for a party. We sat in a circle in the large living room, as Fennario occupied a footstool and held forth for more than an hour, answering questions with earnest and protracted certainty. Acorn sat beside him in an armchair, absolutely silent, listening respectfully. At a certain point, a woman suddenly shifted attention from Fennario, asking Acorn if he would read her favourite poem. The other guests, weary of Fennario, let out a collective, "Yeah, Milton, read a poem!" Quietly, he took the offered book and read with understated passion, his voice soft but vibrant. Finished, he let the book lie closed on his lap without another word. Someone else said, "Would you read another?" and named a favourite. Again, Acorn read, his voice all the more powerful, in that firelit living room, for its unusual restraint. Another request, then another. The beauty of his language and musicality, the force of meaning in his imagery and narratives, the strength of his vision filled the room. He did not need to shout his love and anger that night. He read for Fennario, who grew quiet, whose head bowed lower and lower as he listened. He read for his friends and acquaintances, who grew larger with the world of each poem. I decided to leave while he was still reading, with his voice and words continuing on in my mind as I walked home alone to my apartment on Dorchester, Captain MacDougall's and Grandma Kate's street, in the neighborhood where "Milton's people" had come from.

Such moments—and the friendships, the daily rounds of his Charlottetown hangouts, the trips to the Hoopers and the seashore—declare that Acorn had found fulfilment: he had gone home not only to die, but to be embraced, with an honoured place in circles of friends and family. And there were new acquaintances who recognized the largeness of his humanity, such as Sister Georgina Johnston, who has worked for many years with some of the Island's less fortunate people. She met him when

He was living in his basement apartment on Donwood Drive. He reached out to a young woman who had mental problems and was trying to live in the community. She stayed with him quite awhile. He was so kind to her. I treasured that part of him that reached deep down to be caring. He exemplified that deep compassion for the little ones in society. He seemed to be able to touch and be touched by a person. He did seem kind of depressed at times, but even in his depression he could reach out, and that was a major gift.

I also used to see him in the swimming pool at the Y. I worried about his breathing. He'd go under water and I'd worry he wouldn't come up. He had quite a presence, even there at the pool. Milton Acorn's good news was his presence to people.

Equally certain is another view provided by Jim Hornby, a Charlottetown folklorist and lawyer. In the late 1960s and early 1970s Hornby wrote poetry, edited UPEI's first student newspaper (*The Cadre*), founded the "Bear Party," and became friends with Acorn. Hornby also played the fiddle while Acorn read at the launch of *Captain Neal MacDougal*. "At that point [the '80s] there was a certain feeling around town, I think, that it was wonderful to have this great Canadian poet from the Island, but it wasn't quite so convenient to have him on the premises, wandering around Charlottetown, being who he was, and someone unpredictable, and certainly difficult, and unmistakable, and hard to avoid.... He didn't have enough to do, I felt, in that era. He was at loose ends, and was probably used to a bigger walk-in social scene in Toronto and the hotel."

In 1984 Libby Oughton said that something should be done to help Acorn financially. He had received another Canada Council grant in 1982. But there was no guarantee that future juries would look favourably on his applications. For several years Oughton had been a confidante and patron, welcoming him at Ragweed Press, and taking him for lunch at the Islander Restaurant across the street and for walks on the seashore or for visits to her summer home at Cape Traverse. She learned of the Canadian Writers' Foundation, an organization affiliated at arm's length with the Canadian Authors' Association, which quietly provided annual grants to distinguished older writers in financial need. Eleanor McEachern, one of Acorn's Toronto friends and a long-time member of the CAA, joined with Oughton to help arrange a grant for Acorn, with the cooperation of Commander Little of the CAA and CWF. The grant commenced on 1 January 1985, and Acorn received four quarterly instalments of $500 until his death.

Unfortunately, Acorn's disorganization and occasional paranoia turned Oughton's good deed into another disrupted friendship. Acorn had given her the number of his bank account, so that cheques could be sent from the Writers' Foundation. The number he provided was inaccurate, and the first cheque failed to arrive in his account. Acorn stormed into Ragweed and accused Oughton of arranging this grant only so that she could steal his money. Oughton, who had generously helped Acorn financially, was profoundly distressed. He refused to consider the simple explanation and solution. He was not going to phone the bank and straighten matters out because he maintained Oughton was robbing him. At the time, *The Bare-Eyed Birdwatcher* manuscript was at Ragweed Press, and Oughton hoped to publish this book when Acorn had completed revisions. Acorn demanded the manuscript back, and swore off his association with Ragweed and friendship with Oughton.

Not all Acorn's friendships or associations turned out this way. Kent Martin is able to say, "I never ended up on the outs with Milton. Some people ended up in real fights with him" (Interview). Joe Rosenblatt kept sending his love to Acorn through mutual friends on the Island, yet suffered Acorn's unforgiving wrath because Rosenblatt had challenged his belligerence during the gay rights debate at the poets' meeting. Oughton was the latest to feel devastated by Acorn's darker irrationality and the loss of such a friend and ally in literature and politics. She alerted Acorn's bank to the likely error, and the grant found its recipient. But the damage had been done. Acorn avoided

Ragweed. Oughton was wary of further overtures, but did whatever she could to help and honour Acorn from a distance.

Gool and Woolnough also decided to help Milton financially. Gool arranged to sell Acorn's papers to the National Archives in 1985, with the assistance of archivist Anne Godard. Woolnough and Gool also planned a benefit dinner with readings and music. Invitations were prepared. The plan hinged on support from the provincial government. "Réshard and I went to an official, and we asked if he would support Milton. After all, he was one of the better poets in Canada and the best poet in Prince Edward Island at the time, and he said, 'It's our lowest possible priority.' That's what the guy said, and of course, after Milton died this official was quoted in the paper at length about the great poet Milton had been." The benefit was called off, and as Mary Hooper recalls, "Milton was really quite hurt about that."

On another occasion, Oughton was having lunch at the Islander Restaurant with a high-level official from the province's culture division. We should do something for Milton, she said, the way New Brunswick provided a writer-in-residence position for Alden Nowlan. Agreeing with the judgment of Gool and John Smith in 1977, Oughton acknowledged that Acorn probably couldn't function anymore as a full-fledged writer-in-residence. But with a decent stipend, he could give readings, and meet with younger writers in the cafés, and write—in other words, be recognized with an official stipend for doing what he did every day as a full-time poet. Yes, the official agreed. And Oughton added, with a tinge of sarcasm, we'll probably wait too long, until he's dead, and then heap honours on him. That's right, the official agreed.

Woolnough and Gool had bought a house in Rose Valley not long after Acorn returned permanently to the Island. Surrounded by woods, blessed with birdsong and Woolnough's gardening genius, this rustic retreat appealed to Acorn as much as the seashore. Just up the road were other old friends, Leon and Karen Berrouard.

Raised in Massachusetts of Island parents, Leon was a student in the heady first years of UPEI and a vital presence in the burgeoning literary and alternative newspaper scene. He was among those PEI poets in the 1970s who, led by Gool, had tried to bring poetry readings into Island schools and legion halls, and had gone on a whirlwind tour of Ontario and Maritime universities. Gool's and Woolnough's Square Deal Press had published a collection of Leon's poetry. During his visits to the Island during 1969-71 Acorn found another fellow spirit in Leon and an understanding friend in Karen Berrouard, a native Islander. In the 1980s, with Leon an influential high school English teacher and the Berrouards settled in Rose Valley, Acorn could walk the short distance between the country homes of these long-time and devoted friends.

Woolnough's and Gool's Rose Valley home was a place of contentment for Acorn: "We would sit out there on the deck as happy as anything. Perfectly happy out there all day just watching the action of the birds." Their home also gave Acorn one of his favourite stories. "When we first came to this house," she says,

We had a big wood pile up at the back and I was taking it to the barn. There was a lot of snow. I heard this ungodly racket. I thought, what the hell is that, maybe the cat is in the trap. Then I heard this screech from hell. That year had been an odd year because we had deep snow and then melts, and the trees were full of apples which had frozen and defrosted quite a few times, and had become complete applejacks with alcohol. I saw in the tree this gigantic raven, absolutely drunk, and he couldn't sit up on the branch. He would make this ungodly noise every time he fell forward. He stayed there for three days absolutely pissed out of his feathers. That was Milton's favourite story. I don't know how many times I told him, and of course, I would make the screech, which he loved, then he would start screeching, the two of us screeching away like ravens.

If Acorn had spent more time in places like Rose Valley and sitting among his stacks of notebooks and books on Donwood Drive, and obeying the doctor's orders, his health might not have declined so rapidly between 1984 and 1986. "He wasn't drinking, of course," says Woolnough, "but he would have donuts and stuff, he was absolutely naughty." The diabetic had a sweet tooth. One long-time acquaintance remembers seeing him at Tim Horton's Donuts on University Avenue almost every day for several months during the late 1970s. When Tim Horton's opened an outlet downtown, he was there in the 1980s. But his sweet tooth was not so hard on his system as the loss of his mother. And there was the wear and tear of his restlessness, his need to visit Toronto and connect with literary friends and events there.

On 6 February 1983, he read for Words Alive at the Havana Restaurant in Toronto. A segment of this reading appears in Kent Martin's film, and even if Acorn as a performer was now less focused, lucid, and galvanizing than he had been in the 1960s and 70s, some of the potency, passion, wit, and charm that made him such a popular performer-poet were still in evidence.

That year, McClelland & Stewart published *Dig Up My Heart: Selected Poems 1952-83*, selected by his old friend Al Purdy. The publication of a "selected" by the largest Canadian-owned publisher was one more major honour.

He read at Grossman's Tavern on 24 June 1984, an event that marked the fourteenth anniversary of his People's Poet Award. After the Sunday afternoon reading, Acorn went to the home of James Deahl and Gilda Mekler. After supper, sitting on the front porch, "Acorn began to have heart pains and began to look very, very ill. Deahl took Acorn in a taxi to Toronto Western Hospital where Acorn was placed in the cardiac care area. Acorn stayed in the hospital for two weeks with severe heart problems. He then fled and refused to return to Toronto Western despite the pleas of his doctor. Acorn returned to PEI via Air Canada on July 8th" (Deahl *Chronology*).

Back in Charlottetown, he began spending more time with another new friend, Valerie LaPointe, a former lab technician. She remembers meeting Acorn "around 81 or 82," while the Hoopers and Woolnough first became aware of LaPointe as one of Acorn's companions in 1984 or 85. She first met him at Pat's Rose and Grey during an argument on abortion. Later she took him to Johnny's Mayfair in search of cigars. Once they became closer, "over a couple of years," Acorn would arrive at her apartment around five-thirty or six o'clock in the morning "and bring his little bag of porridge for me to cook up. He had a number of medications and he'd forget, go to take them and take double, and later on I was trying to help moderate his medication."

LaPointe was another companion—like Purdy, Phelan, Cedric Smith, Woolnough and Gool, the Berrouards, Wells, Deahl, Oughton, and, of course, the Hoopers—who could endure or defuse Acorn's need to indulge in monologues, tirades, and blustery posturing, and who could engage in the kind of mutually satisfying dialogue that other acquaintants found too sporadic or impossible. "When I first met him," LaPointe recalls,

There was the ranting and raving. Milton had this outer play acting personality that got all the attention he needed to get himself recognized as a poet. He needed a hook, and I think Milton developed this character because inside he was very insecure and shy and needed protection. He was a different person at home than he was when he went out. If you saw Milton sitting there and his eyes were closed you'd think he's off in his own world. But he'd tell me, "The most important thing is to listen to people." If he was not listening to people at his own table, he was listening to another table, or just waiting for someone's reaction. He'd test people, say something just to get a reaction, to see what is really inside you. And you didn't always have to agree with Milton. The more you agreed, he wasn't expecting that.

She remembers his Donwood apartment "after his mother died. It would be quite messy, cigar butts and dishes all over the place. But his books and papers, there was not a thumb print or splash or anything on them. The papers he was typing out, so very neat, it was amazing." Acorn began "trying to move in" to LaPointe's apartment, taking his books, having a bath, and then letting his clothes pile up. LaPointe wasn't the first woman, as we have seen, who refused to wash his clothes. Besides, Mary Hooper provided that service for her brother.

LaPointe accompanied Acorn to Brackley Beach on the North Shore, to China Point where—in his ancestral mythology—"his Indian princess grandmother lived," and to Savage Harbour for a week in a cottage where "we'd root around for sticks and stones along the beach, and sit and talk about the clouds in the sky" (Interview). There, Acorn talked about "redoing" *The Road to Charlottetown*, "saying that struggle is not ending, is not over yet. People are too complacent and they have to be made aware of what is happening to the Island and Canada for that matter. We come from a very strong stock of people with backbone, but he was beginning to wonder where the backbone is these days. But it was more on nature that we talked. He really was close to nature, and he liked to go on drives and see the beauty of the Island" (LaPointe Interview).

These pastoral interludes and the companionship he found with LaPointe and others, however, were undercut by his worsening health and a growing despair. He decided he had to move again, and Mary and Garth hauled his voluminous library to a tiny apartment on Palmer's Lane, where he was hemmed in by books, with no space to work.[30] After a few months he moved to his final home, an apartment on Dorchester Street near the waterfront. He had returned to the neighbourhood of Captain MacDougall and the street where Grandma Kate had grown up.

"At that time he was getting older and sicker," says Woolnough. "He got very disappointed with the world." He began sleeping in the backyard, on the ground in a sleeping bag with no cover, rain or shine. He was not a young man then. Réshard would go over because he was really concerned. It would be pouring rain and he would be out there lying on the ground in a soaking bag. Réshard would bring him home and we would try to get him warmed up, but he was really upset, upset with the way the world was going and realizing that he was old and getting sick and that there was very little he could do about it. Also, this Indian thing about lying on the ground had something to do with it, but he took it to ridiculous lengths and didn't take care of himself at all. That was the beginning of him really going, and I thought he would be dying.

In light of Acorn's seriously failing health and his sorrow that he could not have a family, Jim Hornby's final recollection of him in 1986 is poignant: "The last thing I really remember of Milton is I met him in the Bank of Montreal and I had my son who was probably two, and he was quite taken with my son. And the next time we met he asked me something about my son. He seemed to be quite taken with him."

Still in need of that "bigger ... scene" Hornby mentioned, and despite ill health, Acorn gave a reading in Ottawa on 19 July 1985, and was in Toronto later in 1985 seeking a publisher for *The Bare-Eyed Birdwatcher*. Meanwhile, James Deahl was negotiating a publishing arrangement for *Whisky Jack*, another of Acorn's manuscripts-in-progress. *Whisky Jack* would be published posthumously by HMS Press in October 1986, and 14 of its 28 poems are in the manuscript of *The Bare-Eyed Birdwatcher*. A sample of *Whisky Jack*'s titles demonstrates the devotion to nature, and especially to birds, which became even stronger in his last years: "The Raven Conceit," "The War of the Sparrows," "The Great Blue Heron," "Hummingbird," "Wild Strawberries," "The Canadian Moon."

With *Whisky Jack* taken on by HMS Press and *The Bare-Eyed Birdwatcher* virtually complete and awaiting a publisher, Acorn was concentrating on two other manuscripts in addition to the uncompleted *The Sonnets of Martin Dorion*, which he had begun in 1979: *The Sunnybrook Poems* and *Codex Maximus*. The manuscript of *The Sunnybrook Poems* is dated 1985, and contains poems on diverse subjects, including the lead poem, "Sunnybrook Hospital," dated 20 October 1985, with these lines about the veterans hospitalized there:

> I've been accused of trying to make Sunnybrook
> A home away from home as was my right.

> After the war it was a sacred trust
> When those who survived maimed had the right
> To live as tall there as possible
> According to present circumstances.
> Woe to those who trusted sacred trusts!

The power to call forth and craft compelling, memorable language was deserting Acorn. More often than not, the verses in *The Sunnybrook Poems* consist of prosaic declarations and undistinctive tropes. Yet the energy of his passionate beliefs and commitments persists in these last manuscripts, hardly mitigated by his growing illness and bouts of despair, and his output of new poems and drafts remained remarkable.

In a draft of the introduction to the manuscript of *The Sonnets of Martin Dorion*, Acorn wrote,

The first Sonnet of Martin Dorion was pinned on the wall of the Lick'n Chicken Cafe on Bloor Street ... and dated 20 March 1979. A certain familiarity of tone, unusual confidence of expression alerted me to the possibility that I had rediscovered an old "voice" or "muse". I traced it back to the poem "Offshore Breeze" ... and then a whole series began to develop. The man soon identified himself as an Acadien, writing in English.... I remained unaware of this entity until some years later myself and the Perth County Conspiracy (Does Not Exist) under the aegis of a sound man named Karl recorded the poem somewhere in Perth County.... Then when it was replayed a remarkable hard voice, utterly unlike my own, that of a large man absolutely pickled in salt manifested itself.... This gigantic man was Martin Dorion.

This is still vintage Acorn: fabulous myth-maker, A-1 bullshitter, self-aware wit, and ingenuous devotee of his Maritime heritage. This is the Acorn who could still invoke, with the power of poetic persuasion, his psychic connections with Acadian forerunners and seafaring ancestors. This is the poet who could still, in Kent Martin's film, summon from the centre of his deteriorating self the powerful presence and voice in an Island field overlooking the sea: "All the stories that are here, all the stories of this little island.... The spirits you see, you feel—pardon me, I'm sorry, I don't see the spirits here, I feel them. They are not creepy at all, they're very seldom creepy, I should say. They're warm, kindly, interested, they're listening. They know what's going on, and all that there is in the precincts of this little island. I never want to die. I want to tell all, all, all. There's no end to it."

Martin observes that "he had real guts. The demons he was struggling with were formidable, and he really tried to deal with them. He could have been a real recluse with a mind like his. But he kept himself publicly engaged" (Interview).

In contrast, a draft preface in the *Codex Maximus* manuscript is indicative of the rambling, obsessive, disjointed quality of much of his prose writing, correspondence, and conversation in his final years:

CODEX MAXIMUS, the name of this slim volume, means THE GREATEST BOOK. In a way it is my greatest book because whereas previously I wrote mainly for fun, taking care only to tell the truth, now I'm mad. I regard the institution of a massacre of infants (to which most of the so-called Canadian so-called Left has succumbed) to be a personal insult; besides a horror I think of daily. The Socialism remains but after all life comes first. Of course I know that the real Greatest Book was written by the Prophet Mohhammad hundreds of years ago. Jesus, continually harassed by the Boars, wrote no books. Consider my borrowing of a title belonging to him (bless him) to be a complement, not a declaration of rivalry.

Referring to *Codex Maximus*, LaPointe says, "He felt that when he finished that, it would be his last. He was going to try to get a grant to go to New Zealand or Australia for Halley's Comet, and that was going to be part of his *Codex Maximus*. I got the travel information. I was going to be his secretary-driver. When he came back from the League meeting in 1986, after being in the hospital, he says, 'Well, I don't know whether we are going to make it to Australia and New Zealand for Halley's Comet.'"

The 1986 annual meeting of the League of Canadian Poets was held during May in Toronto. The occasion drew Acorn for his penultimate trip off the Island. The year before, the League's membership, preferring to honour Acorn's virtues and overlook the unpleasantries, had elected him to life membership. Acorn, however, was not in attendance. He had avoided League meetings since the 1981 debacle. That bitter experience was rolled into his lifelong difficulty with organizations: his need for camaraderie and social action at odds with his insecurity, suspicion, and quickness to anger. He had even warned LaPointe's 17-year-old-son in Charlottetown, "I want you to stay out of that group downtown, you know, the arts people. They'll change you. It's a difficult scene, it's dirty business, you know." Now that the Island art scene was sizable and maturing—and honouring him in the process—Acorn's paranoia associated with Toronto and Vancouver was trickling over onto Charlottetown.

Acorn nonetheless decided to attend the 1986 League meeting, perhaps sensing that it might be his final opportunity to be among a large gathering of the nation's poets. He wanted LaPointe to accompany him to Toronto: "He was a little bit afraid. So it was all set, and I was going to go. All of a sudden he got really upset. He says, 'No. I know what will happen. You get down there with those people in Toronto and those guys will change you. You won't come back.' He was afraid. 'I'll lose you in Toronto.'" It was as if the childhood memories of being taunted and attacked by bullies had merged with the sadness over his failed marriage, bitter quarrels, and damaged friendships in the adult world of politics and art, causing an upwelling of apprehension and resentment.

Acorn wavered about going, then showed up the day of his scheduled flight at LaPointe's apartment. "It was a beautiful sunny day and I was out in my bathing suit in the backyard. He was all dressed up, suit and everything, but he didn't have a bag or anything. We were there for ages, and then he started reciting poetry, quite loud. We had a great time and I said, 'Milton, don't you have to get a flight today?' 'Well, yeah, but Mary's taking care of it.'" Mary Hooper, however, didn't know where LaPointe lived, and she and Garth had been driving around town. "He was hiding in the backyard," LaPointe says, "and he was in good spirits, and he was asking me to marry him. He'd been on this thing for a couple of years, and finally I said no, he wanted a family, and I had a hard enough time taking care of myself." The Hoopers found LaPointe's residence with minutes to spare. "He had this little smile when they found him," says LaPointe. "He was at the car, so I told him that if he wanted a family he'd have better luck in Toronto. I guess he did, but he ended up in the hospital." Mary and Garth had his suitcase and ticket, and made a mad dash to the airport.

At the start of the League meeting, Acorn ran into Glen Sorestad, the Saskatchewan poet and publisher of Thistledown Books. As editor, publisher, and benevolent spirit, Sorestad has played the same enabling role for Prairie poets as Fred Cogswell had with Fiddlehead Poetry Books for decades in the Maritimes and Libby Oughton with Ragweed Press in the 1980s.[31] Sorestad asked Acorn, "How are you doing?"

"I'm dying, Glen," he answered. "I'm dying."

Over a hundred poets crowded into the League meeting. It was a difficult year: although the League was rapidly developing an impressive management and fundraising scheme, a $38,000 deficit and freezes to government funding inevitably bred tense moments during the business meeting. During one of those moments, Milton Acorn rose to speak. There was a communal sucking in of breath, a tangible stiffening of everyone present, as the chair recognized Acorn. Rather than ranting or raving, however, he burst forth brilliantly—the Acorn of irony and supple wit, imaginative metaphor, and pithy observation. He made his colleagues laugh with delight, and reminded the meeting of the real purpose of all this business on the floor: the creation and declaration of poetry. When he finished and sat down, the applause rang out, partly in relief that Acorn had not ignited another powderkeg, but mainly in appreciation of Acorn at his best, and for his reminder of what poets are ultimately about. Thereafter, he sat in silence, glowing.

But soon after, his declining health took him to Sunnybrook Hospital in Toronto for tests. Doctors determined he should stay in hospital for treatment and rest. He was befriended by Eleanor McEachern, who moved Acorn's books, notebooks, and clothes into his hospital room. She also loaned him a number of her books. "A lot of his belongings, including some of his books and journals and my books, were stolen from the hospital. At that time he was writing an historical play [revisions of *The Road to Charlottetown*] about Charlottetown. He also got his last reading in Toronto, at the Toronto Press Club with Al Purdy and poet Phil Hall. He checked himself out against the doctors' advice, and stayed with me the night before the reading. The night of the reading, he was proud. He had to have an expensive cigar. 'I can't see Al Purdy without having an expensive cigar,' he said."

Riding the crest of another Toronto reading, a reunion with Purdy, and a visit with James Deahl and Gilda Mekler, he returned to the Island in June. Whatever despair and resignation he felt was still powerfully countered by his overwhelming devotion to poetry. His faith in poetry's potential to ask the right questions and proclaim the best answers did not waver. Neither did his determination to shape all the poetry he could out of his aging voice. He had told Deahl during his May visit in Toronto, "I've no goals for my poetry today. I've done all of it. Poetry is the music of life. Poetry is the language of life. Poetry is the first of the literary arts. I'm just going to write more poetry" (Deahl "Acorn" 54).

Thus he kept filling his notebooks with fragments and drafts, notes and ideas. Thus he went back to Toronto "to arrange the publication of *The Uncollected Acorn*. Joyce Wayne of Deneau Publishers and Acorn and Deahl discussed the book project. It was decided that Deahl would edit and Deneau would publish *The Uncollected Acorn*" (Deahl *Chronology*). In August, Unfinished Monument Press decided to publish *A Stand of Jackpine*, a chapbook containing 24 "jackpine sonnets," 12 each by Acorn and Deahl.32

He was in worse physical and emotional shape when he returned to Charlottetown. "He would come into the gallery and burst into tears. First it would be something he had read in *The Globe and Mail* about the Americans, the environment, whatever, and then he'd just cry and cry and I'd console him. I'd try to encourage him, but he was like Queequeg in *Moby Dick*, his intention to die" (Woolnough).

He checked into Queen Elizabeth Hospital in Charlottetown. "You knew he was on the way out," says Woolnough. "He sort of backed out of life. He told me he didn't want to go on. He just didn't see the point of it. Then he stopped eating and I said, 'You have to eat.' And he said, 'I don't see any point in it.' He got thin really fast. He did it with intention, nothing to do with diabetes, it had to do with disappointment in the world."

One day in mid-August, Robert Acorn was visiting his brother in hospital. "He always impressed on me, if I come and he's asleep, never turn around and go. Wake him up. So that's what I was trying to do. He didn't look right to me. His eyes were half open, half closed. I went out to the desk and asked, 'Is Milton tranquillized?' 'No. No more than usual.' I said, 'His eyes are half-open.' She said, 'Oh, he always sleeps like that.' Well, I never saw it before. Back in his room I said, 'Milton, I'm here. Do you want to talk to me? Do you want to wake up and talk to me?' He said, 'Too bad.' That was the last I ever heard from him."

According to one writer, "Finally, on August 20, 1986, the Great Marxist called for an Anglican priest. Milton renounced his Godless ways and accepted Jesus Christ as his personal Saviour" (Gudgeon 157). No one who was present during Acorn's final days, however, remembers Milton asking for a priest or embracing Jesus. Mary says that he was a "religious person," but that he "wouldn't have said 'personal saviour.' That's not part of our vocabulary."

Eleanor McEachern had gone down from Toronto to visit Acorn. She went to his apartment on Dorchester Street, and someone there told her that Milton had died the day before, August 20, in the hospital. She sat on the curb outside his building and cried.

Heart failure. A complication of diabetes.

Cheryl Cashman heard the news in Nelson, BC, from playwright George Ryga. "He said I should make a play of Milton's poems, and spoke of him in the past tense. I was stunned. 'Didn't you know?' he asked. My reaction was real anger. I felt he was a casualty. Another older artist swept off the chessboard. He could have been a Pablo Neruda, instead of his poetry petering out. My gut reaction was that he was another goddamned Canadian casualty."

The funeral was held in St. Peter's Anglican Church in Charlottetown. The casket was an impressive assemblage of brass and expensive wood—the last resting place for Milton's body was definitely more opulent than his room at the Waverly Hotel or his Dorchester apartment. The dignified funeral mass was an appropriate memorial for his Anglican relatives, and it might have appealed to that part of Acorn which sometimes valued the beauty of religious ceremony and the pomp associated with female pharaohs and Zulu warrior dances. The church setting seemed more incongruous to those friends keenly aware of his attitude toward institutionalized religion and his conception of the deity. Most odd was the thought of Milton Acorn shut up in a box. The outspoken poet with the clarion voice not just restrained, as he had been on occasion by the careful shepherding of professors at university readings or officials at government ceremonies, but laid down and sealed tight. At one point in the ceremony, Libby Oughton leaned over to me and said, "Milton must be outraged. I bet any moment he'll sit up, throw the lid back, and tell us what he has to say about all this." Kent Martin recalls, "On the one hand I don't think he would have been really upset with the religious service. He had that religious streak to him. But the minister, who looked like a High Anglican priest from central casting, a Friar Tuck, said some things that made me think the coffin lid might fly up and Milton come out enraged" (Interview).

Sadly, Acorn was not interred in the People's Cemetery on St. Peter's Road. He was buried in St. Peter's Cemetery a short distance away on the same street, among the bones and tombstones of his parents and other ancestors. As the coffin was lowered into the ground, Réshard Gool wept so profoundly he was unable to read from Milton's poems. Hilda Woolnough, too. Mary and Garth Hooper, Robert Acorn, and others listened while Libby Oughton read, and then while

I read one of Milton's own favourite poems, "The Squall," an eloquent manifesto set in the context of his beloved Island:

> When the squall comes running down the bay,
> Its waves like hounds on slanting leashes of rain
> Bugling their way...and you're in it;
> If you want more experience at this game
> Pull well and slant well. Your aim
> Is another helping of life. You've got to win it.
> * * * * *
> How odd, when you think of it, that a man rows
>   backwards.
> What experience, deduction and sophistication
> There had to be before men dared row backwards
> Taking direction from where they'd been
> With only quick-snatched glances at where they're going.
>
> Each strongbacked wave bucks under you, alive
> Young-muscled, wanting to toss you in orbit
> While whitecaps snap like violin-strings
> As if to end this scene with a sudden exit.
>
> Fearfulness is a danger. So's fearlessness.
> You've got to get that mood which balances you
> As if you were a bird in the builder's hand;
> For the boat was built in consideration
> Not only of storms...of gales too.
>
> Though you might cut the waves with your prow
> It'll do no good if you head straight to sea.
> You've got to make a nice calculation
> Of where you're going, where you want to be,
> What you need, and possibility;
> Remembering how you've survived many things
> To get into the habit of living.
>   (*Selected* 156-57)

Libby Oughton threw her pen down to the coffin. A piper then began to play, struggling against a stiffening wind.

EPILOGUE
DIG UP MY HEART

> and history, which is yet to begin,
> will exceed this, exalt this
> as a poem erases and rewrites its poet.
> — "Knowing I Live in a Dark Age"

AS LIBBY OUGHTON had wryly predicted, recognition of Acorn rapidly grew on the Island. Now that the man was gone, people could celebrate his virtues and creations without having to deal with his more difficult traits. A group of friends formed an ad hoc committee to fundraise for a statue. These friends knew that Acorn could have used the recognition more while he was alive, but felt a fitting memorial was still in order. The provincial government now was willing to commit $2,000 toward this purpose. Joseph Sherman suggested a life-size wooden sculpture by John Hooper, a New Brunswick artist who had carved a series of figures placed around the wharf in Saint John. This was affordable, and Acorn could be placed on a favourite street corner or bench at Confederation Centre, amid the daily life of his people. The committee's majority worried about vandalism, for instance, kids carving their initials. Milton would love that, Sherman said. But the committee also wanted something grander, bronze, to be exact. Bronze is vastly more expensive. The project died.

In February 1987 Valerie LaPointe was attending a week-long workshop on social activism. Toward the end of the week, she announced that she would start a festival in honour of Milton Acorn. It would be both a literary festival and an extension of Acorn's political activism and morality. This festival would bear witness to the need for social conscience. The first annual Milton Acorn Festival was held in August of that year. Perhaps the most stirring performance occurred when Frank Ledwell, the final reader, rose just after midnight and declaimed Acorn's "I Shout Love" with all the passionate conviction Milton had written into its lines. Over the next few years, with LaPointe as coordinator and many Islanders volunteering their services, the event grew into the week-long National Milton Acorn Festival, with performances by writers and musicians, including such old friends as Patrick Lane, bill bissett, and James Deahl. A Mi'kmaq sweet grass ceremony, poems against racism by school children, a Milton Acorn tribute by Cedric Smith, and readings from Acorn's poetry became features of the festival.

Also in 1987 the first Milton Acorn Poetry Competition was held on the Island. The winner, appropriately, was native Islander Wendell MacLaine, a carpenter and cabinet-maker by trade, a long-time social activist, and the brother of Brent MacLaine, who had lived in the "air force lady's" house just after Acorn. In 1988 the contest became part of the annual Island Literary Competition. In Toronto, Ted Plantos, James Deahl, and other Acorn friends founded in 1987 the annual Milton Acorn People's Poet Award for a published book that best represents the spirit of Milton Acorn and his poetry. Later, Deahl and Mekler would establish the Acorn-Rukeyser Chapbook Contest and be involved with the Milton Acorn Memorial People's Poetry Awards. In 1997 the Acorn-Livesay Festival and Festival Poetry Contest would be launched in Ontario.

LaPointe claims that, fulfilling one of Acorn's wishes, she entered and won a competition in 1987 to name the provincial tree—the red oak. Ken Mayhew of the PEI Department of Forestry, who was involved in the process of selecting the "official tree emblem," explains that it was not a competition. Rather, people submitted nominations, accompanied by a petition with the names of other supporters: "LaPointe submitted a nomination on behalf of Acorn to the attempt to proclaim a provincial tree. However, there were several other nominations for the red oak, based on its historical connections with PEI. Many people thought it was already the provincial tree because an oak is on the flag. However, the English oak is on the flag and the coat of arms, which was done in England probably around the 1850s. There were about ten different Island trees nominated, and multiple nominations for some species. Approximately 20-25 people signed LaPointe's petition." Acorn's wish was fulfilled by a 1987 amendment to the Provincial Emblems Act which named the red oak the official tree emblem.

After Acorn's death there were memorial readings and, of course, a wake. A memorial reading was held 23 August 1986, in Toronto at The Fallout Shelter with readings by James Deahl, Gerry Shikatani, and Michael Wurster, and jazz music by Bill Smith. "Acorn's Wake" took place 22 March 1987 in Toronto at Grossman's Tavern that afternoon and at Theatre Passe Muraille in the evening, and was filmed by Island filmmaker Brian Pollard. Cedric Smith was host, and performers included Mary Hooper and Robert Acorn, poets Al Purdy, bill bissett, and Robert Priest, and actors Eric Peterson and Susan Hogan. Valerie LaPointe "was in Grossman's ... along with hundreds of his other admirers and friends. Poets, editors, musicians, playwrights, actors, songwriters, publishers.... Later that evening, varied memories and experiences of Milton were related as his reality—big-hearted, gentle, angry, passionate, deeply human and often difficult to manage—was shared" ("Celebrating" 4).

The obituary tributes appeared, primarily in left-wing journals: *ThisMagazine, Canadian Dimension, New Maritimes*. Ted Plantos's *Cross-Canada Writers' Quarterly*, long attentive to working-class writing, published a special Milton Acorn issue edited by James Deahl. In the two years after Milton's death, Deahl became a one-man editorial industry on behalf of Acorn's manuscripts and memories. *Whisky Jack* came out in October 1986. On 16 March 1987, *A Stand of Jackpine* was published. *The Uncollected Acorn*, edited by Deahl, appeared two days later. Also edited by Deahl, *I Shout Love and Other Poems*, selections from Acorn's first four publications and the revised 1970 version of "I Shout Love," was published by Aya Press on 4 August 1987. The following day, Unfinished Monument Press published *The Northern Red Oak*, a collection of poems about and for Acorn by other writers, again edited by Deahl. On 22 November 1988, *Hundred Proof Earth*, edited by Deahl, came out from Aya Press.

All these publications would not change the view of most critics and readers that Acorn's best poetry had been written earlier in his career and published in *I've Tasted My Blood* and *The Island Means Minago*, with a smaller number of impressive poems appearing in *More Poems for People, Jackpine Sonnets*, and the later books.

How would Acorn have felt about this posthumous floodtide of books? He wrote prolifically, but he published with a good deal of discretion, and only when he felt a poem was ready, having undergone as many as 60 drafts. Perhaps he would have laughed at all this adulation after his death. As one obituary insists, "And let's not forget that Milton had a big laugh, one that rattled his whole body, almost demonically" (MacKay 42). Yet laughter would not be all. He would surely have had something trenchant, perhaps heartbreaking, to say about the proliferating volumes, contests, and festivals with his name attached. From another tribute: "If you took his gruff, blustering manner as true, you would miss the sensitivity of his love poetry. If he appeared lost in his head, what he wrote about himself was funny and compelling, often cutting so close to the bone it could make you wince to sense his revealing courage.... Poetry was the muscle that held together the secrets of his torn heart" (Wayne 18).

Not all tributes after his death were uncritical. Tom Wayman, the younger poet who had assumed the leadership of the "work poetry" movement well before Acorn's death, wrote that Acorn "accepted the title of 'People's Poet' even though it must have been clear even to him that the award was not presented by 'the people' in any manifestation but by his fellow *poets*. In actuality this made him the '*Poets*' People's Poet'—a label with a different significance than the official title. The award was advantageous to the mainstream literary practitioners since these men and women, having assigned socially-conscious verse to one chosen individual, were now free to get on with creating 'real' poetry" (39).

Much earlier, Acorn had been attacked for his bardic-political self-image (Davey *From Here* 27-28), and Jewinski argues that, ironically, "Acorn was always awed by the notion of the 'Bard,'" which "implicitly celebrates the 'wise man' of a culture and elevates him above his 'class'" (35). There is some truth in Wayman's critical assessment: "Praising Acorn as the solitary neglected artistic genius helped reinforce the stereotype that art is the preserve of rare and eccentric individuals incapable of being understood by the insensitive majority. It follows from this stereotype that the production of art cannot be the activity of normal people like you and I" (39).

These comments, though, seem almost oblivious of the substantial influence Acorn (along with writers such as Livesay, Layton, Nowlan, and Purdy) have had on so many poets and other artists— not to become impoverished, misunderstood eccentrics but to write in an accessible language and poetic about the richness of ordinary life, the daily concerns of that great majority of humanity he referred to as the working class. Acorn helped a great deal to remind poets, readers and listeners, teachers and students, critics and scholars that "real" poetry includes poems about work, the lives of working people, political and economic reality, war, and the dynamic struggles of a people's history.

Yes, there was a risk that the anointment of a "People's Poet" might tokenize "work poetry" or "people's poetry" in this one individual. In fact, this did not happen. Instead, many fine poets—Wayman included—followed the lead provided by Acorn, Purdy, Livesay, and others, and expanded the repertoire of "real" poetry.

Thankfully, Wayman concluded that "despite Romanticism's impact on Acorn, he was unquestionably a pioneer. With considerable energy—sometimes bordering on the manic—he did crowbar a hole in the wall that separates literature from the working life which engages the minds, bodies and most waking moments of the overwhelming majority of the adult population" (39). Other readers and critics, as well, could be more receptive to, or at least less disturbed by, his "Romanticism." Terry Barker, for instance, in "Acorn—The Last Romantic Loyalist?," notes that "since his traumatic experience with the CLM [Canadian Liberation Movement], Acorn has increasingly reverted to the 'spilled religion' of Romanticism, which has always formed the spiritual substructure of his thought" (56).

Gwendolyn MacEwan wrote a remarkable tribute to his influence:

Milton was the first true poet I knew, and during the short time we were together in the early Sixties, I was pulled forward, both as a person and as a poet, by the sheer intensity of the man, into a world of love and anger, rage and joy, conviction and doubt, human folly and human truth. His mind could accommodate elephants and dinosaurs, while a tiny winged insect on his arm could distract him and shut out the world for a moment of wonder and incredulity. He could carry on a scathing argument with some fellow poet on world politics, then stop short in mid-sentence, mesmerized by a bird he'd spotted in a tree. He was, to quote Irving Layton's poem, 'A quiet madman, never far from tears'—and although Milton was often far from quiet, he could plunge from heights of oratory to bottomless valleys of despair. He enraged some, bewildered others, and never tolerated fools. You could go for years without seeing him, and yet he'll always be there somehow, a great craggy presence at the back of your mind, a gnarled tree in silouhette on the horizon. He has earned this new, untroubled sleep, and no one who has seen or heard him, even for a moment, will forget him. ("To Milton")

Would Acorn and his poetry have been better known, more popular and unforgettable, on Prince Edward Island if he had been less "different"? Probably. Had he been less irascible, and more able to play the role of colourful and lovable poet, he might have become something like the Robbie Burns of PEI or the Island's equivalent of Farley Mowat, Alden Nowlan, or W.O. Mitchell. Imagine a Milton Acorn who was not too radical or not too vocal about his radicalism. He should preferably drink with local dignitaries, tell funny stories with the right kind of off-colour humour, wear a kilt or Lederhosen on occasion, and consume schnitzel and haggis, scotch and lager, in honour of his Scots and German ancestry. He would speak to high school graduations.

That was not Milton Acorn. Unfortunately, his manner and appearance too often were a barrier between Islanders and his poetic vision, passion, and voice. But the fault was sometimes in the beholder: in his compatriots' unwillingness to see beyond stained shirt and dishevelled hair, to filter the noise and hear the poems, to enter into his clear, lovely, and sometimes painfully challenging perceptions of our lives, our world.

It is not that surprising, then, that Prince Edward Island has not, officially and commercially, done more to immortalize and exploit Milton Acorn and his poems. Obviously, Acorn has received more posthumous attention than the vast majority of poets and other artists in Canada. But the PEI Department of Tourism has not yet co-opted his myth. It might happen. Even the troublesome aspects of his personality are splendid ingredients, at this safe remove from the man. Most heroes, mythic figures of the past, had their flaws, vices, bothersome traits, to go with their promotable virtues and achievements.

The poetic accomplishment is certainly there, in abundance and variety, for an Island that wants to trumpet and market its blessings. Poems about the Island's beauty and history, harbours and farms, birds and woods, carpenters and waitresses, rebel farmers and landlords' agents, war veterans and fiddlers, sea captains and a naked goddess. A cynic or a purist might detest the idea of Acorn's "Charlottetown Harbour" on a large waterfront plaque, of "The Island" or "Islanders" printed, framed, and hung in government offices and tourist information centres. But Acorn wrote his poetry for the people, not for cynics or purists.

Those with a limited view of what "real" poetry is about might not want "I've Tasted My Blood" on posters in school hallways; and some of the Island's economic and political élite might prefer to ignore "Incident From the Land Struggle" and "The Figure in the Landscape Made the Landscape." Acorn, however, wrote about all facets of "the Island way of life"—not just tableaus of landscape and residents that could safely go on the covers of phonebooks. The Island way of life includes: people who fought and died in war; the pleasures and pain of work; violence in Islanders' communities and homes; the blessing and curse of alcohol; the ongoing class divisions of rich, middle class, and poor; social privilege and deprivation; generosity and greed; conscience and complacency; hypocrisy and virtue; spiritual longing and doubt. This, too, is the Island of Milton Acorn's poetry, which is not all sweetness and light—even if it is "a visible sample of Heaven."

But no one familiar with Acorn's poetry could ever accuse him of cynicism, bitterness, negativity, or excessive emphasis on the evil side of human conduct and intention. If depression afflicted Acorn at times during his life and despair took hold of him in his final months, it had no place in his poetry. Moral outrage, political indignation, personal anger: yes. But these were underwritten by his extraordinary hope, love, and—as he says in "I've Tasted My Blood"— "my deepest prayer." He was not capable of apathy, fatalism, or a retreat into postmodern paradox and irony-for-its-own sake. If anything, he believed in "the people," the "masses," the "working class," and "a better future than even the optimists among us would dare." Even most of his political poems call for—and believe resoundingly in—strength, endurance, courage, faith, human betterment as history proceeds, and, of course, love.

Love of humanity. Love of the cab drivers and union organizers. Love of Bull the road foreman and Stan the retired carpenter. Of his mother, sisters, father, brother, godson. Of his friends fallen in battle. Of the women he loved but couldn't stop "from going away." Of the farmers who "made the landscape" of Prince Edward Island. Of the red soil and the roads leading to the sea. Of those who plied the sea in schooners. Of the young poets who could hear the sound in their poems and whose sound was music. He loved his friends. And the ravens and crows. His love reached out to his ancestry and heritage, to justice and equality, to a world in which greed, racism, violence, tyranny, and oppression must dwindle as humanity evolves. His love stretched out toward the "Hands" that touched him. He shouted his love to "This glorious age / When the ancient rule of classes is hit / And hit again." He willed himself to be part of "History's greatest change."

"It comes to the question," said Acorn, when asked if humanity was evolving up or down: "Can man imagine anything greater than himself?" (Barker et al. 173).

Acorn's life was dedicated to imagining for us a humanity greater than what we have been and are. In the end, he slept in the rain and cried because we could not be better, sooner, and in farewell to his brother said, "Too bad." He did all, however, that any one person could do. His imagination was more generous and caring than we perhaps deserved. Although he wrote energetically after *Captain Neal MacDougal & the Naked Goddess*, it may be that, with that book and its final poem, "The Completion of the Fiddle," his work was complete. And ours had begun:

> The fiddle's incomplete without the dance;
> My darling. Let's hook fingers to complete
> By motion to the calls, the sweet riddle
> Of the tune now wriggling in the soft wind
> On top of which the bright moon goes riding;
> For if no happy bottoms prance and spin
> Upon the planks and polish what's it all worth—
> That round of steamed, shaped, rehardened wood
> Varnished as it's put about a hollow
> From which a tune may radiate its mirth
> By merry rub of gut against gut?
> The candles flicker and the stars twinkle
> All to be parts of the completed fiddle!

NOTES

1. This story was told to me by a UPEI student after class one day in the late 1980s. I can't recall her name.
2. Unreferenced quotations are from personal interviews with the indicated person.
3. See Wayman's two collections of essays: *Inside Job: Essays on the New Work Writing,* Madeira Park, BC: Harbour, 1983, and *A Country Not Considered: Canada, Culture, Work,* Concord, ON.: Anansi, 1993. He has edited several anthologies of work poetry, including *A Government Job at Last,* Vancouver: McLeod Books, 1975, and *Going for Coffee,* Madeira Park, BC: Harbour, 1981.
4. "Hessian" is the name attached, somewhat loosely, to the 29 thousand Germans who served as auxiliary forces with the British in the American colonies and fought for the British during the American Revolution. Many were from Hesse, but thousands were from neighbouring realms. Around 12 thousand settled permanently in the United States and Canada after the American victory. German Loyalists are an important part of Maritime history, and their descendants feature prominently in the development of many Maritime communities. Acorn, Haydn, and Schurman are only a few of the distinguished German loyalist names in Island history. See: "The German Issue" of *The Abegweit Review,* vol. 5, no. 2, Spring 1989, edited by Lothar Zimmermann.

5. It is a lovely coincidence that when the PEI Literary Awards were initiated in the mid-1980s, the first new categories were the Milton Acorn Poetry Competition and the Carl Sentner Short Fiction Competition. Sentner was an Island fiction writer and CBC employee who died shortly before Acorn's death. Sentner is another German Loyalist name.
6. Mary Hooper and Robert Acorn Jr. were interviewed at length in the summer of 1992, and Mary Hooper was interviewed again in 1994 and 1996 to clarify certain information. In February 1997 I again interviewed Mary and Robert regarding sections of Chris Gudgeon's 1996 biography, *Out of This World: The Natural History of Milton Acorn*. Quotations from these interviews are cited as M. Hooper or R. Acorn, or attributed to Mary Hooper or Robert Acorn, without a date. Mary's husband Garth was present during the interviews with Mary and contributed information. Their son David Hooper was interviewed separately. Quotations from Mary Hooper's written tributes to her brother are indicated as such in citations.
7. The term "myth," of course, can embrace a vast territory of traditions, tales, motifs, figures, rituals, and beliefs, and the meaning of "myth" and "mythic figure" can change with context, from the sacred to the profane, from prehistory to contemporary pop culture, from the benevolent to the malignant.
8. Legions of historians, journalists, military campaigners, missionaries, and politicians as well as poets have reported and interpreted "history" according to their values and biases—ethnic, racial, gender, class, religious, moral, ideological, and methodological. This is why many contemporary historians now refer to their field and the results of their research as "historiography"—the writing of history—rather than "history." Historiography acknowledges that any researcher-writer is not fully and flawlessly discovering and transmitting what "really" happened. Rather, the historian or historiographer attempts to discern and relate the most reliable version, given the limitations of research and the background, resources, and perspectives of the researcher-writer. Literary writers, of course, have more "poetic license" than the historiographer, and can imaginatively conjure and rearrange historical events to more effectively communicate their sense of human experience. Imaginative interpretation, however, has been a dominant element in

historical accounts over the centuries, and is hardly confined to literary writers, although most "historians" in the past would hardly agree that their observations were made through the lenses of their cultural conditioning or that their interpretations were imaginatively constructed according to their value systems.

As Stephen Slemon observes, "history is a mode of discourse that is culturally motivated and ideologically conditioned; it is a mirror of contemporary concerns and dominant, institutionalized practices. It consists not of things, but of words" (159). Slemon continues to note that "history is not a set of immovable past achievements but a discourse, open, as are all discursive practices, to reinterpretation" (164), that is, to the "process of transforming received concepts of history and tradition" (162). A poet such as Milton Acorn was engaged in a process of interpretation common to countless authors of historical accounts. His historically based poems rely on an imaginative interrogation of received history, on an amalgam of fact and invention. The historiographer's work may assist in the explication of Acorn's poems and the reader's determination of their significance.

9. Records of former civilian employees of the federal government are destroyed 80 years after the birth date of the person. Hence, no records of Helen Acorn's federal government employment are available.
10. School records of former students on PEI are confidential, and access to their contents is denied even to researchers and members of the subject's immediate family. As a result, I was unable to gain specific information about Acorn's academic achievements.
11. Although publicly funded and nonsectarian, Prince of Wales College was the academy that most Protestants attended in moving beyond matriculation. Catholics attended St. Dunstan's University, a private institution.
12. Chris Gudgeon states that Acorn wrote and passed his civil service examinations in 1946. In light of Acorn's employment as a civil servant in Moncton with the Unemployment Insurance Commission commencing on 22 July 1944, it is clear that Acorn wrote the examinations well before 1946.
13. Robert Grimm also comments on the use of sulpha-based drugs for the treatment of ear infections: "During the Second World War, the sulpha-based antimicrobials were introduced for the management of infections. If the blast had blown out Acorn's ear

drums, as there is a natural bacterial flora living in the ear canal ... they would have been granted access to the middle ear cavity and directly into the air cell structure of the mastoid to set up a nasty infection viz. the old mastoiditis.... It is possible that if the use of a sulpha compound failed to cure Acorn's putative mastoiditis, and his infection dragged on for several years (not uncommon in this ear), he may have received streptomycin, which in turn may have added to his troubles" (Letter).

14. Joseph Heller's great satirical novel set in World War II, *Catch-22*, centres on this same reality: that soldiers have more than one enemy to contend with, and that their leaders—high-ranking officers, politicians, bureaucrats, industrialists, and financiers—are as great a threat as the designated "enemy."

15. Official documentation of Milton Acorn's employment with the Federal Government of Canada was provided by the Personnel Records Unit, Researcher Services Division, National Archives of Canada, in correspondence dated 3 October 1994, and prepared by Claire Leblanc, Research and Public Inquiries Officer. Records of Acorn's employment at the PEI Provincial Hospital, the old fertilizer wharf, and the CNR yard in Charlottetown may no longer exist. The old provincial hospital has been closed for years, and its employment records appear to have been destroyed. This is most likely the case with records of employment from the government wharfs and CNR yard. As well, no archival storage of local union membership rolls from the 1940s-50s was discovered during research for this book. Until a forgotten cache of such records is discovered in an Island attic or storeroom, there are no documents that precisely date Acorn's employment at several Charlottetown jobs, including his work as a labourer on construction sites.

16. Acorn was a middle-class child who became a socialist and communist. Nowlan grew up in formidable poverty in rural Nova Scotia and eventually became a close friend of Tory premier Richard Hatfield, a reader and patron of poetry. The poems of Acorn and Nowlan, I believe, have a great deal in common in their devotion to working people and the poor. Acorn, however, is on record saying that "it's true he was of working class origin, but his mind never was, and his life never was. However, Nowlan was a mighty good poet. But not working class, it was not among his interests" (Burrill 6). Supporters of

Acorn's verdict might insist that his political convictions, along with the class-struggle rhetoric and stance of certain poems, legitimize his poetry as "working class." Another view is that Nowlan's poems are equally, if not more, of the "working class" and everyday experience, and even more effective without the ideological baggage that sometimes weighs Acorn's poetry down. The correspondence between Acorn and Nowlan in the Acorn collection at the National Archives indicates a mutual respect and affection, which their differences never affected and which never waned.

17. An appreciative treatment of the history and culture of harness racing on Prince Edward Island, including a detailed account of the Charlottetown Driving Park, may be found in Charles Duerden's *Sulkies, Silks, Cups and Saucers: A Retrospective of the Charlottetown Driving Park*, Charlottetown: Ragweed Press, 1988.

18. The University of Prince Edward Island was established in 1969, an amalgamation of St. Dunstan's University and Prince of Wales College into the new public university.

19. Crawford (1850-87) is best remembered for her narrative and mytho-poetic poems, written in the 1880s. Also a prose writer, she is considered the first major English-Canadian woman poet. Lampman (1861-99) was one of the four "Confederation Poets." Long admired for his nature poems, with their distinctive adaptation of Romantic, especially Wordsworthian, conventions and concerns to his personal and Canadian context, Lampman has attracted contemporary readers to the radical social criticism in his later poetry. In his lyricism and nature poetry, and especially his poetic critique of capitalism, Lampman was an important influence on Acorn. Marriott (1913-97) published "The wind, our enemy," a long narrative poem about the effect of the Depression and the drought during the 1930s on the Prairies. Livesay (1909-96) is one of the most significant figures in Canadian literature—for her poetry, feminism, advocacy of other writers, and social activism on many fronts for much of the century.

20. Robert Heilbroner, in his classic study of economic thinkers and systems *The Worldly Philosophers*, stressed that capitalism developed gradually and unevenly from the 15th century on, and did not appear at the beginning of prehistoric communities or historical civilizations, as some proponents of capitalism maintain. To claim that "capitalism is natural," as Robert Fulford did in *The Globe and*

Mail in 1994, is to be dreadfully ignorant of biology and anthropology, as well as economic history. It also reveals ignorance of a central premise argued by Adam Smith—the "father" of modern capitalist theory—in his classic *An Inquiry Into the Wealth of Nations*: left to their own devices in an unregulated and unfettered marketplace, capitalist owners will ruin all but a handful of triumphant survivors in a competitive frenzy driven by greed, and will devastate society.

Moreover, capitalism alters, evolves, and manifests itself differently depending on the region and era. If humans are fortunate enough to survive that long, capitalism is unlikely to be around in anything resembling its present forms five hundred years from now. In an episode of the TV series *Star Trek: The Next Generation*, Captain Picard tells humans from the past—who were frozen cryogenically and rescued and thawed three hundred years later by the starship *Enterprise*—that material needs are no longer an issue in the Federation. Everyone has enough. Accumulation of excess wealth and fear of financial ruin and impoverishment were eliminated long ago. Milton Acorn could have written the script.

21. For a more extensive account of Acorn's relationship with MacEwan, see Rosemary Sullivan's *Shadow Maker: The Life of Gwendolyn MacEwan*, Toronto: HarperCollins, 1995.
22. Several years after Acorn's death, Jack LeClair, a Charlottetown photographer, was walking home along King Street. Outside Jardine's Auction Warehouse a few doors from his house, he noticed a photo scrapbook on a pile of rubbish. He took the scrapbook home, where his wife, Karen Mair, a CBC broadcaster, recognized it as Milton Acorn memorabilia. Mair phoned Robert Acorn and the Hoopers, who arrived at Jardine's just as the garbage truck pulled up. The garbageman was startled by this group rummaging frantically through the rubbish, and agreed to return later. They found valuable photographs, letters, newspaper clippings, and drafts of several poems.
23. The source of this review is at present unknown. I found a copy of the review in Mary Hooper's personal Milton Acorn files, but this single page did not contain periodical information. My search at the Metropolitan Toronto Library and National Archives was fruitless. I sent a copy to Dennis Lee, who could not recall the source. Moreover, Lee's official bibliographer has no record of this piece. I then sent the review to Tanya Prince, a

Master's student in the Faculty of Information Studies at the University of Toronto, whom I hired to track down several articles. She, too, was thwarted. Identification of this source will be most welcome.

24. Bowering's award-winning books were *Rocky Mountain Foot* and *The Gangs of Kosmos*.

25. Two decades later, with the Confederation Bridge between PEI and the mainland opened on 1 June 1997, the debate appears to have been decided in favour of Premier Campbell's Development Plan. Tourism is heavily promoted as a major part of the Island economy, and is, indeed, central to the "Island way of life," with the Island's pastoral identity commercialized in proliferating ways. Industrial development in the form of food processing is actively supported by the provincial government, and by much of the farming community, with some reservations about corporate control by the Irving and McCain conglomerates. Nevertheless, the widespread apprehensions of Islanders which were expressed by the Brothers and Sisters of Cornelius Howatt and manifested in support for Premier MacLean's Rural Renaissance are very much alive today in the concern that tourism and manufacturing sustain, rather than supplant, the Island's traditional charm and sense of community.

26. Eugene A. Forsey writes in *The Canadian Encyclopedia*, "Padlock Act (Act Respecting Communistic Propaganda), a 1937 Quebec statute empowering the attorney general to close, for one year, any building used for propagating 'communism or bolshevism' (undefined)" (1601).

27. As two postcolonial scholars explain, "colonialism, the conquest and direct control of other people's lands, is a particular phase in the history of imperialism, which is now best understood as the globalization of the capitalist mode of production" (Williams and Chrisman 2). Postcolonial scholars also distinguish among different kinds of colonialism. For instance, "*Imperial colonization* ... involves large-scale, territorial domination" such as British rule in India and the USSR's domination of Eastern Europe; "*deep settler colonization* [domination of the native majority by the minority colonists] prevailed ... in Algeria, Kenya, Zimbabwe and Vietnam." "*Break-away settler colonies*" include Canada, the United States, Australia, New Zealand, and South Africa (McClintock 295). One can argue that Canadian history began

with imperial colonization by England and France and developed into break-away settler colonization.
28. For an authoritative treatment of this subject, see Ian Ross Robertson's book-length study, *The Tenant League of Prince Edward Island 1864-1867: Leasehold Tenure in the New World*, Toronto: University of Toronto Press, 1996.
29. Like some Marxists of his generation, Acorn admired Stalin for certain achievements of the USSR—its rapid industrialization and its contribution to the defeat of Fascism, for example—while rationalizing or denying the price paid under Stalinist oppression and brutality. Acorn could point out that a much higher price in human suffering has been paid over the centuries for capitalist enterprise, but he was hard pressed to agree that capitalist abuses, however enormous, did not justify Stalinist abuses.
30. Acorn had a lifelong love affair with books, that is, with the book as object and possession, as well as with the book's contents. In his later years, as his financial situation somewhat improved, he believed in buying hardcover editions, rather than paperbacks, to better support author and publisher. His rented rooms and apartments were filled with books, and after his death Mary and Garth Hooper inherited an impressive collection which they hope to turn into a memorial library. As Garth says, "I moved his books so many times, I figured when he died I'd take them."
31. Two other prominent publishers of contemporary Atlantic Canadian poetry should be mentioned. The Nova Scotian Lesley Choyce, a prolific writer as well as publisher, founded and edited for years the invaluable literary journal *Pottersfield Portfolio*, and established and runs Pottersfield Press. In Newfoundland, Clyde Rose, founder and publisher of Breakwater Books, has befriended and published some of Newfoundland's finest poets.
32. Deahl believes the "jackpine sonnet" is a distinctly Canadian form developed by Acorn. "A jackpine sonnet, as I define it, is an irregular sonnet of 13 or 17 lines. The lines are about ten syllables long and do not rhyme. In the hands of its greatest proponent it is a loose, rangy, sonnet that can also be 14 lines and may rhyme. Mine tend to be more formal, more like the traditional sonnet" (Deahl "Introduction").

WORKS CITED

MILTON ACORN PAPERS AT THE NATIONAL ARCHIVES OF CANADA

These papers are organized in 54 volumes: general correspondence (vols. 1-3); family correspondence (vol. 4); miscellaneous correspondence (vol. 5); biographical and personal material: documents relating to Acorn's honours and awards, interviews, entries in biographical dictionaries (vol. 5); financial records (vol. 5); subject files: material relating to poetry, poetry magazines, political organizations, and a variety of general subjects (vols. 5-7); manuscripts: poetry: published collections: original (vols. 7-10); manuscripts: poetry: unpublished collections: original (vols. 10-11); manuscripts: poetry: uncollected published and unpublished (vols. 11-21); manuscripts: poetry: fragmentary: original (vols. 21-22); manuscripts: fiction: original (vols. 22-24); manuscripts: plays: *The Road to Charlottetown* (vols. 24-25); manuscripts: non-fiction: original (vols. 25-26); manuscripts: miscellaneous notes and sketches (vol. 26); manuscripts: notebooks (vols. 27-52); general and family correspondence (vol. 53); manuscripts: poetry: poems published in periodicals (vol. 54).

Most of the items in the Acorn papers at the National Archives were received in 1985. Later additions include the unpublished manuscript *Sonnets of Martin Dorian*, received from Deneau Publishers in 1986, the unpublished manuscript of his collaboration with bill bissett, *i want 2 tell yu love*, received in 1988, and material from Mary Hooper, received in 1986 after Acorn's death and in 1993 after the 1992 discovery of Acorn papers and memorabilia on a Charlottetown street.

A catalogue of the National Archives collection is available to researchers at the PEI Public Archives. This catalogue provides a list of correspondents, individual poems, and other documents in the collection. Researchers may also be interested in the small collection (113 pages) of Acorn papers at Simon Fraser University.

Anyone who wishes to donate Acorn papers to the collection in Ottawa should contact Anne Godard at the National Archives.

MILTON ACORN MANUSCRIPTS: PUBLISHED AND UNPUBLISHED

Against a League of Liars. Toronto: Hawkshead Press, 1960.
The Bare-Eyed Birdwatcher. Unpublished manuscript. National Archives of Canada.
The Brain's the Target. Toronto: Ryerson Press, 1960.
Captain Neal MacDougal & the Naked Goddess. Charlottetown: Ragweed Press, 1982.
Codex Maximus. Unpublished manuscript. National Archives of Canada.
Dig Up My Heart: Selected Poems 1952-83. Toronto: McClelland & Stewart, 1983, 1994.
"Goddam it Prince Edward Island Needs that Causeway." *Notes For a Native Land.* Ed. Andy Wainwright. Ottawa: Oberon, 1969, 113-18.
"Grey Girl's Gallop." *New Frontiers* (Winter 1953):36-39.
Hundred Proof Earth. Toronto: Aya Press, 1988.
In Love and Anger. Montreal: self-published, 1956.
I Shout Love and other poems. Ed. James Deahl. Toronto: Aya Press, 1987.
The Island Means Minago. Toronto: NC Press, 1975.
"I was a communist for my own damn satisfaction." *evidence* 5 (1962):32-38.
I've Tasted My Blood: Poems 1956 to 1968. Toronto: McGraw-Hill Ryerson, 1969.
Jackpine Sonnets. Toronto: Steel Rail, 1977.
Jawbreakers. Toronto: Contact Press, 1963.
More Poems for People. Toronto: NC Press, 1973.
"On the Wheel." *The Broad-Axe* (August 1971):3-4.

Sonnets of Martin Dorion. Unpublished manuscript. National Archives of Canada.
A Stand of Jackpine. Toronto: Unfinished Monument Press, 1987.
The Sunnybrook Poems. Unpublished manuscript. National Archives of Canada.
The Uncollected Acorn. Ed. James Deahl. Toronto: Deneau, 1987.
Whiskey Jack. Toronto: HMS, 1986.
"A Worried But Easy Habit." *The Canadian Forum* (June 1959):61.

OTHER ACORN MANUSCRIPTS

"The Assembly Line." Unpublished essay. Unpaginated.
Hooper, Mary. "Memoirs." Unpublished essay. Unpaginated.
"My Brother Milton." Unpublished essay. Unpaginated.
"Red Light!" Unpublished essay. Unpaginated.

ACORN INTERVIEWS AND LETTERS

Acorn, Helen. Letters to Milton Acorn. 22 March 1962, 4 October 1962, 15 November 1962, 7 February 1965.
Acorn, Milton. Letters to Helen Acorn. 12 April 1953, 7 May 1953, 3 July 1956, 21 October 1956, 17 March 1961, 1 January 1964, 16 August 1965, 17 January 1969, ("Probably the AA ..."), undated. National Archives of Canada.
———Letter to Robert Acorn, Jr. 8 May 1954. National Archives of Canada.
———Letter to Cid Corman. 8 February 1961. National Archives of Canada.
———Letters to Louise Harvey. 29 November 1954, 14 May 1955, 6 July 1955. National Archives of Canada.
———Letter to Mary Hooper. 17 March 1952. National Archives of Canada.
———Letter to Mary and Garth Hooper. Undated, c. 1952-53. National Archives of Canada.
———Letter to Irving Layton. 16 December 1978. National Archives of Canada.
———Letter to the League of Canadian Poets. 26 August 1971. National Archives of Canada.
———Letter to Dennis Lee. Undated, c. 1981. National Archives of Canada.

———Letter to Dorothy Livesay. 21 March 1974. National Archives of Canada.
Acorn, Milton. Letters to Gwendolyn MacEwan. 1 April 1962, 20 August 1965. National Archives of Canada.
———Letter to Stephanie Nynych. 19 February 1969. National Archives of Canada.
———Letters to Al Purdy. Undated 'A', c. 1958, Undated 'B', c. 1958, 21 October 1963, 11 January 1964, 4 May 1974, 24 September 1982. National Archives of Canada.
———Letter to Raymond Souster. 31 July 1969. National Archives of Canada.
———Letter to Joe Wallace. 11 May 1955. National Archives of Canada.
Barker, Terry, Aileen LeRoux, and James Deahl. "An Interview With Milton Acorn." *intrinsic!* (Spring 1979):161-76.
Burrill, Gary. "An Afternoon With Milton Acorn." *New Maritimes* (May 1984):4-7.
Deahl, James. "WQ Interview with Milton Acorn." *Cross-Canada Writers' Quarterly* 8.3/4 (1986):3-4, 52-54.
Hornby, Jim. "Milton Acorn Talks About Poetry, Politics and Milton Acorn." *Cadre* (April 1970):8-9.
MacDonald, Helen. Interview. 7 October 1969. PEI Archives.
Pearce, Jon. "The Idea of a Poem: an Interview with Milton Acorn." *Canadian Poetry: Studies, Documents, Reviews* 21 (Fall/Winter 1987):93-102.

ARCHIVAL AND MANUSCRIPT SOURCES: ACORN COLLECTION

McCormich, Root. CN Telegram. 4 October 1960. National Archives of Canada.
MacEwan, Gwendolyn. Letter to Milton Acorn. Undated, 1962. National Archives of Canada.
Purdy, Al. Letter to Milton Acorn. 5 December 1962. National Archives of Canada.

ARCHIVAL AND MANUSCRIPT SOURCES: GOVERNMENT DOCUMENTS

Feasby, W.R., ed. *Official History of the Canadian Medical Services*. Vol. 3. Ottawa: Minister of National Defence, 1956.
PEI *Registry of Ships 1787-1914*. Public Archives and Records Office of PEI.

PERSONAL INTERVIEWS AND LETTERS

Acorn, Robert. Personal interviews. 25 July 1992, 10 February 1997.
Arsenault, Leo. Personal interview. 17 July 1997.
bissett, bill. Letter to the author. 9 November 1994.
Cashman, Cheryl. Personal interview. 4 January 1995.
Deahl, James. Letters to the author. 16 August 1992, 12 November 1994.
Dickson, Agnes. Personal interview. 28 October 1994.
Flynn, Joe. Personal interview. 17 July 1994.
Grimm, Robert J. Letter to the author. 21 May 1995.
Harrison, Elaine. Personal interview. 22 March 1995.
Hooper, David. Personal interview. 24 August 1993.
Hooper, Garth. Personal interviews. 18 July 1992, 7 November 1994, 10 February 1997.
Hooper, Mary. Letter to the author. 4 February 1994.
———Personal interviews. 18 July 1992, 7 November 1994, 10 February 1997.
Hornby, Jim. Personal interview. 9 January 1995.
Johnston, Georgina. Personal interview. 18 January 1995.
Kemp, Penn. Letter to the author. 9 July 1997.
Kennedy, Karen. Personal interview. 25 September 1994.
Lane, Patrick. Personal interview. 18 January 1995.
LaPointe, Valerie. Personal interview. 25 July 1992.
Ledwell, Bill. Personal interview. 29 November 1994.
Ledwell, Frank. Personal interview. 28 October 1994.
MacDonald, Edward. Letter to the author. 6 December 1996.
McEachern, Eleanor. Personal interview. 19 November 1994.
MacLaine, Brent. Personal interview. 26 October 1994.
McLeod, Dan. Letter to the author. 26 July 1994.
Martin, Kent. Personal interview. 23 January 1995.
Mayhew, Ken. Personal interview. c. 1995.
Partridge, Gertrude. Personal interview. 25 July 1994.
Phelan, Reg. Personal interview. 1 August 1994.
Pound, Fred. Personal interview. 23 October 1994.
Purdy, Al. Letter to the author. 12 June 1992.
Rosenblatt, Joe. Letter to the author. 4 November 1994.
Shama, Peter. Personal interview. 23 October 1994.
Sherman, Joseph. Personal interview. 9 November 1994.
Shields, William. Personal interview. 21 August 1994.

Smith, John. Personal interview. 28 July 1992.
Sorestad, Glen. Personal interview. 13 September 1994.
Steiger, George. Personal interview. 25 July 1994.
Sullivan, Rosemary. Personal interview. 17 April 1995.
Turgeon, Frank. Letter to Frank Ledwell. No date. Used by permission of the author.
Wells, Andy. Personal interview. 13 March 1995.
Wheler, Eleanor. Personal interview. 22 March 1995.
Woolnough, Hilda. Personal interview. 15 August 1992.

PUBLISHED AND UNPUBLISHED SECONDARY SOURCES

Avakumovic, Ivan. *The Communist Party in Canada: A History.* Toronto: McClelland & Stewart, 1975.
Baglole, Harry. "Drawing Lots." *Horizon Canada* 5.55 (1985-87 [volumes undated]):1297-1303.
———"William Cooper." *Dictionary of Canadian Biography*, vol. 9. Toronto: University of Toronto Press, 1976, 155-58.
———and David Weale. *Cornelius Howatt: Superstar!* Charlottetown: Williams and Crue, 1974.
Baldick, Chris. *The Concise Oxford Dictionary of Literary Terms.* New York: Oxford University Press, 1990.
Balingall's Directory of Prince Edward Island, 1914. Charlottetown: G. Ballinger Publishing, 1914.
Barker, Terry. "Acorn—The Last Romantic Loyalist?" *Cross-Canada Writers' Quarterly* 8.3/4 (1986):12, 56-57.
Bartley, Jan. "Gwendolyn MacEwan." *Canadian Writers and Their Works.* Poetry series. Eds. Robert Lecker, Jack David, and Ellen Quigley. Vol. 9. Toronto: ECW Press, 1985, 231-71.
Bowering, George. "A singing hydrant doesn't slum." Review of *I've Tasted My Blood*, by Milton Acorn. *The Globe Magazine*, 14 June 1969:20.
Callbeck, Lorne C. *The Cradle of Confederation.* Fredericton: Brunswick Press, 1964.
Cogswell, Fred. "Reviews." *The Fiddlehead* 49 (Summer 1961):58.
Compton, Anne. "Milton Acorn's PEI Poems: An Ecological Approach." Paper presented at the international conference Message in a Bottle: The Literature of Small Islands, Charlottetown, PEI, June 1998.
"Contribution Made By Grants Committee." *The Guardian*, 22 May 1970:2.

Dash, J. Michael. "Edward Kamau Brathwaite." *West Indian Literature*. Ed. Bruce King. 2nd ed. London: MacMillan, 1995, 194-208.

Davey, Frank. *From Here to There: A Guide to Canadian Literature Since 1960*. Erin, ON: Press Porcépic, 1974.

———"Tish." *The Oxford Companion to Canadian Literature*. Gen. ed. William Toye. Toronto: Oxford University Press, 1983, 790-91.

Davies, Gwendolyn. *Studies in Maritime Literary History 1760-1930*. Fredericton: Acadiensis Press, 1991.

Deahl, James. "Acorn and the Revolutionary Mind." *Cross-Canada Writers' Quarterly* 8.3/4 (1986):13, 58.

———*In Memoriam: Milton Acorn 1923-1986*. London: HMS Press, 1991.

———Introduction. *A Stand of Jackpine*. By Milton Acorn and James Deahl. Toronto: Unfinished Monument Press, 1987.

———*Milton Acorn: A Chronology*. Unpublished.

Dudek, Louis. "Books Reviewed." *The Canadian Forum* (August 1957):114.

Duerden, Charles. *Sulkies, Silks, Cups and Saucers: A Retrospective of the Charlottetown Driving Park*. Charlottetown: Ragweed Press, 1988.

Dzeguze, Kaspars. "Praise and prize for poet Acorn." *The Globe and Mail*, 18 May 1970:20.

Eksteins, Modris. *Rites of Spring: The Great War and the Birth of the Modern Age*. Toronto: Lester & Orpen Dennys, 1989.

"Epic night for poetry lovers." *The Telegram* (Toronto), 13 June 1969:45.

Ferry, Antony. "Ah, Our Night Life Is Coming of Age." *Toronto Star*, 18 November 1960:34.

Finnigan, Joan. "Canadian Poetry Finds Its Voice in a Golden Age." *The Globe Magazine*, 20 January 1962:11-14.

Forsey, Eugene A. "Padlock Act." *The Canadian Encyclopedia*. Vol 3. Edmonton: Hurtig, 1988, 1601.

Frederick's Prince Edward Island Directory, 1889-1890. Charlottetown: The Frederick's Publishing Co., 1889.

Fulford, Robert. "Who speaks for capitalism?" *The Globe and Mail*, 4 January 95:A9.

Gnarowski, Michael. "Milton Acorn: A Review in Retrospect." *Culture* 25 (1964):119-29.

Gudgeon, Chris. *Out of This World: The Natural History of Milton Acorn*. Vancouver: Arsenal Pulp Press, 1996.

Holman, H.T. "The Belfast Riot." *The Island Magazine* 14 (Fall-Winter 1983):3-7.

Horne, Shirley. "Milton Acorn—The People's Poet; But How Many People." *Journal-Pioneer,* 30 July 1977:1.

Hosek, Chaviva. "Poetry in English 1950-1982." *The Oxford Companion to Canadian Literature.* Gen. ed. William Toye. Toronto: Oxford University Press, 1983, 660-69.

Jewinski, Ed. "Milton Acorn." *Canadian Writers and Their Works.* Poetry series. Eds. Robert Lecker, Jack David, and Ellen Quigley. Vol. 7. Toronto: ECW Press, 1990, 21-74.

Jones, Orlo, and Doris Haslam, eds. *An Island Refuge.* Charlottetown: Abegweit Branch of the United Empire Loyalists, 1983.

LaPointe, Valerie. "Celebrating the Carpenter-Poet." *New Maritimes* (July/August 1989):4-5.

Lecker, Robert, ed. *Canadian Canons: Essays in Literary Value.* Toronto: University of Toronto Press, 1991.

Lee, Dennis. Review of *I've Tasted My Blood,* by Milton Acorn. Source unknown.

"Little Theatre Studio Night." *The Charlottetown Patriot,* 25 February 1955:5.

Livesay, Dorothy. "Search For a Style: The Poetry of Milton Acorn." *Canadian Literature* 40 (Spring 1969):33-42.

McAlpine's Prince Edward Island Directory, 1887-1888. Charlottetown: Charles D. McAlpine, 1887.

McAlpine's Prince Edward Island Directory, 1900. Charlottetown and St. John: C.D. McAlpine, 1889.

McAlpine's Prince Edward Island Directory, 1904. St. John: McAlpine Publishing Co., 1904.

McAlpine's Prince Edward Island Directory, 1909. Halifax: McAlpine Publishing Co., 1909.

McClintock, Anne. "The Angel of Progress: Pitfalls of the Term 'Post-colonialism.'" *Colonial Discourse and Post-Colonial Theory.* Eds. Patrick Williams and Laura Chrisman. New York: Columbia University Press, 1994, 291-304.

MacEwan, Gwendolyn. "To Milton." *Cross-Canada Writers' Quarterly* 8.3/4 (1986):9.

MacFarlane, David. "The People's Choice." *Books In Canada* (June-July 1981):3-5.

MacIntyre, Walter. "Island Born Poet to Have Work Published." *The Guardian,* 12 June 1968:5.

MacKay, Jock. "Hey You Milton Acorn." *Canadian Dimension* (July-August 1987):41-42.

Maple Leaf Magazine (August 1929):252.

Marchand, Blaine. "'People's Poet' Milton Acorn forever cares about his peers." *The Ottawa Citizen*, 14 July 1977:70.

Marshall, Tom. *Harsh and Lovely Land: The Major Canadian Poets and the Making of a Canadian Tradition.* Vancouver: UBC Press, 1979.

Martin, Kent. Director. *In Love and Anger: Milton Acorn—Poet.* National Film Board of Canada. 1984.

Meyer, Bruce, and Brian O'Riordan, eds. "Milton Acorn: In the Cause of the Working-Class." *In Their Own Words*. Toronto: House of Anansi, 1984.

Milne, David. "Politics in a Beleaguered Garden." *The Garden Transformed.* Eds. Verner Smitheram, David Milne, and Satadal Dasgupta. Charlottetown: Ragweed Press, 1982, 39-72.

"Native Poet Milton Acorn Is Heard in Reading Tonight." *The Guardian*, 7 October 1969:5.

P.E.I. Register, 24 February 1929.

"Police Stop Poetry Reading: No Poetic License." *The Telegram* (Toronto), 16 July 1962:1.

Pollock, Zailig. "Milton Acorn." *The Oxford Companion to Canadian Literature*. Gen. ed. William Toye. Toronto: Oxford University Press, 1983, 4-5.

Purdy, Al. "In love and anger." *Books In Canada* (October 1986):16-18.

———Introduction. *I've Tasted My Blood*. By Milton Acorn. Toronto: McGraw-Hill Ryerson, 1969.

———Introduction. *Whiskey Jack*. By Milton Acorn. London: HMS Press, 1986.

Rawlyk, George A. "Maritime Provinces." *The Canadian Encyclopedia*. Vol. 2. Edmonton: Hurtig, 1988, 1306.

Richmond, John. "Laureate crowned in Toronto tavern." *The Montreal Star*, 23 May 1970:4.

——— "Milton Acorn, a taste of real poetry." *The Montreal Star*, 2 August 1969.

Robb, Andrew. "Third Party Experience on the Island." *The Garden Transformed.* Eds. Verner Smitheram, David Milne, and Satadal Dasgupta. Charlottetown: Ragweed Press, 1982, 73-79.

Roberts, Gildas. *Chemical Eric*. St. John's: Belvoir Books, 1974.

Robertson, Ian Ross. "Introduction." *Island Land Commission of 1860*. Fredericton: Acadiensis Press, 1988.

Robertson, Ian Ross. "Historical Writing on Prince Edward Island since 1975." *Acadiensis* 17.1 (Autumn 1988):157-83.

———*The Tenant League of Prince Edward Island 1864-1867: Leasehold Tenure in the New World.* Toronto: University of Toronto Press, 1996.

Rosenblatt, Joe. "Remembering another Acorn." *The Globe and Mail*, 14 May 1994:D7.

Said, Edward W. *Culture and Imperialism.* New York: Knopf, 1993.

Sharpe, Errol. *A People's History of P.E.I.* Toronto: Steel Rail, 1976.

Slemon, Stephen. "Post-Colonial Allegory and the Transformation of History." *Journal of Commonwealth Literature* 23:1 (1988):157-68.

Smith, Don B. "'I Always Wanted to be a Fighter Pilot': Reflections upon Two Women in Canadian Military Aviation, 1942-1992." Unpublished paper. 1992.

Smith, John. Citation for Acorn's honorary doctorate, 1977.

Sullivan, Rosemary. *Shadow Maker: The Life of Gwendolyn MacEwan.* Toronto: HarperCollins, 1995.

Sypnowich, Peter. "Colleagues plan fund to honor poet passed over for literary award." *Toronto Star*, 15 April 1970:35.

Teare's Directory and Hand Book of Prince Eward Island, 1880-81. Charlottetown: Teare & Co., 1880.

Van Steen, Marcus. "People's Poet at crusty best." *The Ottawa Citizen*, 16 July 1977:29.

Wayman, Tom. "Fighter in Amber: An Appreciation of Milton Acorn." *Canadian Dimension* (July-August 1987):38-39.

Wayne, Joyce. "Shouting Love: Milton Acorn Remembered." *ThisMagazine* (December 1988):12-18.

Weale, David, and Harry Baglole. *The Island and Confederation: The End Of An Era.* Charlottetown: Williams and Crue, 1973.

Weaver, Robert. "Songs of the road have a new destination in the 1960s." Review of *I've Tasted My Blood*, by Milton Acorn. *Toronto Star*, 7 June 1969:15.

Williams, Patrick, and Laura Chrisman. "Colonial Discourse and Post-Colonial Theory: An Introduction." *Colonial Discourse and Post-Colonial Theory: A Reader.* Eds. Patrick Williams and Laura Chrisman. New York: Columbia University Press, 1994, 1-20.

Zimmermann, Lothar. "By Way of Introduction." *The Abegweit Review: A German Issue* 5.2 (Spring 1989):5-14.

INDEX

A

aboriginal peoples 13, 15, 40, 152, 179, 193-94, 238
Acadians 15, 35, 180, 196
Acorn, Charles 15, 218
Acorn, George 14, 217
Acorn, Gilbert 16
Acorn, Helen Carbonell 11, 29, 31, 32-35, 37-38, 41-43, 49, 50, 81, 82, 94, 97-98, 123, 124-25, 140, 150, 153-55, 178, 182, 218, 223-24, 228
Acorn, Helen [daughter] 11, 106
Acorn, Katherine 11, 42, 48, 57
Acorn, Milton
  aboriginals 13, 15, 40, 152, 179, 194, 238
  Acadians 15, 35, 180, 195
  acting 79-80, 95
  alcohol 19, 124, 125, 135-36, 144, 176-77, 229-30
  Anglicanism 17, 19, 217-18, 245
  Bell's disease 133

birdwatching 98, 225-27, 236
carpentry 67-72, 80, 104, 110
class and class struggle 8, 10, 12-13, 27, 45, 69-70, 79, 85, 88-93, 108-09, 144-45, 168, 187, 193-202, 205, 212, 255
communism, Marxism, and socialism 44-45, 51, 71, 76-78, 88-91, 93, 107-10, 165, 168
diabetes 230
disability pension 83, 94-95, 98
divorce 126
education 42-44, 53, 54
employment 69-72, 84, 86, 94, 96
feminism 220-22
fiction writing 9, 79-81, 93, 157
fixed link 204-05
Governor-General's Award 136, 157-60, 162, 165, 206-07
honorary doctorate 3, 208
marriage and separation 121-28, 131, 134, 135
mental illness 83, 94, 125-26,

Acorn, Milton (*cont'd*)
    129, 139, 141, 144, 149
    military experience 54-56, 59
    mythmaker 23-25
    nationalism 9, 62, 147, 161-62, 186-87, 192-95
    People's Poet Award 4, 17, 24, 48, 114, 136, 152, 160-65, 187, 237, 252-53
    psychic ability 181-82, 240-41
    regionalism 8-9, 113-14, 165, 168-69, 189-94, 205, 113-14
    relationship with father 20, 50-52, 57-58, 77, 83-84, 92, 115-17
    relationship with mother 32, 49-50, 78, 143-44, 176, 179
    relationships with women 78, 93-96, 120-28, 131, 143-44, 173-74, 177-79, 210-11, 227-28
    religion and spirituality 217-21, 225-28, 240-41, 244
    romanticism 7-8, 253
    sexuality 78, 120, 124, 143-44, 227-28
    son 96, 228
    war injury 54-57, 68
Acorn, Milton
    Articles: "Goddam It ... Causeway," 204-05
    "I was a communist ... satisfaction," 44-45, 91-92
    Drama: *The Road to Charlottetown,* 185, 189, 193, 202, 207-08, 210 238, 243
    Books: *Against a League of Liars,* 95, 114, 139
    The Brain's the Target, 114, 116, 139
    Captain Neal MacDougal & the Naked Goddess, 20, 136, 216-22, 233, 256
    Dig Up My Heart: Selected Poems 1952-83, 170, 206, 226, 229, 237
    58 Poems by Milton Acorn, 135
    Hundred Proof Earth, 251
    Jackpine Sonnets, 211-12, 218, 251
    I Shout Love and Other Poems, 251
    In Love and Anger, 4, 5, 103, 103-06, 114
    The Island Means Minago, 21-22, 23-24, 40-41, 176, 178, 185-86, 189-206, 251
    I've Tasted My Blood, 4, 89, 129, 136, 153, 155-57, 160-61, 187, 188, 194, 251
    Jawbreakers, 135
    A Stand of Jackpine, 244, 251
    More Poems For People, 186-87, 251
    The Uncollected Acorn, 244, 251
    Whisky Jack, 239, 251
    Unpublished manuscripts:
    The Bare-Eyed Birdwatcher, 27, 226, 234, 239
    Codex Maximus, 239, 241
    The Sonnets of Martin Dorion, 239-40
    The Sunnybrook Poems, 239-40
    Poems: "Annie's Son," 114
    "At El Cortijo," 88, 114
    "Belle," 114
    "The Bronze Piper," 60-62
    "Charlottetown Harbour," 74-75, 100, 111, 114, 189, 205
    "The Completion of the Fiddle," 256
    "Daddy," 22-23
    "The Dead," 63-65
    "E.T. Carbonell," 27
    "The Execution ... Pierce," 197
    "The Fights," 114

Poems: (*cont'd*)
"The Figure ... Landscape," 9, 205-06
"First Wife Sonnet," 132
"For Mao and Others," 23
"Grey Girl's Gallop," 86-88, 106-07
"Hotel Fire," 190
"Hummingbird," 114, 239
"I, Milton Acorn," 12, 40, 46-47, 130-31, 218
"I Shout Love," 105, 161, 250
"In Addition," 90-91
"Incident from the Land Struggle," 197-98
"The Island," 39-40, 104, 111, 114, 205
"Islanders," 100, 111, 114, 190
"It's All in Mother's Head," 224
"I've Gone and Stained ... Love," 73-74
"I've Tasted My Blood," 32, 40, 46-47, 58-59, 111, 152, 255
"Knowing I Live in a Dark Age," 8
"Letter to My Redheaded Son," 33, 95-96, 114
"Libertad," 114
"Live with Me ... Moon," 131-32
"Lumumba Arrested," 23
"Non-Prayer," 218
"Offshore Breeze," 189, 240
"Old Property," 100, 114, 189-90
"One Day Kennedy ... Alcatraz," 23
"Our True/False National Anthem," 187
"Parting," 132
"Pastoral," 225
"Picasso's 'Seated Athlete With Child,'" 114
"Poem," 32-33

"Rabbie Still Be With Us," 63
"Rent Collection," 197-98
"The Retired Carpenter," 74
"The Schooner," 20-21, 190
"The Second World War," 59-60
"Self-Portrait," 52-53, 133
"The Squall," 190, 246
"Sunnybrook Hospital," 239-40
"They've Murdered Two Workers," 84
"To My Little Sister ... Illness," 106-07
"The Trout Pond," 116, 190
"What I Know of God Is This," 218-19
"Why a Carpenter Wears His Watch," 72-73
"William Cooper," 198-200
"A Worried But Easy Habit," 115-16
"You Growing," 132-33
Acorn, Robert Fairclough 11, 17-20, 41-42, 50-52, 57-58, 69, 77, 106, 115-16, 141, 150, 218, 223
Acorn, Robert, Jr., 11, 19, 29, 31, 44, 46, 48-52, 54, 57-58, 69-70, 76, 79-82, 87, 94, 96, 98, 106, 229-30, 244, 245, 251
Advance Mattress Coffee House 143
Allan Gardens protest 134
Anglican Young People's Association 79
Arsenault, Adrien 79-80, 97, 151, 153
Atwood, Margaret 111, 120, 122, 160

B

Baglole, Harry 167, 169-70, 190-91, 195-96, 197-200, 222
Barometer Rising [MacLennan] 62-63, 159

Beat poets 134, 138-39
Belfast Riot 21
The Bear House 175
Berrouard, Leon and Karen 235-36
bissett, bill 142-43, 157, 250
Black Mountain movement 138-39, 147
Bohemian Embassy 119, 121, 124, 133-34, 143
Booth, Luella 134, 173-74
Bowering, George 129, 138-39, 157-58
Broad-Axe 92, 176
Brothers and Sisters of Cornelius Howatt 167
Bryant, Stanley 18, 69-70, 74, 77, 83
Burke, Brian ii, 33

C

Campbell, Premier Alex 161, 166-69
Campbell, Robert 153
Canada Council of the Arts 6, 141, 153, 157, 163, 213, 234
Canadian Broadcasting Corp. 115, 164, 230
The Canadian Forum 111, 115, 121, 139
Canadian Liberation Movement 186-87
Canadian Poets' Award (People's Poet Award) 4, 17, 24, 48, 114, 136, 152, 160-65, 187, 237, 252-53
Canadian Writers' Foundation 234
Carbonell, E.T. 26-30, 218
Carbonell, Kate [neé Macdougall] 29-31, 181, 218, 233, 238
Cashman, Cheryl 210-11, 212, 245
Chemical Eric [Roberts] 155
Clarke, George Elliott 75, 89

class and class struggle 8, 10-12, 27, 45, 79, 85, 88-93, 109, 111, 144-45, 168, 193-202, 205
Cogswell, Fred 135, 216, 242
Cohen, Leonard 96, 99, 111-13, 115, 161
Colombo, John Robert 114, 136
colonialism 9, 13, 190-97, 200-03, 205; and neocolonialism 9, 62-63, 159, 168, 186-87, 191-92, 205
communism 51, 71, 76-78, 88-91, 107-10, 168
Confederation 6, 9, 75-76, 190, 195, 200-01, 203, 205
Cooper, William 185, 198-200, 203
Cornelius Howatt: Superstar! 167

D

Dawson Creek, B.C. 152
Deahl, James 91, 93, 99-100, 170, 174, 186-88, 211, 212-13, 216, 219-20, 237, 239, 243, 250-51
Dougan, Harold 54, 58, 64, 94
Dudek, Louis 99, 100, 105, 108

E

Eichorn [Acorn], John 13-14, 77, 196, 217
Eichorn, Mary 13-14
Eichorn, Matthias von 13-14, 217
Eichorn, Matthias, Jr. 13

F

Fairclough, Mary 15, 181
Fairclough, Robert 15, 16-17
Fennario, David 232
The Fiddlehead 111, 135, 139
Findley, Timothy 62
Foster, Bert 81

G

The Georgia Straight 1, 139, 146-47
German-American Loyalists 14
Go Preachers 16

Gool, Réshard 7, 163, 167, 170-72, 174-77, 209, 221, 235-37, 239, 245
Governor-General's Award 128, 129, 157, 162, 189, 190, 206-07, 210, 230
Great George Street Gallery 7, 170, 221-22, 230-32
Grossman's Tavern 160
Gustafson, Ralph 41, 111

H

Harris, Robert 120, 206
Harrison, Elaine 7, 170, 180-81, 223
Harvey, Louise 80, 93-96
Hennessey, Michael 7
home place 9, 40-41
Hooper, David 13, 15-20, 26-27, 29, 31, 35, 50-52, 96-98, 106, 123, 150, 181-82, 217, 224-25, 230
Hooper, Garth 15, 18, 26, 34, 71, 85, 93, 170, 224, 237, 242, 245
Hooper, Mary 11-12, 15, 17, 19, 27, 31, 33-35, 37-39, 41-42, 44-47, 50-51, 53-57, 71-72, 80, 83-85, 93-94, 96, 115, 123, 150, 154, 170, 177, 207, 212, 219, 223-27, 229, 237-38, 242, 245, 251
Hornby, Jim 157, 233, 239

I-J

The Island and Confederation 190
The Island Magazine 170
Jago, Martha 15-16
Jones, Premier Walter 77-78

K

Kerr [Booth], Luella 134, 174-75
Kessler, Deirdre 4, 7, 170
Klein, A.M. 53, 89, 99-100, 102
Kroetsch, Robert 40

L

Labour Progressive Party 86, 88, 107
Lampman, Archibald 99, 102, 211
Land Question 24, 185-91, 195-203, 207-08
Lane, Patrick 89, 143-46, 152, 157, 163, 174, 250
Lane, Red 111, 141, 143-44, 157
LaPointe, Valerie 231, 237-38, 241-42, 249-51
Large, Gloria "Sally" 163, 170, 177-78, 212
Layton, Irving 53, 96, 99, 102-04, 111-13, 135-36, 158, 160-61, 178-79, 252
League of Canadian Poets 115, 179, 228-29, 241-43
Ledwell, Frank 7, 96-97, 150-51, 153-54, 175, 250
Lee, Dennis 156, 229
Leslie, Kenneth 89
Little, Jim and Connie 151
Little Theatre 79, 95
Livesay, Dorothy 89, 99-100, 102, 111, 135, 160, 187-88, 252-53
Lowther, Pat 145-46
Loyalist refugees 4-5, 14

M

MacDougall, Capt. Neil 20-23, 25-26, 29, 216, 218, 233, 238
MacEwan, Gwendolyn 120-31, 134, 141, 144, 157, 160, 228, 253
MacInnis, John 29-31
MacLaine, Brent 163, 178, 250
MacLaine, Wendell 250
MacLean, Angus 169
MacLennan, Hugh 62-63, 159
MacLeod, Alistair 75
MacPhail, Andrew 7
Mandel, Eli 158, 160

Marlatt, Daphne 40
Marriott, Anne 99-100
Martin, Kent 222, 234, 245
  and *In Love and Anger* 32-33,
  37-39, 51, 105, 107, 128, 164,
  188, 219, 222-23, 226, 228, 236,
  240-41
McEachern, Eleanor 234, 243,
  244-45
McFarlane, Myra 144
McLachlan, Alexander 89
McLeod, Dan 139, 146-47
Mi'Kmaq 13, 15, 40
Milton Acorn Festival 7, 250
modernism 100-03, 112
Moment 110, 122, 135
Moncton 70, 79
Montgomery, L.M. 4, 7, 48
Montreal and poetry 99-102
Musick, Peter 13, 15
myth 23
mythopoetic writing 23-26

N-O

National Film Board 120
nationalism 6, 9, 23, 62, 102-03,
  112, 158-59, 186-87, 192-95, 206
New Frontiers 86-87
New Glasgow, PEI 117, 120
The Northern Red Oak 251
Nowlan, Alden 77, 82, 89, 100, 111,
  153, 157, 235, 252, 254
Oughton, Libby 127, 180, 216,
  221-22, 234-35, 237, 242,
  245-46, 249

P-Q

Page, P.K. 99-100, 111
Partridge, Gertrude & Glen 93, 182
Peace River District 152
A People's History of P.E.I. 202

People's Poet Award 4, 17, 24, 48,
  114, 136, 160-65, 187, 237,
  252-53
Perth County Conspiracy 185-86,
  240
Phelan, Reg 47-48, 135-36, 149-50,
  175-76, 178, 179-80, 189, 237
Pierce, Lorne 113-14
poetics of place 102-03
postcolonial theory 191-93
Pratt, E.J. 102
Prince Edward Island
  artistic environment 5-7, 10, 82,
  151-53, 170-73, 174-75, 183-84,
  221-22, 250, 254
  Confederation 6, 9, 75-76, 190,
  195, 205
  Development Plan 165-69
  garden myth 75, 165-70
  German-American Loyalists 14
  Land Question and Tenants'
  Revolt 9, 24, 185, 190-91,
  195-203, 205, 207-08
  tourism 193, 203-06
psychic ability 31, 181-82, 240-41
Purdy, Al 80, 89-90, 96, 99, 102-06,
  107-15, 119, 122, 125-26,
  135-36, 139, 141, 152-53, 155,
  160, 173, 174, 188, 229, 237,
  243, 251-53
Purdy, Henry and Gertie 151

R

Ragweed Press 7, 127, 170, 216,
  221-22, 228, 234-35, 242
regionalism 6, 9-10, 102-03, 112-14,
  189-93, and postcolonialism 6,
  25, 191-93, 205
resistive regionalism 192
Rogers, Stan 75
romanticism 7-8, 253

INDEX 279

Rosenblatt, Joe 119-20, 128-29,
    134-36, 146, 160, 174, 228, 234
S
Sabine, Caroline 15
science fiction 49, 80
Scott, F.R. 89, 99-100, 111, 135,
    153, 228-29
Seattle 143
Sentner, Anne 14
Sept-Iles 84
Sharpe, Errol 202
Sherman, Joseph 7, 163, 229, 249
Smith, A.J.M. 99-100, 139
Smith, Cedric 172, 175, 185-86,
    207-08, 210, 237, 250-51
Smith, John 7, 154, 163, 170, 172,
    208-09, 213, 215, 221, 226-27
    235
Sorestad, Glen 242
Souster, Raymond 89, 99, 102, 135
St. Lawrence Centre 153
Stewart, Elizabeth 21, 26
Steinfeld, J.J. 7
Sunnybrook Hospital 125-26, 243
T-V
Tallman, Warren 158
Tenants' Revolt 185, 190-91,
    195-203, 207-08
Theatre PEI 170
Tish 138-39

Toronto
    and marriage 128
    and poetry 120-21
Toronto Island 123
Turgeon, Frank 181
University of Prince Edward Island 3,
    153, 208-09
Vancouver and poetry 138-39
W-Z
Waldoboro, Maine 13
Wallace, Joe 86, 89, 100, 135
The Wars [Findley] 62
Waverly Hotel 162, 188, 209-10, 245
Wayman, Tom 12, 74, 89, 91,
    252-53
Weale, David 167, 169, 190-91, 195
Weaver, Robert 156, 158
Wells, Andy 164-69, 173, 237
Williams, Eleanor 14, 180-81
Wiseman, Adele 180-81
Woolnough, Hilda 4, 7, 96, 127,
    153, 162-63, 170-78, 187, 204,
    210, 221, 230-31, 235-37,
    238-39, 244, 245
working class 11-12, 23, 45, 79, 85,
    88-93, 112, 145, 187, 211-12,
    252, 255
World War I 17-18, 76, 101, 150
World War II 18, 30, 42, 54, 58-64,
    101